Square Mile of Murder

Four of the world's greatest murder cases took
place within one square mile of the city of
Glasgow. And this square mile included some of
the most fashionable areas of the new Victorian
West End.

The cases include the trial of Madeleine Smith
who was found Not Proven of poisoning her
persistent lover Emile L'Angelier by arsenic
administered in late-night cocoa; Dr Edward
Pritchard who took professional pleasure in the
lingering deaths he prescribed for his wife and
mother-in-law; Jessie McLachlan whose case is
considered by some authorities to be the finest in
the world; and Oscar Slater who spent nearly
twenty years in prison for a crime he did not
commit.

Jack House throws new light on these fascinating
and classic murder cases.

To the Abiding Memory of
William Roughead
Criminologist Extraordinary

Square Mile of Murder

by JACK HOUSE

RICHARD DREW PUBLISHING

GLASGOW

SQUARE MILE OF MURDER
ISBN 0 904002 11 X

First published in 1961 by W. & R. Chambers
New edition published 1984 by Richard Drew Publishing Limited
6 Clairmont Gardens, Glasgow G3 7LW, Scotland

Copyright © 1961, 1975 and 1984 by Jack House

Made and printed in Great Britain by Cox & Wyman Ltd.,
Reading

Contents

The Square Mile

Most people imagine that murder in Glasgow usually takes place in the East End of the city in the depths of winter. It's just the opposite. All the best Glasgow murders have taken place in the West End in the spring or the summer. Not only that, but Glasgow can boast (if that is the right word) that four of the world's greatest murder cases took place within one square mile of the city.

There may be other towns which can rival Glasgow in the number of murders in any one square mile. I should think that the Notting Hill district of London might well have a square mile that could beat Glasgow's in quantity. But when it comes to quality, what murder cases can compare with those involving 'that prodigious damsel', Madeleine Smith; Jessie McLachlan, whose case is considered by some authorities to be the finest in the world; Dr Edward William Pritchard, the 'human crocodile'; and Oscar Slater, to my mind the greatest of all murder cases anywhere?

Three of these cases are Victorian. Madeleine Smith was put on trial in 1857, Jessie McLachlan in 1862 and Dr Pritchard in 1865. But, although Oscar Slater was not condemned until 1909, the spirit of his case is also Victorian. For the one thread that links all these cases is respectability. Respectability saved Madeleine Smith and doomed Jessie McLachlan and Oscar Slater. And respectability was the reason that Dr Pritchard got away with one murder and nearly got away with two more.

Glasgow in Victorian days was an intensely respectable city. Today Glasgow has an ill-deserved reputation for crime. For one person who knows that Glasgow has the only perfectly preserved Gothic Cathedral on the mainland of Scotland, a thousand will know of the existence of the Gorbals. I have met people who are actually afraid to go to Glasgow because of what they have read in the newspapers. Indeed, it's possible that the reason for Glasgow's bad reputation is the energy and enterprise of its newspaper reporters. As one authority has said, 'You've only got to flash a razor in Glasgow to get onto the front page.'

Now Victorian Glasgow (and Edwardian Glasgow too) was a much worse place than the city today. But respectability ruled the roost and, although three world-famous murders took place within eight years, nobody suggested that Gasgow was a city of crime.

The square mile of murder lies around Charing Cross, which was once a clearly defined place, dominated by the old Grand Hotel. But the Grand Hotel has gone and, instead, there are motorways and what is nowadays called 'landscaping'. The heroes and heroines of this book would simply not know the old place. They would hardly recognise Sauchiehall Street, most of which is now, as they glibly say, 'pedestrianised'. However, it's still reasonably true to repeat what I wrote when this book was first published fourteen years ago that our square mile is situated where Sauchiehall Street is coming to an end as a shopping centre and giving way to well-built terraces which were private houses in Victorian days but are now given over mainly to offices, restaurants, consulting rooms, clubs and hair-dressing establishments. In the middle of the nineteenth century Glasgow, which at one time seemed to be spreading east, suddenly decided to go west, in a residential sense. So most of the buildings in our square mile of murder were houses and terraces and tenements.

Madeleine Smith lived in Blythswood Square, which is just off Sauchiehall Street. If she poisoned Pierre Emile L'Angelier (as I think she did) she accomplished the deed there. Jessie McLachlan was charged with the murder of

8

her dearest friend in a house at 17 Sandyford Place, which is part of Sauchiehall Street. Dr Pritchard committed one murder in Berkeley Terrace, just round the corner from Sandyford Place, and his next two were done in Sauchiehall Street, quite near Blythswood Square. Oscar Slater lived in a building which can be seen from Charing Cross, and the woman he was accused of killing had her home only a few minutes' walk away.

What makes our square mile of murder so fascinating is that, in these four cases, we can be sure of only one murderer. That is our human crocodile, Dr Pritchard, the last man to be hanged in public in Glasgow. He confessed to two of his three murders before he went to the scaffold.

But Madeleine Smith was found Not Proven (that peculiarly Scottish verdict) of poisoning L'Angelier, and to this day there are people who think she didn't do it. Jessie McLachlan served fifteen years in prison for a murder so remarkable that no one will ever know the truth of it. And Oscar Slater served nineteen years for a murder that he did not commit. Then who did kill Miss Marion Gilchrist?

One man knew more about these four murders than anyone else, and I must pay tribute to him now. He was probably the greatest criminologist in the world – William Roughead, Writer to the Signet in Edinburgh. He edited the series of Notable British Trials published by William Hodge and Co., and he collected all sorts of things connected with our square mile of murder. He wrote brilliantly of each case and no one who writes of these murders today can put down a word without having studied Roughead.

And now come with me into gaslit Glasgow and we shall see how a little respectability goes a long, long way.

A Kiss, a Fond Embrace

The Case of Madeleine Smith

The Reigning Belle

On St Valentine's Day, 1855, the reigning belle of Glasgow received a single red rose. The reigning belle was small, dark, flashing-eyed and inclined to be a bit plump. She was eighteen years of age and her name was Madeleine Hamilton Smith. She lived with her father, a well-to-do architect, and the rest of the Smith family in a terrace house in India Street, now in the middle of Glasgow, but then considered to be in the West End.

Madeleine had been to school in England and she found, when she returned to Glasgow, that she did not like the town. However, she tried to get over her dislike by going to parties, balls and assemblies, and such was her vitality and vivacity that she actually succeeded in going to five dances in one night. She was certainly the belle of the ball.

Since all Valentines are anonymous, there was no note with the red rose. But Madeleine may well have wondered if it came from that dashing foreign-looking gentleman who seemed to make a habit of sauntering up and down Sauchiehall Street when Madeleine and her sister Bessie were sauntering up and down Sauchiehall Street too.

The foreign-looking gentleman was named Pierre Emile L'Angelier and he claimed to be a Frenchman. In fact, he had been born in Jersey in the Channel Islands, but his father was a French nurseryman who left France during the revolution of 1830 and settled in Jersey. L'Angelier, like

Madeleine, was the eldest of five children. He was dandified in his dress, wore a fine twirling moustache, was very proud of his small feet, could play the guitar, and, again like Madeleine, was a little on the plump side. He was a clerk in a seedsman's office in Bothwell Street and he was getting ten shillings a week in salary. He was ten years older than Madeleine.

A few weeks after she had received the rose, Madeleine Smith was introduced to Pierre Emile L'Angelier. L'Angelier had asked a friend of his who knew Madeleine to come walking with him in Sauchiehall Street so that, if they met, he could be introduced. So Robert Baird and L'Angelier walked up and down Sauchiehall Street until they spied Madeleine and Bessie, and the fateful introduction was made.

Out of that meeting has come endless speculation – also four books, four plays (including a television one), and a film. And James Bridie used the Madeleine Smith story in his first stage success, *A Sleeping Clergyman*. Miss F. Tennyson Jesse says (in her Introduction to the Madeleine Smith case in *Notable British Trials*) that 'Madeleine Smith was born before her time. She had all the profound physical passion with which the northern woman so often makes her southern sister seem insipid; and this passion, of the essence of her being, was a thing supposed at that particular date not to exist in a "nice" woman.' But I must say that in my opinion Pierre Emile L'Angelier died because Madeleine wanted to become respectable.

However, as the best writers say, we anticipate. Madeleine and Bessie Smith were introduced to the dashing foreigner with the twirling moustache and the fancy waistcoat. Apparently Bessie Smith, two years younger than Madeleine and rather plain and fat, thought L'Angelier was interested in her. Madeleine knew better. She contrived to have several meetings with L'Angelier and was much impressed by his foreign background. He was very proud of his family descent and, at the drop of a chapeau, would talk of the counts, marquises, and dukes of the old French nobility to whom he was related.

The fact that he was getting but ten shillings a week from the Bothwell Street seedsmen would make him all the more romantic. As we might say today, he was a Cinderella man to Madeleine. He had a high-flown way of talking and he was very strong for the straight and narrow path. Right away he made it plain to Madeleine that he did not approve of her parties and dances and flirting. But also he sent her another red rose.

Madeleine's father, the architect James Smith, had built himself a country house at Rhu on the Gareloch. It was the time when all well-to-do Glasgow men were building houses on the Clyde coast. You can still see them 'doon the watter' today, although most of them have been turned into boarding houses and private hotels. James Smith not only built Rowaleyn at Rhu: he designed it. And as soon as the spring came along, the family moved down to Rhu and came up to Glasgow only when business or society demanded.

So, soon after Madeleine met L'Angelier, the Smith family moved to Rowaleyn. It was the beginning of April, 1855, and Madeleine wrote her first letter to L'Angelier. No one knows how many letters she wrote to him, but 198 were found in his lodgings and in his office desk when he was found dead from arsenic poisoning. Of these, sixty were read at Madeleine's trial. The first was sent to L'Angelier's business address, 10 Bothwell Street.

'My dear Emile,' wrote Madeleine from Rhu, and I use her own spelling throughout these letters, 'I do not feel as if I were writing you for the first time. Though our intercourse has been very short, yet we have become as familiar friends. May we long continue so. And ere lang may you be a friend of Papa's is my most earnest desire. We feel it rather dull here after the excitement of a Town's Life. But then we have much more time to devote to study and improvement. I often wish you were near us, we could take such charming

13

walks. One enjoys walking with a pleasant companion, and where could we find one equal to yourself?

'I am trying to break myself off all my *very* bad habits, it is you I have to thank for this, which I do sincerely from my heart. Your flower is fading.

> *I never cast a flower away,*
> *The gift of one who cared for me,*
> *A little flower, a faded flower,*
> *But it was done reluctantly.*

'I wish I understood Botany for your sake, as I might send you some specimens of moss. But alas! I know nothing of that study. We shall be in Town next week. We are going to the Ball on the 20th of this month, so we will be several times in Glasgow before that. Papa and Mama are not going to Town next Sunday. So of course you do *not* come to Row. We shall not expect you. Bessie desires me to remember her to you. Write on Wednesday or Thursday. I must now say adieu. With kind love, believe me, yours very sincerely,

Madeleine.'

This high-flown style was not to last. L'Angelier wrote back to Madeleine. We don't know what he said because Madeleine either destroyed his letters or sent them back to him. Perhaps she didn't like his epistolary style. Or perhaps she didn't want anyone to find them in her escritoire. At any rate, in her next letter Madeleine was proposing a subterfuge to allow her to meet L'Angelier. And apparently sister Bessie had discovered in some way that the dashing foreigner was paying court to Madeleine, and so was, naturally, jealous of her. It would be rather hard on a girl to be the sister of the belle of the ball. Bessie tried to get her own back in a small way by shortening Madeleine's name to 'Lena'. Her father objected to this but, oddly enough, long after Madeleine had stood her trial and left her family to rot, she assumed the name that Bessie had given her. She was buried as Lena and not Madeleine.

Here, then, is Madeleine's second letter to L'Angelier.

'My dear Emile,
    'Many thanks for your kind epistle. We are to be in town
tomorrow (Wednesday). Bessie said I was not to let you
know. But I must tell you why! Well, some friend was *kind*
enough to tell papa that you were in the habit of walking
with us. Papa was very angry with me for walking with a
Gentleman unknown to him. I told him he had been
introduced, and I saw no harm in it. Bessie joins with Papa
and blames me for the whole affair. She does not know I am
writing you, so dont mention it. We are to call at our old
quarters in the Square on Wednesday about quarter past 12
o'c. So if you could be in Mr McCall's Lodgings – see us
come out of Mrs Ramsay's – come after us – say you are
astonished to see us in Town without letting you know –
and we shall see how Bessie acts. She says she is not going
to write you. We are to be in Town all night. We are to be
with Mrs Anderson. Rest assured I shall not mention to
anyone that you have written me. I know from experience
that the world is not lenient in its observations. But I don't
care for the world's remarks so long as my own heart tells
me I am doing nothing wrong. Only if the day is fine expect
us to-morrow. Not a word of this letter. Adieu till we meet.
Believe me, yours most sincerely,

                                    Madeleine.'

    Well, the romance started, but it looked as if it was going
to end in a couple of weeks. Bessie tattled to her papa and
the stern Mr Smith soon discovered that this young man
was not only a foreigner but a penniless clerk in Huggins,
the seedsmen in Bothwell Street. He was completely unsuit-
able as a suitor for Madeleine's hand. Mrs Smith treated
the affair more in sorrow than in anger. She was something
of a hypochondriac, and left the running of the household to
Madeleine. Between her father's admonitions and her
mother's tears, Madeleine was forced to make an agonising
reappraisal of the situation.

She wrote to L'Angelier, this time at his lodgings in the Botanic Gardens out along Great Western Road. L'Angelier either lost or destroyed part of this letter, but enough remains to show us that Madeleine had decided to end the acquaintance.

On April 18th, 1855, she wrote:

'My Dear Emile,

'I now perform the promise I made in parting to write you soon. We are to be in Glasgow to-morrow (Thursday). But as my time shall not be at my own disposal, I cannot fix any time to see you. Chance may throw you in my way.

'I think you will agree with me in what I intend proposing, viz., That for the present the correspondence had better *stop*. I know your good feeling will not take this unkind, it is meant quite the reverse. By continuing to correspond harm may arise. In *dis*continuing it nothing can be said. It would have afforded me great pleasure to have placed your name on—'

And that is all we have. We do know, however, that though the correspondence may have stopped, the sweethearts still met. L'Angelier took to hanging around India Street and, if the coast was clear, Madeleine would let him into the house, particularly into the laundry.

Meanwhile Pierre Emile had made a close and constant friend of an elderly maiden lady, Miss Mary Arthur Perry. She lived at 144 Renfrew Street, just behind the Assembly Rooms, and she went to the same church which L'Angelier attended – St Jude's Episcopal. She often invited him to tea and he confided in her that he was deeply in love with Miss Madeleine Smith. So Miss Perry suggested that L'Angelier should bring his loved one round to tea some day. And eventually, when Madeleine could manage it, she would have her assignations with L'Angelier at 144 Renfrew Street, while Miss Perry remained discreetly out of the way. By this time Madeleine was calling herself 'Mimi' to L'Angelier and

Miss Perry. When she wrote as Mimi, she was quite a different person from Madeleine.

Madeleine versus Mimi

In the middle of July, 1855, the Victorian father laid down the law again. He discovered that the liaison between his daughter and the Frenchman was not over, and now forbade Madeleine to see L'Angelier. She wrote to him and also to Miss Perry. We don't have her letter to L'Angelier, but her note to Miss Perry explains it all:

'Dearest Miss Perry,

'Many kind thanks for all your kindness to me. Emile will tell you I have bid him adieu. My Papa would not give his consent, so I am in duty bound to obey him. Comfort dear Emile. It is a heavy blow to us both. I had hoped some day to have been happy with him, but alas it was not intended. We were doomed to be disappointed. You have been a kind friend to him. Oh! Continue so. I hope and trust he may prosper in the step he is about to take. I am glad now that he is leaving this country, for it would have caused me great pain to have met him. Think my conduct not unkind. I have a father to please, and a kind father too. Farewell, dear Miss Perry, and with much love believe me, yours most sincerely,

Mimi.'

At this time L'Angelier had been talking of going to Lima to seek his fortune. He was very conscious of the difference between his rank as a ten-bob-a-week clerk and Madeleine's as the eldest daughter of a wealthy architect. We do know that there was discovered among his possessions a letter, or a copy of a letter, which puts his point of view. When it came to the murder trial, the judges would not allow this letter to be read.

The rejected document says:

17

'Glasgow, 10 Bothwell Street
19th July, '55

'In the first place, I did not deserve to be treated as you have done. How you astonish me by writing such a note without condescending to explain the reasons why your father refuses his consent. He must have reasons, and I am not allowed to clare myself of accusations.'

[As with Madeleine's letters, I am adhering to L'Angelier's own spelling.]

'I should have written you before, but I preferred waiting untill I got over surprise your last letter caused me, and also to be able to write you in a calm and a collected manner, free from any animosity whatever.

'Never, dear Madeleine, could I have believed you were capable of such conduct. I thought and believed you unfit for such a step. I believe you true to your word and to your *honour*. I will put questions to you which answer to yourself. What would you think if even one of your servants had played with any one's affections as you have done, or what would you say to hear that any lady friends had done what you have – or what am I to – of you now? What is your opinion of your own self after those solemn vows you uttered and wrote to me. Shew my letters to any one, Madeleine, I don't care who, and if any find that I mislead you I will free you from all blame. I warned you repeatedly not to be rash in your engagement and vows to me, but you persisted in that false and deceitful flirtation, playing with affections which you knew to be pure and undivided, and knowing at the same time that at a word from your father you would break all your engagement.

'You have deceived your father as you have deceived me. You never told him how solemnly you bound yourself to me, or if you had, for the honour of his daughter he could not have asked to break off an engagement as yours. Madeleine, you have truly acted wrong. May this be a lesson to you never to trifle with any again. I wish you every happiness. I shall be truly happy to hear you are happy with another. You desire and now you are at liberty to recognise me or cut me just as you wish – but I give you my word of honour I shall act always as a Gentleman towards you. We may meet yet, as my intentions of going to Lima are now at an end. I would have gone for your sake. Yes, I would have sacrificed all to have you with me, and to leave Glasgow and your friends you detested so very much. Think what your father would say if I sent him your letters for a perusal. Do you think he could sanction your breaking your promises. No, Madeleine, I leave your conscience to speak for itself.

'I flatter myself he can only accuse me of a want of fortune. But he must remember he too had to begin the world with dark clouds around him.

'I cannot put it into my mind that yet you are at the bottom of all this.'

Whether L'Angelier ever sent this letter, or one like it, to Madeleine or not, it does represent his attitude to the whole affair. Almost every writer who has dealt with the Madeleine Smith case has portrayed the unfortunate Emile as a perfidious wretch who, once he got Madeleine into his power, threatened to blackmail her. I do not see him that way at all. He was priggish in the extreme, but Madeleine obviously enjoyed for a time being lectured, not to say hectored. I think of L'Angelier as a foreign Nobody who wanted to become an accepted Somebody. I think he was genuinely in love with Madeleine, but he wanted also to be received as an equal in the Smith household. In fact, I think L'Angelier was more sinned against than sinning.

At any rate, this second attempt of Madeleine's to finish the affair ended like the first. She became Mimi once again, and L'Angelier visited her at Rhu when the family was on holiday, and her servant, Christina Haggart, helped in the clandestine arrangements both at Rhu and at the town house in India Street. And Miss Perry, of course, was always ready to oblige.

The romance prospered so well now that on December 3rd, 1855, Madeleine posted this letter to her beloved. it was one of those which shocked the Victorians terribly. Madeleine, you see, was honest about sex. I should imagine she shocked L'Angelier too. At any rate, this is what she wrote:

Tuesday, 2 o'c

'My own darling husband,

'I am afraid I may be too late to write you this eveng., so as all are out I shall do it now, my sweet one. I did not expect the pleasure of seeing you last evng., of being *fondeled* by you, dear, dear Emile. Our Cook was ill, and went to bed at 10 – that was the reason I could see you – but I trust ere long to have a long, long interview with you, sweet one of my soul, my love, my all, my own best beloved. I hope you slept well last evng., and find yourself better today. I was at St. Vincent Street to-day. B/ and M/ are gone to call for the Houldsworths and some others. Never fear me, I love you well, my own sweet darling Emile. Do go to Edr. and visit the Lanes – also, my sweet love, go to the Ball given to the Officers. I think you should consult Dr McFarlan – that is, go and see him, get him to sound you, tell you what is wrong with you. Ask for him to prescribe for you – and if you have any love for your Mimi follow his advice, and oh! sweet love, follow the Md. advice – be good for once, and I am sure you will be well. Is it not horrid cold weather? I did, my love, so pity you standing in the cold last night, but I could not get Janet to sleep – little stupid thing. This is a horrid scroll, as I have been stoped twice with that bore – visiter. My own sweet beloved, I can say nothing as to our marriage, as it is not certain when they may go from home, or when I may go to Edr. it is uncertain. My beloved, will we require to be married (if it is in Edr.) in Edr. or will it do here. You know I know nothing of these things. I fear the Banns in Glasgow, there are so many people know me. If I had any other name but Madeleine it might pass – but it is not a very common one. But we must manage in some way to be united ere we leave Town . . . . Much much love kisses tender long embraces kisses love. I am thy own thy ever fond thy own dear loving wife thy

Mimi L'Angelier.'

Yes, Madeleine, as they say, could write a letter. Perhaps I should explain one or two details in this one. She refers to being at St Vincent Street. Mr Smith's office was at 124 St Vincent Street, which is parallel to Bothwell Street where her sweet pet worked. B/ and M/ were Bessie and Mama, and Edr. was Edinburgh. The reference to 'little stupid thing' Janet is important. Both at the house in India Street and in Blythswood Square later, Madeleine shared a bedroom with her little sister. Fortunately for the lovers, Janet was a sound sleeper.

On April 29th, 1856, Madeleine wrote a special letter to 'My own, my beloved Emile' for his birthday, that very day. 'My beloved,' she said, 'may you have very, very many happy returns of this day – and each year may you find yourself happier and better than the last and may each year find you more prosperous than the last. I trust, darling, that on your next birthday I may be with you to wish you many happy returns in person.'

But Pierre Emile L'Angelier was destined never to have another birthday. A year after Madeleine Smith wrote those loving words, she was confined in Glasgow prison, charged with the murder of L'Angelier. But then, in the spring of 1856, she was still writing passionate letters which ended customarily with 'A kiss. A fond embrace'. As usual, the Smith family had gone to Rhu, and Madeleine had to make special arrangements to receive L'Angelier's letters and also to see him occasionally in the garden of Rowaleyn. In the first place, she arranged that his letters should be sent to a 'Miss Bruce', care of the local Post Office, and Christina Haggart, the servant, collected them. In the second place, she had to be very careful about their meetings in the garden because two attempts had been made to burgle Rowaleyn, and a watch was being kept on the place. But Madeleine was a very determined young woman.

Her romance was reaching its zenith when she wrote to her own, beloved Emile at the beginning of May to invite him back to Rowaleyn. She suggested that if, by any chance, her father was on the boat that Emile should get off at Helensburgh. This was the Gareloch pier just before Rhu, and it wouldn't take an active young man long to get from Helensburgh to Rowaleyn. Madeleine goes on:

'Well, beloved, you shall come to the gate (you know it) and wait till I come. And then, oh happiness wont I kiss you, my love, my own beloved Emile, my husband dear. I don't think there is any risk. Well, Tuesday, 6th May. The Gate, half-past 10. You understand, darling. I hope you are well – no cold. Take care of yourself. I have nothing new to tell you. I have been rather busy all this week. I shall expect you to have a letter for me. The weather is so fine. I have been a great deal out this week, looking after out door arrange-ments. I have got a new employment – The "Hen Yard". I go there every morning. You can fancy me every morning at 10 o'c seeing the Hens being fed and feeding my donkey. I don't get on very fast with it – I fear it has little affection – do for it what I shall it only appears to know me, and come to me when I call. My beloved Emile, I feel so delighted at the idea of seeing you I cannot write. I hope you will be able to tell me that you shall get married in Spt. Darling, I love you, and shall for ever remain true. Nothing shall cause me to break my vows to you. As you say, we are Man and Wife. So we are, my pet. We shall, I trust, for ever remain so. It shall be the happiest day of my life the day that unites us never more to separate. I trust and pray we shall for ever remain happy and loving. But there is no fear of that, we are sure to do so, love – are we not? But I must stop, as P/ wishes me to go and read the Papers to him – it is 11 o'c night. So if I dont write any more, forgive me love. Beloved of my soul, a fond embrace, a dear kiss till we meet. We

shall have more than one love dearest from thy own thy ever
devoted & loving wife thine for ever,

> Minie.'

Victorian blushes

Well, L'Angelier found the gate all right. He found it so well
and so often that at last these two lovers consummated their
love in the garden at Rhu. Although, when it came to her
trial, Madeleine preserved a remarkable composure, it was
observed that she bowed her head and seemed to blush as
certain of her letters were read out in court. She bowed and
blushed for this one. It was sent to Pierre Emile L'Angelier
in the wedding month of June.

'My own, my beloved husband,
  'I trust to God you got home safe, and were not much the
worse of being out. Thank you, my love for coming so far to
see your Mimi. It is truly a pleasure to see you, my Emile.
Beloved, if we did wrong last night it was in the excitement
of our love. Yes, beloved, I did truly love you with my soul.
I was happy, it was a pleasure to be with you. Oh if we
could have remained, never more to have parted. But we
must hope that the time shall come. I must have been very
stupid to you last night. But everything goes out of my head
when I see you, my darling, my love. I often think I must be
very, very stupid in your eyes. You must be disappointed
with me. I wonder you like me in the least. But I trust and
pray the day may come when you shall like me better.
Beloved, we shall wait till you are quite ready. I shall see
and speak to Jack on Sunday. I shall consider about telling
Mama. But I don't see any hope from her – I know her
mind. You, of course, cannot judge of my parents. You know
them not . . . . Darling, Emile, did I seem cold to you last
night. Darling I love you. Yes, my own Emile, love you with
my heart and soul. Am I not your wife. Yes I am. And you
may rest assured after what has passed I cannot be the wife

23

of any other but dear, dear Emile. No, now it would be a sin . . . .

'I did not bleed in the least last night – but I had a good deal of pain during the night. Tell me, pet, were you angry at me for allowing you to do what you did – was it very bad of me. We should, I suppose, have waited till we were married. I shall always remember last night. Will we not often talk of our evening meetings after we are married. Why do you say in your letter – "If we are NOT married" I would not regret knowing you. Beloved, have you a doubt but that we shall be married some day. I shall write dear Mary soon. What would she say if she knew we were so intimate – lose all her good opinion of us both – would she not.

'Adieu again, my husband. God bless you and make you well. And may you yet be very, very happy with your Mimi as your little wife. Kindest love, fond embrace, and kisses from thy own true and ever devoted Mimi. Thy faithful

Wife.'

It was this absolute honesty about sex on Madeleine's part that worried the Victorians so much when her letters were read in court and then published. And it worried her lover too. One wonders, when L'Angelier's reply to Madeleine is read, who seduced whom? Once again, his letter was not read in court, because it was considered to be only a copy of a letter and there was no proof that such a letter had ever been actually sent. But it is in his handwriting, and undoubtedly it shows his feelings after the seduction and her letter.

'My dearest and beloved Wife Mimi,' he wrote, 'Since I saw you I have been wretchedly sad. Would to God we had not met that night. – I would have been happier. I am sad at what we did, I regret it very much. Why, Mimi, did you give way after your promises? My pet, it is a pity. Think of the consequences if I were never to marry you. What reproaches I should have, Mimi. I never shall be happy

24

again. If I ever meet you again, love, it must be as at first. I will never again repeat what I did until we are regularly married. Try your friends once more – tell your determination – say nothing will change you, that you have thought seriously of it – and on that I shall firmly fix speaking to Huggins for Sepr. Unless you do something of that sort, Heaven only knows when I shall marry you. Unless you do, dearest, I shall have to leave the country; truly dearest, I am in such a state of mind I do not care if I were dead. We did wrong. God forgive us for it. Mimi, we have loved blindly. It is your parents' fault if shame is the result; they are to blame for it all.'

Well, we can see that everybody was to blame but L'Angelier! However, he writes on, mixing passion with trivia in just the way that Madeleine does.

'I got home quite safe after leaving you,' he says, 'but I think I did my cold no good. I was fearfully excited the whole night. I was truly happy with you, my pet; too much so, for I am now too sad. I wish from the bottom of my heart we had never parted. Though we have sined, ask earnestly God's forgiveness and blessings that all the obstacles in our way may be removed from us. I was disappointed, my love, at the little you had to say but I can understand why. You are not stupid, Mimi, and if you disappoint me in information, and I have cause to reproach you of it, you will have no one to blame but yourself, as I have given you warning long enough to improve yourself. Sometimes I do think you take no notice of my wishes and my desires, but say yes for a mere matter of form.

'Mimi, unless Huggins helps me I cannot see how I shall be able to marry you for years. What misery to have such a future in one's mind. Do speak to your brother, open your heart to him, and try and win his friendship. Tell him if he loves you to take your part. And besides, my dear, if once you can trust, how pleasant it would be for you and me to meet. I could come over to Helensburgh when you would be

25

riding or driving, or of a Sunday (though I stoped with the Whites) I could join you in a walk of a Sunday afternoon. Mimi, dearest, you must take a bold step to be my wife. I entreat you, pet, by the love you have for me, Mimi do speak to your mother – tell her it is the last time you shall ever speak of me to her. You are right, Mimi, you cannot be the wife of any one else than me. I shall ever blame myself for what has taken place. I never never can be happy until you are my own, my dear fond wife. Oh! Mimi, be bold for once, do not fear them – tell them you are my wife before God. Do not let them leave you without being married, for I cannot answer what would happen. My conscience reproaches me of a sin that marriage can only efface . . . .

'We must not be separated at all next winter, for I know, Mimi, that you will be as giddy as last. You will be going to public balls, and that I cannot endure. On my honour, dearest, sooner than see you or hear of you running about as you did last, I would leave Glasgow myself. Though I have truly forgiven you, I do not forget the misery I endured for your sake. You know yourself how ill it made me – if not, Mary can tell you, my pet.

'Dearest Mimi, let us meet again soon, but not as last time. See if you can plan anything for the Queen's birthday. I intend to be in Helensburgh some night to cross over with Miss White to Greenock. I could refuse stoping with them, and come up to see you, but I cannot fix the day, and as I do not know how to let you know except by sending a newspaper to B/, and the evening after the date of the newspaper would be the evening I would come, or tell me a better arrangement. Do you not think it would be best to meet you at the top of the Garden, same as last Summer? Remember, if the newspaper answers be sure and repeat the arrangement, that I may see we agree.

'My dear wife, I could not take you to Lima. No European woman could live there. Besides, I would live 3 or 4 thousand miles from it, far from any white people, and no Drs. if you were ill or getting a baby. No if we marry I must stay in Glasgow until I get enough to live elsewhere. Besides, it would cost £300 alone for our bare passage money. I do not understand, my pet, your not bleeding for every woman having her virginity must bleed. You must have done so some other time. Try to remember if you never hurt yourself in washing, &c. I am sorry you felt pain. I hope you are better. I trust, dearest, you will not be— Be sure and tell me immediately you are ill next time, and if at your regular period. I was not angry at your allowing me. Mimi, but I am sad it happened. You had no resolution. We should indeed have waited till we were married, Mimi. It was very bad indeed. I shall look with regret on that night. No, nothing except our Marriage will efface it from my memory. Mimi, only fancy it was know. My dear, my pet, you would be dishonoured, and that by me! Oh! Why was I born, my pet? I dread lest some great obstacle prevents our marriage. If Mary did know it, what should you be in her eyes?

'My Sisters' names are Anastie and Elmire. I cannot help doubting your word about flirting. You promised me the same thing before you left for Edin., and you did nothing else during your stay there. You cared more for your friends than for me. I do trust you will give me no cause to find fault again with you on that score, but I doubt very much the sincerity of your promise. Mimi, the least thing I hear of you doing, that day shall be the last of our *tie*, that I swear. You are my wife, and I have the right to expect from you the behaviour of a married woman – or else you have no honour in you; and more, you have no right to go any where but where a woman could go with her husband. Oh! Mimi, let your conduct make me happy. Remember when you are good how truly happy it makes Emile – but remember this, and if you love me you will do nothing wrong. Dearest, your letter to Mary was very pretty and good. I thought a great deal of it, and I liked its seriousness. Fancy how happy I was when Mary told me the other day how Mimi was improving fast; she could tell it by her letters.'

And then, written down at the foot of the page:

'For Gods sake burn this, Mimi, for fear any thing happening to you, do dearest.'

Before we condemn L'Angelier too heartily for this odd letter, in which real feelings are hidden in priggish regret and self-abasement and blame on others are mixed with admonitions on 'improvement', we should remember that this was typical of the Victorian climate. L'Angelier was completely Victorian. Madeleine, on the other hand, could have fitted into today's society without the slightest difficulty. No wonder, as we shall see later, George Bernard Shaw liked her. Certainly, Madeleine must have been completely infatuated with L'Angelier or she would never have permitted him to lecture her like this, and especially at such a time, Tennyson Jesse suggests that Madeleine was a masochist and delighted in being L'Angelier's 'slave', for the time being.

The romance went on, but it did not last to the end of the year – on Madeleine's side, at any rate. While she was so much in love Madeleine wrote to Miss Perry, 'My dear friend, it shall be my constant endeavour to practise economy for Emile's sake. I proposed Lodgings, because I thought they would be less expensive than a house, and if there should be a little discomfort attending our residing in lodgings, we must just put up with it for a time. In time Emile's income shall increase. I dont fear but that we shall get on very well – with economy. I have taken the charge of Mama's house for the last two years.'

Eligible Bachelor Appears

The time came when dear Emile's salary was raised from 10s. a week to £1 a week, but such a flush of fortune came too late. Madeleine, having spent her sexual passion, was now disgusted with the whole affair. But still, in that lovely June of 1856, Madeleine could write to L'Angelier:

'I am longing to see you, sweet pet – to kiss and pet you. Oh! for the day when I could do so at any time. I fear we shall spoil each other when we are married, we shall be so loving and kind. We shall be so happy, happy in our own little room – no one to annoy us, to disturb us . . . . If it were not for these thoughts I should be sad, miserable, and weary of this cold, unfeeling thoughtless world. Wealth is the ruling passion. Love is a second consideration, when it should be the first, the most important . . . . True and constant shall I prove. Dont fear me. I shall be thine. Dont give ear to any reports you may hear. There are several I hear going about regarding me going to get married – regard them not. A kiss dear love from thy devoted and loving, much attached wife, thine own

Mimi.'

These reports that Madeleine mentioned had some substance. She was being courted, at a distance, by an eligible Glasgow bachelor – Billy Minnoch. Mr Minnoch moved in Glasgow society so he often met Madeleine. He had £3000 a year. James Smith approved of him highly and Mrs Smith, when she was well enough to attend to the affairs of the world, liked him too. But Madeleine still preferred her sweet pet Emile with his £1 a week.

'Oh! how I love that name of Mimi,' she wrote to him. 'You shall always call me by that name – and, dearest Emile, if ever we should have a daughter I should like you to allow me to call her Mimi for her father's sake.' And she ended this particular letter, 'I dont think I am any stouter, but you can judge when you next see me; but I must go to bed, as I feel cold – so good night. Would to God it were to be by your side – I would feel well and happy then. I think I would be wishing you to *love* me if I were with you – but I dont suppose you would refuse me. For I know you will like to *love* your Mimi. Adieu, sweet, love, kind pet husband my own true Emile. I am thine for ever, thy wife, thy devoted, thy own true

Mimi L'Angelier.'

Madeleine underscored the word 'love' three times in that letter. That shocked the Lord Justice Clerk at her trial, when he talked about the 'criminal intimacy' between the two lovers. As if defending this charge in advance, Madeleine wrote, 'Our intimacy has not been *criminal*, and I am your wife before God – so it has been no sin – our loving each other.'

But then Mr Minnoch pops up again in the correspondence. 'Minnoch was here again to-day,' wrote Madeleine to Emile from Rhu. '*Only* left on Saturday and back to-day again. He was here for four hours. He brought a fellow Weymiss with him. I think he might have a little better feeling than come so soon knowing that every one down here has heard the report regarding myself and him – even for the people on our own place. P/ and M/ were much displeased at him – they said nothing, but M/ said it was enough to make people think there was something in the report. Say nothing to him in passing – it will only make him rude if you say something.'

As the summer went on, the prospect of marriage in September grew smaller. Billy Minnoch was still paying polite addresses at Rowaleyn, but Pierre Emile L'Angelier was seeing Madeleine in the garden at night. Once more he was threatening to throw up his job with the seedsmen in Glasgow and go to England or Africa or Australia. He claimed to Madeleine that he had applied for a job in Australia and, after he left Rhu that night, she wrote:

'Would you leave me to end my days in misery. For I can never be the wife of another after our intimacy. But, sweet love, I do not regret that – never did, and never shall. Emile, you were not pleased because I would not let you *love* me last night. Your last visit you said "You would not do it again till we were married." I said to myself at the time well, I shall not let Emile do this again. It was a punishment to myself to be deprived of your *loving me*, for it is a pleasure, no one can deny that. It is but human nature. Is it not every one that *loves* of the same mind? Yes, I did feel so ashamed after you left of having allowed you to see (any name you please to insert). But as you said at the time, I was your wife.'

Well, Emile might be tasting some of the joys of love, but Minnoch was really winning the day. Madeleine's letters to L'Angelier started to cool off. The protestations of undying love did not seem so spontaneous. And in one letter she wrote, 'I did tell you at one time that I did not like William Minnoch, but he was so pleasant that he quite raised himself in my estimation. I wrote to his sisters to see if they would come and visit us next week, also him, but they can not.'

Then, at the end of September, she wrote again from Rhu:

'What cold weather we have had. Mr. Minnoch has been here since Friday – he is most agreeable – I think – we shall see him very often this winter – he says we shall – and P/ being so fond of him I am sure he shall ask him often.' There is a P.S. to this letter which says, 'I have just got word of the death of my old sweetheart in Edr. for which I am not in the least sorry – love again to you sweet love. Adieu, ever yours,

Mimi.'

Madeleine was ruthless as well as romantic. We shall see what happened when she got word of the death of her Glasgow sweetheart. And sixty years later she could not even remember his Christian name. When she discussed her case with H. B. Irving, she referred to her sweet pet, Emile, as Louis!

Her reference to seeing Billy Minnoch very often was certainly justified. James Smith had decided to give up their house in India Street and flit to fashionable Blythswood Square, a garden surrounded by terrace houses. He had taken No. 7 Blythswood Square, which looked much more imposing from the outside than it really was. There was a fine pillared entrance up a flight of stairs and anyone seeing the house would assume that the basement, the ground floor and the two storeys above were all the Smiths' house. In fact, James Smith owned only the ground floor and the basement. Round the corner in Mains Street there was a close entrance which led to the two flats above. And the first flat belonged to Billy Minnoch.

There really wasn't too much accommodation for the Smith family of seven and their three servants, and once again Madeleine and Janet had to share a bedroom, this time in the basement, along with the servants.

L'Angelier, by the way, had changed his dwelling too: he had left the grey house in the Botanic Gardens and now had a room with a Mrs Jenkins in Franklin Place, part of Great Western Road near St George's Cross. It was much nearer Madeleine's home than the house in Botanic Gardens.

To 11 Franklin Place Madeleine wrote a letter from Rowaleyn on a day in October. The opening of that letter tells its meaning clearly.

'My dear Emile,

'The day is cold so I shall not go out – so I shall spend a little time in writing you. Our meeting last night was peculiar. Emile you are not reasonable. I do not wonder at your not loving me as you once did. Emile I am not worthy of you. You deserve a better wife than I. I see misery before me this winter. I would to God we were not to be so near to Mr. M. You shall hear all stories and believe them. You will say I am indifferent because I shall not be able to see you much . . . .

'Our letters I dont see how I am to do. M. will watch every post. I intended to speak to you of all this last night – but we were so engaged otherways. I do hope that you got home safe, and that you have got no cold – tell me love. I could not sleep all night. I thought of your unhappy appearance – you shed tears love – but I did not. Yes, you must think me cool – but it is my nature. I never did love anyone till I loved you – and I shall never love another.

Love, Emile, my sweet darling, causes unhappiness in more ways than one. I know you will, I feel sure you will, quarrel with me this winter . . . .

'I sometimes fancy you are disappointed with me. I am not what you once thought I was. I am too much of a child to please you. I am too fond of amusement to suit your fancy. I am too indifferent, and I do not mind what the world says, not on the least – I never did.'

And Madeleine never did, not once up to her death at the age of ninety-two. She was truly William Roughead's 'prodigious damsel'. But in this letter she was still trying to wriggle out of her liaison with L'Angelier.

'I promised to marry you knowing I would never have my father's consent,' she went on. 'I would be obliged to marry you in a clandestine way. I knew you were poor. All these I did not mind. I trust we have days of happiness before us – but God knows we have days of misery too. Emile, my own, my ever dear husband, I have suffered much on your account from my family. They have laughed at my love for you – they taunted me regarding you. I was watched all last winter. I was not allowed out by myself for fear I should meet you – but if I can I shall cheat them this winter. I shall avoid you at first, and that may cause them to allow me out myself. I shall write to you as often as I can – but it cannot be three times a week as it has been . . . .

'I have come to the conclusion that you do not know me. If you were with me long you would know me better – it is only those I love that I am indifferent too – even my Dog – which I love – sometimes I hate it, and for no reason – it is only a fancy which I cannot help.'

And then the Smiths moved up to their new house in Blythswood Square, and Madeleine discovered a way to keep the correspondence going. You'll recollect that her problem was to *receive* letters. They would be noticed in the post. She saw that the basement bedroom she shared with

Janet had two windows facing on to Mains (now Blyths-wood) Street. These windows were set very low on the street level, and part of them were under that level. They were protected by bars. Madeleine worked out that Emile could drop a letter behind these bars and she could open the window and get hold of it. In her correspondence with Emile she was now blowing hot and cold. The love affair for her was ending, but it still had its moments.

'Sweet love,' she wrote, 'I have thought more of you for this last fortnight than I ever did – you are my constant thought. Emile is the only name ever on my lips. A fond embrace, sweet darling. Did you go to the concert? . . . I looked at every one but could not see my husband. Mr. M. was there with his horrid old sister – but I only bowed to them. I have not seen any of them yet. I dont understand why P/ has not asked him to dinner yet.'

'Mr. M', of course, was Billy Minnoch. Madeleine goes on to improve on the letter arrangement.

'Sweet love,' she says again, 'you should get those brown envelopes – they would not be so much seen as white ones put down into my window. You should just stoop down to tie your shoe, and then slip it in . . . .

'Well, dearest love of a husband, I am going to bid you goodnight. Would you were beside me, and I would fall asleep on your bosom, dearest love. What would I not give to place my head on your breast, kiss and fondel you – and then I am sure you would kindly *love* me – but some night I hope soon we may enjoy each other – what delightful happiness to be *loved* by a dear, sweet husband – our love then shall be more than we shall be able to express. I can fancy the first night we spend in each other's arms. Emile, my love, my all, my husband, if you were here now I am sure I would allow you to *love* me – I could not resist you, my love, my own beloved Emile. I have been ordered by the Dr. since I came to town to take a fearful thing called "Peice

Meal'', such a nasty thing, I am to take at Luncheon. I dont
think I have tasted breakfast for two months. But I dont
think I can take this Meal. I shall rather take Cocoa. But
dearest love, fond embraces much love and kisses from your
devoted wife. Your loving and affet. wife,

Mini L'Angelier.'

And, indeed, Madeleine became quite attached to cocoa.
Her bedroom was near the kitchen so it was easy for her to
get some hot water and mix the cocoa in her room.
L'Angelier not only 'posted' notes to her down the window.
He would also wait at the window in the winter darkness
and talk with Madeleine once Janet was safe asleep. Now
and then it was so cold in the street outside that Madeleine
made cocoa and passed a cup through the window to her
shivering swain. One remarkable fact was that the two
windows of her bedroom were next door to the entrance to
Billy Minnoch's flat, and yet the rivals never seem to have
met.

L'Angelier did find it necessary to give cigars to the
policeman on the Blythswood Square beat, and that officer
turned a blind eye to the goings on. Likely he thought that
L'Angelier was an admirer of one of the servants in the
Smith household, for usually it was only servants who slept
in the basement.

Madeleine made the point herself when she warned
L'Angelier, 'I hope no one sees you – and, darling, make no
noise at the window. You mistake me. The snobs I spoke off
do not know anything of me. They see a light, and they
fancy it may be the servants room, and they may have some
fun – only you know that I sleep down stairs – I never told
any one, so dont knock again my beloved, but dearest love,
good night.'

But in spite of the promises she gave to L'Angelier,
Madeleine was still the belle of the ball, the reigning beauty
at the theatre and the concert hall. Sweet pet Emile, always

35

ready with an admonition or an accusation, had plenty of ammunition:

'I wept for hours after I received your letter, and this day I have been sad, yes very sad. My Emile, I love you, and only you. I have tried to assure you no other has a place in my heart. It was Minnoch that (I) was at the concert with. You see I would not hide that from you. Emile he is P's friend, and I know he will have him at the house. But need you mind that when I have told you I have no regard for him. It is only you, my Emile, that I love – you should not mind public report.'

But soon after that she is writing 'You would be annoyed at M/ going to the concert with me – I was, for I knew it would vex you, but all this annoyance will soon end, so, darling, dont vex yourself about them. I am glad you promised me not to say anything to him – and you will ask no one to speak to him for you, you know, dear, it would all come back on your wife, so I know, sweet love, you wont annoy him.'

Seats for 'Lucrezia Borgia'

Madeleine's double life was becoming more and more difficult. By now there was what the Victorians called an 'understanding' between her and Billy Minnoch. But at the same time she was allowing L'Angelier to think that they were going to elope and be secretly married. Now and then, when Papa and Mama were out of the way, L'Angelier was let into the Blythswood Square house, either by the back or the area door under the front stairs. And once, at least, he was in the Smith's drawing-room, alone with Madeleine.

By January, 1857, Madeleine's letters were getting shorter and cooler. She introduced Billy Minnoch's name quite frequently, obviously to forestall complaints by L'Angelier. In one letter, written in the middle of that month, she says, 'Mr. M/ dined with us tonight – do you know I think if you knew him you would like him, he is most kind. I like him very much better than I used to do.'

And yet in another letter she writes:

'Emile, my own beloved, you have just left me. Oh, sweet darling, at this moment my heart and soul burns with love for thee, my husband, my own sweet one. Emile, what would I not give at this moment to be your fond wife. My night dress was on when you saw me. Would to God you had been in the same attire . . . . I never felt so restless and so unhappy as I have done for some time past. I would do anything to keep sad thoughts from my mind. But in whatever place some things make me feel sad. A dark spot is in the future. What can it be. Oh God keep it from us. Oh may we be happy – dear darling, pray for our happiness. I weep, now, Emile, to think of our fate. If we could only get married, and all would be well. But alas, alas, I see no chance, no chance of happiness for me.'

That letter was written on January 23rd, 1857. On January 28th Madeleine accepted Billy Minnoch's proposal of marriage. The rest of the Smith family were delighted.

Madeleine could not bring herself to tell the truth to L'Angelier. But she chose the first possible opportunity to break off her engagement with him. Her letters grew colder and colder, and then he sent one back to her. Early in February she wrote:

'I felt truly astonished to have my last letter returned to me. But it will be the last you shall have the opportunity of returning to me. When you are not pleased with the letters I send you, then our correspondence shall be at an end, and as there is coolness on both sides our engagement had better be broken. This may astonish you, but you have more than once returned me my letters, and my mind was made up that I should not stand the same thing again. And you also annoyed me much on Saturday by your conduct in coming so near me. Altogether I think owing to coolness and

37

indifference (nothing else) that we had better for the future consider ourselves as strangers. I trust to your honour as a Gentleman that you will not reveal anything that may have passed between us. I shall feel obliged by your bring me my letters and Likeness on Thursday eveng. at 7 – be at the Area Gate, and C.H. will [take] the parcel from you. On Friday night I shall send you all your letters, Likeness, &ca. I trust you may yet be happy, and get one more worthy of you than I. On Thursday at 7 o.'C. I am &c.

M.

'You may be astonished at this sudden change – but for some time back you must have noticed a coolness in my notes. My love for you has ceased, and that is why I was cool. I did once love you truly, fondly, but for some time back I have lost much of that love. There is no other reason for my conduct, and I think it but fair to let you know this. I might have gone on and become your wife, but I could not have loved you as I ought. My conduct you will condemn, but I did at one time love you with heart and soul. It has cost me much to tell you this – sleepless nights, but it is necessary you should know. If you should remain in Glasgow or go away, I hope you may succeed in all your endeavours. I know you will never injure the character of one you so fondly loved. No Emile, I know you have honour and are a Gentleman. What has passed you will not mention. I know when I ask you that you will comply. Adieu.'

Well, that letter was as fine a piece of wishful thinking as one can imagine. But Madeleine's wish did not come true. No L'Angelier appeared at the area door. And no letter explained his non-appearance. On February 9th she wrote again:

'I attribute it to your having cold that I had no answer to my last note. On Thursday evening you were, I suppose, afraid of the night air. I fear your cold is not better, I again appoint Thursday night first same place, Street Gate, 7 o'c.

M.

'If you can not send me or bring me the parcel on Thursday, please write a note saying when you shall bring it, and address it to C.H. Send it by post.' [C.H. was Christina Haggart].

This time sweet pet Emile did reply. He told Madeleine that he regarded her as his wife and that he would show her letters to her father to prove it. While she had burned almost all of his letters, he had kept most of hers, and particularly those which proved the 'criminal intimacy' between them. Madeleine, in a desperate situation, wrote desperately:

'Monday Night. – Emile, I have just had your note. Emile, for the love you once had for me do nothing till I see you – for God's sake do not bring your once loved Mini to an open shame. Emile, I have deceived you. I have deceived my Mother. God knows she did not boast of any thing I had said of you – for she, poor woman, thought I had broken off with you last Winter. I deceived you by telling you she still knew of our engagement. She did not. This I now confess – and as for wishing for an engagement with another, I do not fancy she ever thought of it. Emile, write to no one, to Papa or any other. Oh, do not till I see you. On Wednesday night – be at the Hamiltons at 12, and I shall open my Shutter, and then you come to the Area Gate, I shall see you.

'It would break my Mother's heart. Oh, Emile, be not harsh to me. I am the most guilty, miserable wretch on the face of the earth. Emile, do not drive me to death. When I ceased to love you, believe me, it was not to love another. I am free from all engagements at present. Emile, for God's sake do not send my letters to Papa. It will be an open rupture. I will leave the house. I will die. Emile, do nothing till I see you. One word to-morrow night at my window to tell me or I shall go mad.

'Tuesday morning. – I am ill. God knows what I have suffered. My punishment is more than I can bear. Do nothing till I see you, for the love of heaven do nothing. I am mad, I am ill.'

39

To this heart-rending cry L'Angelier did reply. He did not appear at Madeleine's window, but at some time during the evening he left a note to say that he would do nothing until he saw her the following night. So at midnight she wrote:

'Emile, I have this night received your note. Oh, it is kind of you to write to me. Emile, no one can know the intense agony of mind I have suffered last night and to-day. Emile, my father's wrath would kill me; you little know his temper. Emile for the love you once had for me do not denounce me to my P/. Emile, if he should read my letters to you – he will put me from him, he will hate me as a guilty wretch. I loved you, and wrote to you in my first ardent love – it was with my deepest love I loved you. It was for your love I adored you. I put on paper what I should not. I was free, because I loved you with my heart. If he or any other one saw those fond letters to you, what would not be said of me. On my bended knees I write you, and ask you as you hope for mercy at the Judgment do not inform on me – do not make me a public shame.'

And so poor Madeleine writes on, page after page, repeating herself, imploring and occasionally writing something more than usually revealing:

'I did love you,' she says, 'and it was my soul's ambition to be your wife. I asked you to tell me my faults. You did so, and it made me cool towards you gradually. When you have found fault with me I have cooled – it was not love for another, for there is no one I love.'

Was she slightly drunk when she wrote this letter? She says, 'I grow mad. I have been ill, very ill, all day. I have had what has given me a false spirit. I had to resort to what I should not have taken, but my brain is on fire. I feel as if death indeed would be sweet.'

But she didn't make clear whose death. What she did,

however, the very next day was to ask the Smith's page boy, William Murray, to get her some prussic acid. She gave him a note saying 'A small phial of prussic acid', and said she wanted it for her hands. Young Murray went to Dr Yeaman's surgery in Sauchiehall Street, but the man behind the counter, after asking who wanted it, told Murray to tell his mistress that she could not get it without a physician's line, for it was rank poison. When the page boy conveyed this message to Madeleine, she just said, 'Very well, never mind.'

That was on Wednesday, February 11th, and it's odd that on the very same day L'Angelier started to keep a sort of diary in a little pocket-book. The diary was produced in court at Madeleine's trial but, like the other writings of L'Angelier that I have mentioned, it was not allowed in evidence. If it had been, the result of the trial might have been quite different.

The first entry reads:

Wed. 11 Feb.—Dined at Mr J. Mitchell's
Saw M. at 12 p.m.
In C.H. Room

And there, in Christina Haggart's room, the great rec-onciliation took place. We know it was a reconciliation (in L'Angelier's view, at all events) because of the way that Madeleine started writing again.

The next entries in L'Angelier's diary are:

Thurs. 12 Feb. – Spent the Even at Pat Kennedy's
Major Stuart and Wife
D. Jameson & family

Frid. 13th Feb. – Saw Mr Phillpot
Mimi
dined at 144 Renfrew St.

That last address was Miss Perry's, of course, and we

may be sure that Emile told the sweethearts' confidante all about the troubles.

Then comes the diary entry:

Sat. 14 Feb. – a letter from M.

And here, sure enough, is the letter:

'Saturday. – My Dear Emile,
    'I have got my finger cut, and can not write, so dear, I wish you would excuse me. I was glad to see you looking so well yesterday. I hope to see you very soon . . . . Write me for next Thursday, and then I shall tell you when I can see you. I want the first time we meet, that you will bring me all my cool letters back – the last four I have written – and I will give you others in their place.
    'Bring them all to me. excuse me more; just now it hurts to write, so with kindest and dearest love, ever believe, yours with love and affection,

M.'

On Tuesday, February 17th, L'Angelier dined once again with Miss Perry at Renfrew Street, and told her than his next meeting with Madeleine was to be on Thursday. And his diary records:

Thurs. 19 Feb. – Saw Mimi
            a few moments
            was very ill during the night

That means he must have seen Madeleine after she had returned from the Opera. On that evening Billy Minnoch took Madeleine and his sister to the theatre. Many years later Sir Compton Mackenzie, working on the script for the film, *Madeleine*, thought it would be interesting to find out what opera Madeleine had seen that night. He asked the help of the late John Dunlop of the Mitchell Library in Glasgow. John Dunlop studied a newspaper for that very night and discovered that Mr Minnoch had taken Miss Madeleine Smith to *Lucrezia Borgia*.

Emile is Unwell

Now, as I have said, L'Angelier lodged with a Mrs Ann Jenkins at 11 Franklin Place, which is about a quarter-hour's walk from Blythswood Square. Mrs Jenkins liked her lodger and she noted that he received a great many letters. The envelopes were inscribed in such a dashing style that she thought they were from a man. But she learned that L'Angelier had an 'intended' and hoped to marry her, and she concluded that these letters were from a woman. L'Angelier kept regular habits, but sometimes he said he was going to be out late, and Mrs Jenkins would give him a key of the flat.

Later in court Mrs Jenkins was to say she couldn't be sure of the date, but it was somewhere about the middle of February and before the 22nd, when she knocked at L'Angelier's door about eight in the morning and got no answer. She knocked a second time, and he said, 'Come in, if you please.' He was still in bed and said, 'I have been very unwell. Look what I have vomited.'

'I think that's bile,' said Mrs Jenkins, looking at the greenish substance. 'Why did you not call on me?'

'On the road coming home,' replied L'Angelier, 'I was seized with a violent pain in my bowels and stomach, and when I was taking off my clothes I lay down upon the carpet. I thought I would have died, and no human eye would have seen me. I was not able to ring the bell.'

After a rest and some tea, and a visit from his fellow lodger, a real Frenchman, L'Angelier recovered sufficiently to go out to see a doctor. The doctor gave him a bottle of medicine, which must have been wonderful stuff for he was able to write in his diary:

Frid. 20 Feb. – Passed two pleasant hours
        with M. in the Drawing Room

The following morning Miss Madeleine Smith left the house in Blythswood Square and took a four minutes' walk

43

to Murdoch Brothers, druggists, in Sauchiehall Street. One Brother, George, was in a backroom when an assistant came in and said a lady wanted to buy sixpenceworth of arsenic. So George Murdoch went out to the counter, recognised Miss Smith and they bowed politely to each other. Mr Murdoch explained that she would have to sign a book and asked what she needed the arsenic for.

'For the garden and country house,' replied Madeleine. Mr. Murdoch knew that Mr Smith had a country house on the Gareloch, so he told his assistant to make up an ounce of arsenic. Madeleine signed the book and left the arsenic to be charged to her father's account, and sent by Blythswood Square along with two dozen bottles of soda water.

L'Angelier's diary entry for that day reads:

> Sat. 21 Feb. – don't feel well
>   went to T. F. Kennedy's

On the day after Madeleine bought the arsenic, L'Angelier entered this in his diary:

> Sun. 22 Feb. – Saw Mimi in Drawing Room
>   Promised me French Bible
>   Taken very ill

About four o'clock on Monday morning L'Angelier rang the bell in his room at 11 Franklin Place. When Mrs Jenkins went in he was vomiting the same kind of stuff as he had before. He complained of the same pains, but added that he was terribly thirsty and that he felt cold. Amadée Thuau, the other lodger, went for a doctor later in the morning and this doctor prescribed powders for the bile.

L'Angelier was well enough to write to his Mimi on Tuesday and tell her of his mysterious illness. On her part, Madeleine paid a return visit to George Murdoch, druggist, and asked if arsenic should not be white. Mr Murdoch explained that the law required him to mix arsenic with some colouring material. At Murdoch's they mixed white arsenic with soot. Madeleine thanked him for the information and went out without buying anything.

Next day she wrote:

'Dearest, Sweet Emile,

'I am sorry to hear you are ill. I hope to god you will soon be better – take care of yourself – do not go to the office this week – just stay at home till Monday. Sweet love it will please me to hear you are well. I have not felt very well these last two days – sick & headache. Every one is complaining: it must be something in the air. I cannot see you Friday, as M/ is not away – but I think Sunday P/ will be away, & I might see you, I think, but I shall let you know. I shall not be at home on Saturday, but I shall try, sweet love, and give you, even if it should be a word. I cannot pass your windows, or I would, as you ask me to do it – do not come and walk about and become ill again.

'You did look bad Sunday night and Monday morning. I think you got sick with walking home so late – and the long want of food, so the next time we meet I shall make you eat a loaf of bread before you go out. I am longing to meet again, sweet love. We shall be so happy. I have a bad pen – excuse this scroll, and B/ is near me. I cannot write at night now. My head aches so, and I am looking so bad that I cannot sit up as I used to do – but I am taking some stuff to bring back the colour. I shall see you soon again. Put up with short notes for a little time. When I feel stronger you shall have long ones. Adieu my love my pet my sweet Emile. A fond dear tender love and sweet embrace. Ever with love,

Yours, Mini.'

Now the Smith family were planning to go for a holiday to Bridge of Allan. Madeleine's fiancée, Billy Minnoch, was to visit them there, and it was understood that the happy date, as Victorian ladies said, would be fixed.

L'Angelier was invited to tea by Miss Perry on March 2nd, and she was surprised to see him looking so ill. His first words were, 'Well, I never expected to have seen you again,

45

I was so ill.' She understood from what he said that he was talking about an illness he had had on February 19th, and he mentioned that it was a cup of chocolate that had made him ill. But he didn't say he had seen Madeleine then, nor where he had got the cup of chocolate.

A week later he had tea with Miss Perry again, and again he talked of Madeline and his illnesses. This time he said, 'I can't think why I was so unwell after getting that coffee and chocolate from her.' And he went on to talk of his love for Madeleine and added, 'It is a perfect fascination, my attachment to that girl. If she were to poison me, I would forgive her.'

'You ought not to allow such thoughts to pass through your mind,' Miss Perry scolded. 'What motive could she have for giving you anything to hurt you?'

'I don't know that,' said L'Angelier. 'Perhaps she might not be sorry to be rid of me.'

Months later, recollecting this conversation, Miss Perry said she didn't think L'Angelier meant this in a sinister sense. She thought he meant that Madeleine would not be sorry to break off her engagement to him.

There had been three significant letters between Madeleine-Mimi-Mini and her sweet pet between L'Angelier's two dates for tea with Miss Perry. First, Madeleine wrote on March 4th:

'Dearest Emile,

'I have just time to give you a line. I could not come to the window as B/ and M/ were there, but I saw you. If you would take my advice, you would go to the south of England for ten days: it would do you much good. In fact, sweet pet, it would make you feel quite well. Do try and do this. You will please me by getting strong and well again.

'I hope you wont go to B. of Allan, as P/ and M/ would say it was I brought you there, and it would make me to feel very unhappy. Stirling you need not go to as it is a nasty dirty little Town. Go to the Isle of Wight. I am exceedingly sorry, love, I cannot see you ere I go – it is impossible, but the first thing I do on my return will be to see you, sweet love. I must stop as it is post time. So adieu, with love, and kisses, and much love.

'I am, with love and affection, ever yours,

Mini.'

To this rather odd epistle, L'Angelier replied right away:

'Glasgow, March 5th, 1857.

'My dear, sweet pet Mimi,

'I feel indeed very vexed that the answer I recd. yesterday to mine of Tuesday to you should prevent me from sending the kind letter I had ready for you. You must not blame me, dear, for this, but really your cold indifferent, and reserved notes, so short, without a particle of love in them (especially after pledging your word you were to write me kindly for those letters you asked me to destroy), and the manner you *evaded* answering the question I put to you in my last, with the reports I hear, fully convince me, Mimi, that there is foundation in your marriage with another; besides, the way you put off our union till September without a just reason is very suspicious. I do not think, Mimi dear, that Mrs Anderson would say your mother told her things she had not, and really I could never believe Mr Houldsworth would be guilty of telling a *falsehood* for mere talking.'

Here L'Angelier was referring to close friends of Billy Minnoch's – indeed, Billy was in partnership with Mr Houldsworth. So we can well imagine what they had been saying.

'No, Mimi,' L'Angelier continued, 'there is a foundation for all this. You often go to Mr M/s house, and common sense would lead any one to believe that if you were not on the footing reports say you are you would avoid going near any of his friends. I know he goes with you, or at least meets you in Stirlingshire. Mimi, dear, place yourself in my position and tell me I am wrong in believing what I hear. I was

47

happy the last time we met – yes, very happy. I was forgetting all the past, but now it is again beginning.

'Mimi, I insist in having an *explicit* answer to the questions you evaded in my last. If you evade answering them this time, I must try some other means of coming to the truth. If not answered in a satisfactory manner, you must not expect I shall again write you personally or meet you when you return home. I do not wish you to answer this at random. I shall wait a day or so if you require it. I know you cannot write me from Stirlingshire, as the time you have to write me a letter is occupied in doing so to others. There was a time you would have found plenty of time.

'Answer me this, Mimi – Who gave you the trinket you showed me. Is it true it was Mr Minnoch. And is it true you are, directly or indirectly, engaged to Mr Minnoch or to any one else but me. These questions I must know.

'The doctor says I must go to B. of A. I cannot travel 500 miles to the I. of W. and 500 back. What is your object in wishing me so very much to go south. I may not go to B. of A. till Wednesday; if I can avoid going I shall do so for your sake. I shall wait to hear from you. I hope, dear, nothing will happen to check the happiness we were again enjoying. May God bless you, Pet, and with many fond and tender embraces believe me with kind love your ever affte. husband,

Emile L'Angelier.'

Madeleine had a busy twenty-four hours after she received that letter. In that time she replied to L'Angelier, bought more arsenic and shepherded her mother and two sisters to Bridge of Allan.

First, her letter:

'My sweet, dear pet,

'I am so sorry you should be so vexed – believe nothing, sweet one, till I tell you myself – it is a report I am sorry about – but it has been six months spoken of. There is one of the same kind about B.'

B. was Bessie, the sister next to Madeleine in age. Poor Bessie was always being dragged into Madeleine's correspondence, usually to show how much superior Emile's Mimi was in every way.

'I wish, love, you could manage to remain in town till we come home, as I know it will be a grand row with me if you are seen there. Could you, sweet love, not wait for my sake till we come home. You might go the 20th or so. I would be so pleased with you if you can do this to please me, my own dear beloved. I shall be very glad to meet you again, and have as happy a meeting as the last.

'I have only been in M/s house once, and that was this week – and I was sent a message because M/ could not go herself. I will tell and answer you all questions when we meet. Adieu, dearest love of my soul – with fond and tender embraces, ever believe me, with love and kisses, to be your own fond, dear, and lovingMini.

'If you do not go to B. of A. till we come home – come up Main St. to-morrow morning, and if you go come your own way.'

Madeleine certainly had a busy Friday. So busy that she was late for her appointment with an old school friend, Mary Jane Buchanan, daughter of Dr Buchanan of Dunbarton. When they were at school in Clapton they had agreed that whichever of them was engaged to be married first was to ask the other to be her bridesmaid. So Madeleine had written to Mary Jane to call at 7 Blythswood Square because she was engaged and the probable date of the wedding was in June.

Mary Jane kept the appointment all right, but Madeleine was out, and she did not return to Blythswood Square until 1.30 p.m., by which time Mary Jane said she had to be going home. So Madeleine suggested that they should walk together from Blythswood Square along Sauchiehall Street in the direction of Dumbarton.

49

When the two girls reached Charing Cross Madeleine said, 'Oh, just stop a minute. I want to go into this shop. Will you go with me?' Mary Jane realised they were outside Currie the chemist. She agreed and in they went. Madeleine asked if she could buy some arsenic and the shop assistant said she must sign for it. 'Oh, I'll sign anything you like,' said Madeleine.

Mary Jane asked Madeleine what she was going to do with arsenic and Madeleine replied that she wanted it to kill rats. The shop assistant said he thought phosphorus would do, but Madeleine said no, she had tried that before and it was unsuccessful. She preferred arsenic and, as the family were going to Bridge of Allan, there was no danger of leaving it lying about the town house as it would be put down in the cellars.

'Would sixpenceworth be a large quantity?' she asked the assistant. He replied that it would kill a great many people, and Madeleine turned to Mary Jane and said, 'but I only want it for rats.'

She signed the book and took the arsenic with her. Mary Jane laughed as they left the shop at the idea of a young lady buying arsenic. Madeleine said nothing, but she laughed too.

And we permit ourselves a wry smile, because there were no rats at 7 Blythswood Square. There *were* rats at Rowaleyn, but they had been dealt with successfully with phosphorus paste. Also Madeleine had not revealed that she already knew what sixpenceworth of arsenic was like, because she had bought it at Murdoch's, farther east along Sauchiehall Street. I can only imagine that Madeleine had changed her shop for arsenic because she had found Murdoch's arsenic didn't do the job to her satisfaction, and also she didn't like arsenic mixed with soot. Currie's arsenic was mixed with indigo.

Well, off went Madeleine to Bridge of Allan with her arsenic. She did not know whether L'Angelier was going to try to see her there or not, but he had passed the Smith

house on Friday morning and you'll recollect Mimi's P.S:
'If you do not go to B. of A. till we come home – come up
Main Street to-morrow morning . . . .'

L'Angelier kept his word. Instead of going straight to
Bridge of Allan, he went to Edinburgh on March 10th for a
few days. If he *had* gone to Bridge of Allan, he might have
been fortunate enough to see Billy Minnoch around the
village. For, on March 12th, Billy and Madeleine arranged
the date of their marriage, the 18th of June.

She had forgotten, no doubt, that she had once written,
'I used to say there were three things I would like to do, first
to run off, second to marry a Frenchman, and three that I
would not marry a man unless he had a moustache.'

This was to be a church wedding, and Billy Minnoch was
decidedly Scots and clean-shaven.

Three days later Madeleine wrote a love letter to her
fiancé, William Minnoch, Esq., 124 St Vincent Street,
Glasgow:

'My dearest William,

'It is but fair, after your kindness to me, that I should
write you a note. The day I part from friends, I always feel
sad. But to part from one I love, as I do you, makes me feel
truly sad and dull. My only consolation is that we may meet
soon. To-morrow we shall be home. I do so wish you were
here to-day. We might take a long walk. Our walk to
Dumblane I shall ever remember with pleasure. That walk
fixed a day on which we are to begin a new life – a life which
I hope may be of happiness and long duration to both of us.
My aim through life shall be to please you and study you.
Dear William, I must conclude, as Mama is ready to go to
Stirling. I do not go with the same pleasure as I did the last
time. I hope you got to Town safe, and found your sisters
well. Accept my warmest kindest love and ever believe me
to be, yours with affecn.,
Monday, Prospect Villa

Madeleine.'

I'm sure that Billy thought Madeleine wrote a very good letter, even if she couldn't spell Dunblane.

And what was sweet pet Emile doing on this happy day for his Mimi? He was visiting Miss Perry's married sister at Portobello. She and her husband had invited him to dinner, but he was not a very good companion. She said afterwards that L'Angelier talked about his health almost the whole time he was with them. And Mr Towers, her husband, recollected that L'Angelier said he had had two attacks of biliousness or jaundice after taking coffee or cocoa. L'Angelier also said he thought he had been poisoned after taking the cocoa and coffee. When Mr Towers asked who would be likely to poison him and why, L'Angelier dropped the subject.

The following day, St Patrick's Day, 1857, L'Angelier left Edinburgh and returned to 11 Franklin Place, and Madeleine left Bridge of Allan and returned to 7 Blythswood Square. The first thing L'Angelier did was to ask Mrs Jenkins if she had got a letter for him. He was very disappointed when she said she had not. He told Mrs Jenkins he'd wait a day and then go to Bridge of Allan.

Next day L'Angelier spent quietly at home, but the awaited letter did not arrive. On her part, Madeleine paid a return visit to Currie's, the Chemists at Charing Cross. She was attended by the same young shop assistant who had sold her sixpenceworth of arsenic when Mary Jane Buchanan was with her. Madeleine told him she wanted another sixpenceworth because it was so good for her purpose – she had found eight or nine large rats lying dead in the basement in Blythswood Square. Mr Currie himself interposed. He wasn't keen on selling arsenic, but when Haliburton, the assistant, explained that Miss Smith had already had some arsenic, Mr Currie, seeing what he described as 'her apparent respectability and frankness', said it was all right.

Mimi and Emile had not written to each other for nearly a fortnight, and Madeleine thought that L'Angelier was still in Glasgow. She didn't know he had been to Edinburgh and was now proposing to go to Bridge of Allan. So, on March 19th she wrote to him, but he had left for his spa before the letter arrived. Mrs Jenkins took it and gave it to Amadée Thuau, who re-addressed it to L'Angelier at Bridge of Allan.

He got it next day and wrote to Miss Perry:

'Bridge of Allan, 20th March.'

'Dear Mary,

I should have written to you before, but I am so lazy writing when away from my ordinary ways. I feel much better, and I hope to be home the middle of next week.

'This is a very stupid place, very dull. I know no one; and besides, it is so very much colder than Edin. I saw your friends at Portobello, and will tell you about them when I see you.

'I should have come to see some one last night, but the letter came too late, so we are both disappointed. Trusting you are quite well, and with kind regards to yourself and sister, Believe me, yours sincerely,

P. Emile L'Angelier.

'I shall be here till Wednesday.'

But the next time Miss Perry was to see her youthful friend he was dead.

The Hidden Hours

Back in Glasgow, on Saturday, March 21st, Mrs Jenkins got another letter for L'Angelier, in the same handwriting as the one on Thursday. Again she handed it to Thuau, and again Thuau re-addressed it to Bridge of Allan.

Mrs Jenkins remembered that, when he left for Bridge of Allan, L'Angelier had said, 'If I get a letter I may be back tonight.' Nevertheless, she was surprised to see her lodger about 8 p.m. on the Sunday. When she asked why he had come home, he said, 'The letter you sent me brought me

home.' He also asked when the letter had arrived, and said
he had walked fifteen miles in getting back from Bridge of
Allan to Glasgow. Then L'Angelier had some tea and toast.
After which he changed his country coat for a town one and
put on his Balmoral.

'If you please,' he said to Mrs Jenkins, 'give me the pass-
key. I am not sure but I may be late.'

She gave him the key and about nine o'clock out he went.
Just at that time the Smith family and their servants were
settling down to family prayers in the drawing-room of 7
Blythswood Square. L'Angelier strolled down from Franklin
Place to Charing Cross, and there he was seen by a man
who knew him by sight only. L'Angelier was dawdling. He
seemed to want to waste time. About 9.20 p.m. he called at
a lodging house in Terrace Street, which once ran between
Bothwell Street and St Vincent Street and was about five
minutes' walk from Blythswood Square. He asked for a Mr
McAlester, who lodged there, but Mr McAlester was not at
home. L'Angelier waited for a moment, as if he would like
to be asked in to wait, but the servant didn't ask him in, and
off he went.

Where did he go from there? No one knows. We can think
what we like, but five hours of L'Angelier's life are completely hidden from us. The next thing we know for a fact is
that the efficient Mrs Jenkins was wakened in her flat at 11
Franklin Place by the door bell ringing 'with great violence'.
The time was 2.30 a.m. Mrs Jenkins threw on her dressing-
gown, went to the front door and called, 'Who's there?'
L'Angelier's voice replied, 'It is I, Mrs Jenkins. Open the
door, if you please.'

L'Angelier was almost bent double. He was clutching his
stomach and he groaned, 'I am very bad. I'm going to have
another vomiting of that bile.' Mrs Jenkins helped him to
his room and he said, 'I thought I never would have got
home, I was so bad on the road.' Then he asked for some
water. Mrs Jenkins gave him a tumbler full and he drank it
empty. He said he thought some tea might help him.

By the time Mrs Jenkins came back with the tea, L'Angelier was half undressed and very ill indeed. He complained of being cold and Mrs Jenkins put hot water jars to his stomach and his feet and covered him with several blankets. About four o'clock in the morning he was so ill that Mrs Jenkins said she would go for his doctor, but L'Angelier said it would be too much trouble for her. At five o'clock, however, he was again so ill that she insisted on going for the nearest doctor, Dr Steven. But when she called, she found that Dr Steven himself was ill. When she explained L'Angelier's symptoms to him. Dr Steven said she was to give him twenty-five drops of laudanum and put a mustard blister on his stomach. When she got back, L'Angelier said he couldn't take laudanum and a mustard blister would be of no use.

By seven o'clock he was so in pain that the kind Mrs Jenkins went for Dr Steven again. This time the doctor rose from his bed of sickness and, when he saw L'Angelier, insisted on applying a mustard poultice. 'Oh, Mrs Jenkins,' said L'Angelier, 'this is the worst attack I ever had. I feel something here,' and he pointed to his forehead.

'It must be something internally,' said Dr Steven. 'I can see nothing wrong.'

'Can you do anything, doctor?' asked L'Angelier.

The doctor said that time and quietness were required, and Mrs Jenkins left the room, signing to the doctor to follow her. Outside she asked what was wrong. The doctor replied by asking, 'Is your lodger a person who tipples?' Mrs Jenkins said he was not. 'Well, he's like a man who tipples,' the doctor said, and the landlady assured him that L'Angelier did not drink. She also said, 'It's strange. This is the second time he has gone out well and returned very ill. I must speak to him and ask the cause.'

The doctor left, saying that he would be back between ten and eleven. When Mrs Jenkins went back to the patient, L'Angelier asked what the doctor thought. 'He thinks you

55

will get over it,' Mrs Jenkins assured him. L'Angelier shook his head. 'I am far worse than the doctor thinks,' he said.

About nine o'clock Mrs Jenkins drew the bedroom curtains open and in the daylight saw that her lodger was looking very ill indeed. She asked him if there was anyone he would like to see, and L'Angelier said he would like Miss Perry of Renfrew Street to visit him. Mrs Jenkins sent her little boy to Miss Perry's house, and kept looking into L'Angelier's room to see that he was all right.

'Oh, if I could get five minutes' sleep,' he said to her, 'I think I would get better.'

The next time she looked in, he seemed to be asleep so, when the doctor called, she said the patient was just newly asleep and it was a pity to waken him. However, the doctor went in. And there was L'Angelier lying dead.

Miss Perry arrived, but Mrs Jenkins had to tell her she was too late. She had supposed, when L'Angelier asked her to get Miss Perry, that this was the woman in his life. So she asked, 'Are you the intended, ma'am?' Miss Perry replied, 'Oh, no! I am only a friend.' Mrs Jenkins said, 'I heard he was going to be married. How sorry the lady will be.'

When L'Angelier's body was laid out, Mrs Jenkins took Miss Perry in to see it. Poor Miss Perry was overwhelmed and cried bitterly and said how sorry she was for his mother. She kissed L'Angelier's forehead several times.

L'Angelier's regular doctor arrived, his fellow lodger Thuau, and William A. Stevenson of Huggins, the seedsmen where L'Angelier had been a clerk. Mrs Jenkins asked Stevenson to take charge, and they started by looking through L'Angelier's clothes, which were thrown over a sofa. In one pocket was a letter, and when Stevenson read it, he said, 'This explains all.'

This was the letter:

'Why my beloved did you not come to me. Oh beloved are you ill. Come to me sweet one. I waited and waited for you but you came not. I shall wait again to-morrow night same hour and arrangement. Do come sweet love my own dear love of a sweetheart. Come beloved and clasp me to your heart. Come and we shall be happy. A kiss fond love. Adieu with tender embraces ever believe me to be your own ever dear fond

Mini.'

We may wonder what Stevenson really meant when he said, 'This explains all.' Afterwards in court he said that he meant that this letter explained why L'Angelier had suddenly left Bridge of Allan and come to Glasgow.

What did it explain to Miss Perry? Well, her next step was to Blythswood Square, to the Smith's house where she had never visited before. She asked to see Mrs Smith. Madeleine received her, shook hands, and asked her to go into the drawing-room if she wished to see Mrs Smith. Madeleine also asked Miss Perry if there was anything wrong and Miss Perry replied, 'I wish to see your mamma and I will acquaint her with the object of my visit.' The object of her visit was to tell Mrs Smith of L'Angelier's death. Why didn't Miss Perry tell Madeleine? Perhaps she felt that would be a work of supererogation.

Mr James Smith had a caller too on that fateful day. The Chancellor to the French Consulate in Glasgow, M. Auguste de Mean, had known L'Angelier for about three years, and he called to tell Mr Smith of the existence of letters written by Madeleine to L'Angelier. He thought Mr Smith should know this in case he wanted to secure his daughter's letters.

The next day was fateful too. Dr Thomson and Dr Steven carried out a post-mortem examination of L'Angelier's body and came to the conclusion that he had died of poisoning. On the Saturday of that week medical experts found enough arsenic in L'Angelier's body to kill forty men.

But we are still at Tuesday, when the news of L'Angelier's unusual death, and the fact that a post-mortem was being held, had got around in Glasgow. Mrs Smith, who had been enjoying ill health for at least two years, stayed in her bed.

Mr Smith took to his bed too. Madeleine carried on running the house and Billy Minnoch doesn't seem to have noticed that anything was wrong.

On Wednesday it was arranged that Billy would take Madeleine to a dinner party at the house of Mr Middleton, minister of the United Presbyterian Church. Her father should have been going, but Billy was to escort her instead. But on Wednesday afternoon Madeleine had an interview that must have given her a poor appetite for dinner. It was with M. de Mean of the French Consulate, and Mrs Smith got up to attend it.

M. de Mean did not beat about the bush. He said that he thought Madeleine must have seen L'Angelier on Sunday because he had come from Bridge of Allan at her special invitation. M. de Mean did not think it likely that, if L'Angelier had committed suicide (that was one of the rumours going around Glasgow), he had done the deed without knowing why she asked him to come to Glasgow. He advised her very seriously to tell the truth if she had seen L'Angelier on that Sunday night, because someone might have seen their meeting.

'I swear to you, Monsieur de Mean,' said Madeleine, 'I have not seen L'Angelier for three weeks.' She also said that L'Angelier had never been in the house, although she used to open her bedroom window at night and talk with him as he stood outside in Main Street.

Well, Billy Minnoch took Madeleine to dine at Mr Middleton's that night. Next morning he called at the Smith's home and James Smith told him that his daughter had left the house. He said it was something to do with an old love affair. Billy took command of the situation. He suggested that Madeleine had probably gone down to Rhu, for there was a servant living in Rowaleyn. Then he and Madeleine's brother Jack set off by train for Greenock. They boarded the steamer for Helensburgh and Rhu, and there was Madeleine on board.

Billy asked her why she had left home and distressed her

friends, and then told her not to reply because there were too many people within earshot. The trio sailed up to Rhu and went to Rowaleyn, where Madeleine said that she had left home because her papa and mama would be so annoyed at what she had done. She did not mention what she had done. Billy ordered a carriage and took Madeleine back to Blythswood Square.

Meanwhile L'Angelier's employer in Bothwell Street, William A. Stevenson, had arranged that Emile should be buried in his family lair in the Ramshorn kirkyard in Ingram Street. The body was buried on the same day that Madeleine ran away. It did not lie there long. Five days later, on March 31st, it was exhumed, because by that time the experts were satisfied that L'Angelier had been poisoned and wanted to carry out a fuller examination.

On the morning of the day L'Angelier's body was exhumed, Billy Minnoch met Madeleine and she asked if he had heard the report that L'Angelier had been poisoned with arsenic. When Billy said he had, she mentioned to him that she had been in the habit of buying arsenic, because she had learned at Clapton School that it was good for the complexion.

That afternoon Madeleine Hamilton Smith was arrested and charged with the murder by poison of Pierre Emile L'Angelier.

She was examined before Archibald Smith, Sheriff-Substitute of Lanarkshire, on that day, and here is her Statement, read out when she came to stand her trial:

'My name is Madeleine Smith. I am a native of Glasgow; twenty-one years of age; and I reside with my father, James Smith, Architect, at No. 7 Blythswood Square, Glasgow. For about the last two years I have been acquainted with P. Emile L'Angelier, who was in the employment of W. B. Huggins & Co., in Bothwell Street, and who lodged at 11 Franklin Place. He recently paid his addresses to me, and I have met with him on a variety of occasions. I learned about his death on the afternoon of Monday, the 23rd of March current, from mamma, to whom it had been mentioned by a lady named Miss Perry, a friend of M. L'Angelier.

'I had not seen M. L'Angelier for about three weeks before his death, and the last time I saw him was on a night about half-past ten o'clock. On that occasion he tapped at my bedroom window, which is on the ground floor, and fronts Mains Street. I talked to him from the window, which is stanchioned outside, and I did not go out to him, nor did he come in to me. This occasion, which, as already said, was about three weeks before his death, was the last time I saw him.

'He was in the habit of writing notes to me, and I was in the habit of replying to him by notes. The first note I wrote to him was on the Friday before his death, viz., Friday, the 20th March current. I now see and identify that note, and the relative envelope, and they are each marked No. 1. In consequence of that note, I expected him to visit me on Saturday night, the 21st current, at my bedroom window, in the same way as formerly mentioned, but he did not come, and sent no notice. There was no tapping at my window on said Saturday night, or on the following night, being Sunday. I went to bed on Sunday night about eleven o'clock, and remained in bed until the usual time of getting up next morning, being eight or nine o'clock.

'In the course of my meetings with L'Angelier, he and I had arranged to get married, and we had, at one time, proposed September last as the time the marriage was to take place, and subsequently, the present month of March was spoken of. It was proposed that we should reside in furnished lodgings; but we had not made any definite arrangements as to time or otherwise.

'He was very unwell for some time, and had gone to the Bridge of Allan for his health; and he complained of sickness, but I have no idea what was the cause of it. I remember giving him some cocoa from my window one night some time ago, but I cannot specify the time particularly. He took the cup in his hand, and barely tasted the contents; and I gave him no bread to it. I was taking some cocoa myself at the time, and had prepared it myself. It was between ten and eleven p.m. when I gave it to him. I am now shown a note or letter, and envelope, which are marked respectively No. 2, and I recognise them as a note or envelope which I wrote to M. L'Angelier, and sent to the post. As I had attributed his sickness to want of food, I proposed, as stated in the note, to give him a loaf of bread, but I said that merely in a joke, and, in point of fact, I never gave him any bread.

'I have bought arsenic on various occasions. The last I bought was a sixpenceworth, which I bought in Currie, the apothecary's, in Sauchiehall Street, and, prior to that, I bought two other quantities of arsenic, for which I paid sixpence each – one of these in Currie's, and the other in Murdoch, the apothecary's shop in Sauchiehall Street. I used it all as a cosmetic, and applied it to my face, neck and arms, diluted with water. The arsenic I got in Currie's shop I got there on Wednesday, the 18th March, and I used it all on one occasion, having put it all in the basin where I was to wash myself. I had been advised to the use of the arsenic in the way I have mentioned by a young lady, the daughter of an actress, and I had also seen the use of it recommended in the newspapers. The young lady's name was Guibilei, and I had met her at school at Clapton, near London.

'I did not wish any of my father's family to be aware that I was using the arsenic, and, therefore, never mentioned it to any of them; and I don't suppose that they or any of the servants ever noticed any of it in the basin. When I bought the arsenic in Murdoch's I am not sure whether I was asked or not what it was for, but I think I said it was for a gardener to kill rats or destroy vermin about flowers, and I only said this because I did not wish them to know that I was going to use it as a cosmetic. I don't remember whether I was asked as to the use I was going to make of the arsenic on the other two occasions, but I likely made the same statement about it as I had done in Murdoch's; and on all the three occasions, as required in the shops, I signed my name to a book in which the sales were entered. On the first occasion I was accompanied by Mary, a daughter of Dr Buchanan, of Dumbarton.

'For several years past Mr Minnoch, of the firm of William Houldsworth & Co., has been coming a good deal about my father's house, and about a month ago Mr Minnoch made a proposal of marriage to me, and I gave him my hand in token of acceptance, but no time for the marriage has yet been fixed, and my object in writing the note No. 1, before mentioned, was to have a meeting with M. L'Angelier to tell him that I was engaged to Mr Minnoch.

'I am now shown two notes and an envelope bearing the Glasgow postmark of 23rd January, which are respectively marked No. 3, and I recognise these as my handwriting, and they were written and sent by me to M. L'Angelier. On the occasion that I gave M. L'Angelier the cocoa, as formerly mentioned, I think that I used, it must have been known to the servants and members of my father's family, as the package containing the cocoa was lying on the mantelpiece in my room, but no one of the family used it except myself, as they did not seem to like it. The water which I used I got hot from the servants. On the night of the 18th, when I used the arsenic last, I was going to a dinner party at Mr Minnoch's house. I never administered, or caused to be administered, to M. L'Angelier arsenic or anything injurious. And this I declare to be truth.'

I don't think you will have any difficulty in identifying Note No. 1 ('Why my beloved did you not come to me.') or No. 2 (written after L'Angelier's first illness). Note No. 3 which Madeleine identified was one of her most passionate letters – the 'night dress' wish – and presumably its importance to the prosecution was to show that Madeleine and L'Angelier had met in the house.

Madeleine's Worst Letter

Exactly three months after she made that statement, Madeleine Smith went on trial at the High Court of Justiciary in Edinburgh. The authorities decided to hold the trial in Edinburgh rather than in Glasgow because feeling was so strong in Mimi's native city. Well-to-do people were inclined to favour Madeleine and think that L'Angelier, the counter-jumper, had committed suicide – or, if by any chance she *had* done it, it was no more than a blackmailing seducer deserved. Not so well-to-do people inclined more to the opinion that here was a rich girl getting rid of a poor but honest lover in order to wed a rich man.

On his part, Billy Minnoch declared that he would wed Madeleine as soon as the trial was over. But Billy, like L'Angelier, was out of his depth where Madeleine was concerned and had no idea of the evidence that was to be produced.

The iron curtain of respectability – well, perhaps that is not the best phrase; in Victorian days it might be said that the silver-plated curtain of respectability was rung down round the Smith family. You might almost have thought that Madeleine Smith was an orphan, so little was said of her family in the trial. Only one member of it was called to give evidence – her thirteen-year-old sister Janet. And yet there were many things that Papa, Mamma, Jack and Bessie could have thrown light on. In fact, neither Mr nor Mrs Smith attended their daughter's trial for life. They stayed in bed. That was the one safe place in Victorian days – as long as you stayed alone in it!

The trial opened in Edinburgh on Tuesday, June 30th, 1857. There were three judges on the bench – the Lord Justice-Clerk (Lord Hope), Lord Ivory and Lord Handyside. The Lord Advocate and Solicitor-General appeared for the Crown against Madeleine Smith, and she was defended by the Dean of Faculty and two advocates (the equivalent of barristers in England). Two hours before the

63

trial started the court was crammed. As one contemporary account said, 'This trial has been for some time looked forward to with intense interest – the prisoner being a young lady lately moving in respectable, if not high society in Glasgow, and the fatal event being the supposed issue of a romantic attachment.'

The trial lasted for nine days and a number of fashionable young men, who were never early enough to get into the court, paraded up and down outside every day, letting spectators understand that they had some 'romantic attachment' to the accused.

As far as the newspaper reporters were concerned, Madeleine seemed to be all things to all men. One said, 'Her countenance is striking, but not pleasant. A projecting brow, a long, prominent nose and a receding chin impart to her features a hawk-like aspect.' And another said of her face, 'We thought it fox-like, unattractive, cunning, deceitful and altogether unprepossessing.'

Many of the newspapers sent artists to the court to sketch the prisoner in the dock. Their pictures vary just as much as the writers' descriptions. One of the artists, for the *Illustrated London Times*, was Charles Doyle, father of Sir Arthur Conan Doyle, who was later to be associated with another case in our Square Mile of Murder.

The description I like best comes from a London edition of the trial, and the reporter found her neither hawk-like nor fox-like, but said:

'Madeleine Smith, a very young lady of short stature and slight form, with features sharp and prominent, and restless and sparkling eye, stepped up the stair into the dock with all the buoyancy with which she might have entered the box of a theatre. During the whole day she maintained a firm and unmoved appearance, her keen and animated expression and healthful complexion evincing how little, outwardly at least, she had suffered by her period of imprisonment and horror of her situation.

'Her head never sank for a moment, and she even seemed to scan the witnesses with a scrutinising glance. Her perfect self-possession, indeed could only be accounted for either by a proud consciousness of innocence, or by her possessing an almost unparalleled amount of self-control. She even sometimes smiled with all the air and grace of a young lady in the drawing-room, as her agents came forward at intervals to communicate with her.

'She was dressed simply, yet elegantly. She wore a brown silk dress with black silk cloak, with a small straw bonnet trimmed with white ribbon, of the fashionable shape, exposing the whole front of her head. She also had lavender-coloured gloves, a white cambric handkerchief, a silver-topped smelling bottle in her hand, which she never used, and a wrapper thrown over her knee. Altogether she had a most attractive appearance, and her very aspect and demeanour seemed to advocate her cause.'

Madeleine was charged with having (1) on two separate occasions in February, 1857, administered arsenic or other poison to Pierre Emile L'Angelier with intent to murder him; and (2) on an occasion in March, 1857, by means of poison, murdered L'Angelier. To this she pleaded Not Guilty 'in audible, though subdued manner'.

A jury of fifteen good men and true were impanelled. They were, of course, all from Edinburgh or the surrounding district. They included three farmers, a merchant, a boot-maker, a currier, a clerk, a cabinetmaker, a cow-feeder, a shoemaker, a teacher, and four gentlemen. Now, after all I have told you, you may have come to the conclusion that this was an open and shut case and that Madeleine was guilty. But that may be because of the chronological way in which I have told the story. The jury did not hear it in that order, nor did they get the letters as they applied to the changing situation. All the sixty letters produced in court were read one after the other. Finally, the jury were not allowed to know what L'Angelier had written to Madeleine, except for one letter, and they were kept in complete ignorance of the entries in L'Angelier's diary.

The Lord Advocate called fifty-seven witnesses. Mrs Jenkins told how her lodger died. Various people gave evidence about L'Angelier's journey from Bridge of Allan to Glasgow on the last Sunday of his life. It appeared that he had walked from Bridge of Allan to Stirling, taken the train to Coatbridge, and walked to Glasgow, as there were no Sunday trains on that line.

William Stevenson, of Huggins, told of the finding of Madeleine's letters in L'Angelier's lodgings and in his office desk. He estimated there might have been three hundred letters altogether.

Then the doctors and the medical experts had their say. The chief expert was Dr Frederick Penny, Professor of Chemistry at the Andersonian College, Glasgow. He gave evidence of the large amount of arsenic in L'Angelier's body. He said he thought it would be highly dangerous to use prussic acid or arsenic as a cosmetic.

But he also said – and this is a statement prized by those who think that Madeleine did *not* do the deed – the dose of arsenic inside L'Angelier must have been of a very unusual size. 'There are cases on record in which large quantities have been found in the stomach,' he said. 'There is one case in which two drachms have been found, that is one hundred and twenty grains.' (The amount inside L'Angelier was nearly eighty-four grains.) 'I cannot tell of any case in which a large quantity has been found in which the arsenic was administered by another party. In the case which I have referred to the poison was voluntarily taken. It would be very difficult to administer a large doze of arsenic in a liquid.'

Later, though, Dr Penny said, 'Cocoa or chocolate are substances in which a considerable doze of arsenic might be conveyed. I have found by actual experiment that when thirty or forty grains of arsenic are put into a cup of warm chocolate, a large portion of the arsenic settles down to the bottom of the cup, and I think a person drinking such chocolate would suspect something when the gritty particles came into his mouth. But when the same or a larger quantity is boiled with the chocolate, instead of stirring it in or mixing it, none of it settles down.'

Madeleine's statement was read in court. At that time an accused person was not allowed to give evidence. Miss Tennyson Jesse says, 'It is not uninteresting to picture what might have transpired had it been possible in those days to put Madeleine Smith herself in the box. How would she have dealt with the question the prosecution must have undoubtedly put to her – the question as to why she wrote that last letter, in terms of passionate love, bidding L'Angelier to come to her? She could not have denied she was wishing to get rid of him, that all her preparations for marriage with Mr Minnoch were going forward . . . . What reason could she have given for writing in those terms except that she wanted an interview with him, and that those terms were the only ones which would bring him? And what answer could she have given as to why she wanted the interview?'

A very good point, except for one thing. In my opinion, the Dean of Faculty would never have allowed Madeleine to go into the witness-box and, if he did not call her, the prosecution could not cross-examine her.

Of course, there's no telling what the 'prodigious damsel' might have done in the witness-box. Her appearance in the dock was formidable enough for the *Ayrshire Express*, whose reporter wrote:

'The personal appearance of Miss Smith . . . . is the point on which most attention seems to be fixed in the court by the spectators with whom it is thronged, and which is most talked of among the less privileged outside world. Eager crowds gather in the early morning at the gaol, and in Parliament Square, to catch a glimpse of the prisoner as she is taken to the court. In the evenings thousands gather in the streets to see the cab in which she is borne back from the

court-room to the prison. Every day sees hundreds at the
door of the court who would willingly expend guineas in
obtaining a look at the young lady. Hundreds are daily
passed in for a few minutes by official friends to get a
glimpse at the prisoner, and may be seen departing with the
air of satisfied curiosity upon their anxious countenances.

'Others, who are privileged to sit in the court through the
whole day, may be seen surveying the slight figure at the
dock with eyes that never weary of gazing upon it, from the
opening of the Diet till its close, while the newspapers, in
the second, and third and fourth editions with which the
town is deluged, stop the press to tell how she looked at a
particular hour, and how for breakfast she had coffee, rolls,
and a mutton chop, which she ate with great apparent
heartiness. In the midst of all this excitement . . . . Madeleine Smith is the only unmoved, cool personage to be seen.'

This was written, of course, before Madeleine's letters
were read in court. She remained quite cool while Augusta
Guibilei (now Mrs Walcot) said that she had been a pupil
teacher at Madeleine's school in Clapton but had never had
any conversation with her about the use of arsenic as a
cosmetic. She did remember once reading an article about
mountaineers taking small quantities of arsenic to improve
their breath, but that was all.

She remained cool while Mr Minnoch told his innocent
story. That was more than Billy did, because after he had
given evidence he followed the lead given by Mr and Mrs
Smith and took to his bed. And she was still cool when
Thomas Fleming Kennedy, the cashier at Huggins, said
that L'Angelier had come to him one morning crying and
saying that Madeleine wanted to break off their engagement.
Mr Kennedy said the lady was not worthy of him and that
he should give up the letters, but L'Angelier replied, 'No, I
won't. She shall never marry another man as long as I live.'
And L'Angelier added, 'Tom, it is an infatuation. She'll be
the death of me.'

Madeleine's letters were read – it took nearly the whole of the fifth day of the trial to read them – and this time she did show signs of emotion. She bowed her head at times, and some people thought she blushed.

On the sixth day the Dean of Faculty opened the case for the defence. He had two main points. One was that L'Angelier was the sort of man who would commit suicide. The other was that the prosecution had not proved that Madeleine and L'Angelier met on any occasion after she had bought arsenic.

A Jersey grocer said he had shared a bed with L'Angelier in the Rainbow Tavern, Edinburgh, in 1852. L'Angelier had told him he was tired of his existence and sometimes spoke of suicide. Once in a letter he said, 'I never was so unhappy in my life. I wish I had the courage to blow my brains out.'

Several witnesses said that L'Angelier was boastful, excitable and talked more about ladies than any other subject. A Dundee bank teller said that L'Angelier, speaking of his various sweethearts, lifted up a long knife and said, if he got a disappointment, he would think nothing of putting that into him. L'Angelier also told this impressionable young man that he had taken arsenic and showed him a white powder in a paper and said this was the stuff.

The defence also produced three chemists who had shops on the road from Coatbridge to Glasgow and they said that, on Sunday, March 22nd, they had sold drugs to a young man who looked like L'Angelier.

The Dean of Faculty also called representatives of two famous Edinburgh magazines, *Blackwood's* and *Chambers's Journal*. An article in *Chambers's Journal* for December, 1851, was entitled 'The Poison-Eaters' and it said, in part:

'In some districts of Lower Austria and in Styria, especially in those mountainous parts bordering on Hungary, there prevails the strange habit of eating arsenic. The peasantry in particular are given to it. They obtain it under the name of Hedri from the travelling hucksters and gatherers of herbs, who, on their side, get it from the glass-blowers, or purchase it from the cow-doctors, quacks, or mountebanks. The poison-eaters have a two-fold aim in their dangerous enjoyment; one of which is to obtain a fresh healthy appearance, and acquire a certain degree of *embonpoint*. On this account, therefore, gay village lads and lasses employ the dangerous agent, that they may become more attractive to each other; and it is really astonishing with what favourable results their endeavours are attended, for it is just the youthful poison-eaters that are, generally speaking, distinguished by a blooming complexion and an appearance of exuberant health.'

Then Janet was called. I quote my contemporary account:

'Janet Smith, sister of the prisoner, thirteen-years-of-age, a sweet-looking girl, whose appearance occasioned much interest, was next examined. She bore a considerable resemblance to the prisoner, but was paler in complexion. She gave her evidence with much composure.'

But about all Janet could say was that she went to bed and fell asleep on the night of Sunday, March 22nd, and thought Madeleine, whose bed she shared, had done the same.

Two doctors said they had tried washing in a mixture of arsenic and water without any ill results. The Lord Advocate said drily that it might be too soon to say whether there would be results or not.

On the seventh day of the trial the Lord Advocate addressed the jury. He talked from ten in the morning to half-past three in the afternoon. It was a fair and good speech, but his case had one great weakness. He could not prove absolutely and without a shadow of a doubt that Madeleine and L'Angelier had met on the night of Sunday, March 22nd, nor on the occasions when he was taken ill.

The Dean of Faculty made a brilliant speech. His opening sentence is still quoted in legal circles as a model one.

Indeed, it has since been used by other defenders in other cases. He said:

'Gentlemen of the Jury, the charge against the prisoner is murder, and the punishment of murder is death; and that simple statement is sufficient to suggest to us the awful solemnity of the occasion which brings you and me face to face.'

He pulled out all the stops in his description of how the pure and innocent Madeleine was seduced by the foul L'Angelier, of how she was tortured by this blackmailer, and of how likely it was that he had committed suicide anyway. Towards the end of his address he said:

'Raise not your rash and impotent hands to rend aside the veil in which Providence has been pleased to shroud the circumstances of this mysterious story. Such an attempt is not within your province, nor the province of any human being. The time may come – it certainly will come – perhaps not before the Great Day in which the secrets of all hearts shall be revealed – and yet it may be that in this world, and during our own lifetime, the secret of this extraordinary story may be brought to light. It may even be that the true perpetrator of this murder, if there was a murder, may be brought before the bar of this very Court.'

And he ended, 'May the Spirit of all Truth guide you to an honest, a just, and a true verdict. But no verdict will be either honest, or just, or true, unless it at once satisfies the reasonable scruples of the severest judgment, and yet leaves undisturbed and unvexed the tenderest conscience among you.'

The audience – I beg your pardon, the spectators in court – gave the Dean of Faculty a loud round of applause.

The Lord Chief Justice started his summing-up after an interval of a quarter of an hour. But he found himself too exhausted to finish it that night, and the trial went on to its ninth day. His summing-up was eminently fair, and no member of the jury could have told from it that some of the documents which had not been admitted as evidence – L'Angelier's diary in particular – had a significant bearing on the case. He was particularly strong on the danger of 'inference' on the part of the jury, and he said, of the alleged meeting of Madeleine and L'Angelier on that last Sunday night:

'You must keep in view that arsenic could only be administered by her if an interview took place with L'Angelier, and that interview, though it may be the result of an inference that may satisfy you morally that it did take place, still rests upon an inference alone; and that inference is to be the ground, and must be the ground, on which a verdict of Guilty is to rest. Gentlemen, you will see, therefore, the necessity of great caution and jealousy in dealing with an inference which you could draw from this one.'

The jury retired about ten minutes past one. When the three judges left the Bench a great hubbub of conversation arose. Everyone in court was arguing and talking excitedly. The one calm, composed person was Madeleine.

Five minutes later a bell rang and it was thought that the jury were returning already. 'A deep thrill of anxiety was visible throughout the court,' says an observer. 'Although the prisoner only slightly turned her head for a moment.' It was a false alarm. About ten minutes later a bell rang again, but again it was a false alarm. Then at thirty-two minutes past one the jury bell did ring and they re-entered the jury box three minutes later. Madeleine did not look in the least affected.

When the judges took their seats the Lord Chief Justice told those in court that, whatever the verdict, there must be no expression of feeling on their part.

The jury had elected their teacher member, Mr Moffat of Edinburgh High School, as foreman and he read out the verdict – Not Guilty on the first charge of administering poison, Not Proven on the second charge, and Not Proven on the charge of murder. (Not Proven is a peculiarly Scottish verdict which means, according to some cynics, 'Go away, and don't do it again!')

The whole court, except, of course, the representatives of the law, erupted into wild applause. Men and women stood on their feet cheering. The cheering was heard by the huge crowd that had gathered in Parliament Square and they cheered back. The judges scowled and the court macers shouted for silence in vain. Then the Lord Justice Clerk pointed to one unlucky man who had caught his eye and ordered him to be taken into custody for contempt of court. When he was arrested, the noise subsided at once.

As the verdict was read out, the Dean of Faculty sank into his seat and put his hands over his face. Others went forward to congratulate Madeleine, but he remained in his seat for some time and left the court without shaking hands with the woman he had defended so brilliantly.

Madeleine herself was more affected by the congratulations than by anything that had happened during the trial. She seemed specifically affected when Miss Aitken, the matron of Edinburgh Prison, took her hand. When she was dismissed from the bar, she was cheered again.

Then a somewhat bewildered individual was brought before the judges. He was the man who had been arrested for cheering in court. The Lord Chief Justice Clerk said that, for the very indecent exhibition of which he had been guilty, under the very eye of the court, they had intended to send him at once to prison. But he seemed to be such a foolish-looking person and, as he had been joined in his indecent behaviour by so many others, the court did not think him fit to be dealt with, and he was accordingly dismissed.

The spectators burst into a roar of laughter at this, and even the judges permitted themselves a slight smile.

The newspapers immediately and confidently gave the votes of the jury. According to the *Caledonian Mercury* – 'After deliberating, there were five for a verdict of guilty, and ten

73

for one of not proven. On the question of an absolute acquittal, there was no diversity of sentiment whatever.

I regret to say that the *Caledonian Mercury* was wrong. The actual vote was two for guilty, and thirteen for not proven. It was learned, though, that most of the jury did think Madeleine was guilty but, in view of what the Lord Justice Clerk had said, felt it would have to be a verdict of Not Proven.

And what did Madeleine Smith think? Four days after the verdict, she wrote to Miss Aitken at Edinburgh prison:

'Dear Miss Aitken,

'You shall be glad to hear that I am well – in fact I am quite well, and my spirits not in the least down. I left Edinburgh and went to Slateford, and got home to Rowaleyn during the night. But, alas, I found Mama in a bad state of health. But I trust in a short time all will be well with her. The others are all well. The feeling in the west is not so good towards me as you kind Edinburgh people showed me. I rather think it shall be necessary for me to leave Scotland for a few months, but Mama is so unwell we do not like to fix anything at present.

'If ever you see Mr. C. Combe tell him that the panel (the accused) was not at all pleased with the verdict. I was delighted with the loud cheer the court gave. I did not feel in the least put about when the jury were out considering whether they should send me home or keep me. I think I must have had several hundred letters, all from gentlemen, some offering me consolation, and some their hearths and homes. My *friend* I know nothing of. I have not seen him. I hear he has been ill, which I don't much care.

'I hope you will give me a note. Thank Miss Bell and Agnes in my name for all their kindness and attention to me. I should like you to send me my Bible and watch to 124 St. Vincent Street, Glasgow, to J. Smith. The country is looking most lovely. As soon as I know my arrangements I

shall let you know where I am to be sent to. With kind love
to yourself and Mr Smith, ever believe me, your sincerely,
                                    Madeleine Smith.'

'Mr C. Combe' was the merchant member of the jury,
and Madeleine knew him slightly. The ill 'friend' was Billy
Minnoch, who, so far from wedding Madeleine, never saw
her again. And, as Tennyson Jesse says, this letter 'is far
more profoundly shocking than any of her violent epistles to
L'Angelier.'

Madeleine Meets G. B. S.

Madeleine dropped out of sight for a while. The *Liverpool
Albion* told its readers that 'Madeleine Smith's father refuses
to see her, and ere this she has left for a foreign land. The
defence has cost somewhere about £4000. A greater sum
than that was subscribed for the purpose by a few leading
Glasgow merchants. One old bachelor . . . . put down £1000
as his own share. Messrs Houldsworth, to which firm
William Minnoch belongs, were, it is said, willing to give
the same measure of assistance; so were the wealthy family
of the Bairds, and a rich uncle of the prisoner, from whom
she has "expectations". The Dean of Faculty's fee was £250,
and a "refresher" of £70 every morning of the trial. Mr
Young, who was associated with the Dean in defence,
received £400 altogether.'

The *Illustrated London Times*, in a leader, said 'We can trace
the results of some of the errors of modern training and
modern morality in the remarkable case of the Trial of
Madeleine Smith.'

And *The Times* (in its best 'Thunderer' style) remarked:

'While it is admitted on all hands that never at any former
period were domestic manners so unexceptionable, we are
shocked with the continual recurrence of attempts by women
against the lives of husbands, paramours and children.
Poisoning especially has become almost a domestic institu-

tion. The friendly arsenic has always been ready in the cottage of the peasant or in the lodging of the mechanic, to rid the impatient wife of a tiresome husband, or the thrifty housewife of parents; or relations, who have become a burden. So, when it was announced that in a higher rank of life a similar crime had been committed, there was interest and excitement, but without surprise. Scotland has been for nearly four months occupied with Miss Madeleine Smith and her lover, and, though there is still sufficient distinction between the two countries to give a Scotch case some difficulty in achieving an English reputation, yet since the commencement of the actual trial the interest of the South has not been less than that which prevailed beyond the Tweed.'

This ineffable leader is only important in its relation to respectability, for if ever respectability triumphed, it did in the case of Madeleine Smith and her family.

For the not so respectable people there were the penny pamphlets which came out after every *cause célèbre*. One entitled *Who Killed L'Angelier?* put forward the idea that he killed himself. But another, *The Story of Minie L'Angelier* (a third spelling of that much loved Christian name), finished by referring to Madeleine's various purchases of arsenic. What, the pamphlet asked, did she say she did with it:

'She washed her hands with it!'

' "What! will these hands ne'er be clean? Here's the smell of the blood still. All the perfumes of Arabia will not sweeten this little hand!" ' A good point. After all, Lady Macbeth was a Scotswoman too.

Before I tell you how Madeleine spent the next seventy years, may we go into the question – how did Pierre Emile L'Angelier die?

Well, there is no doubt that he died of arsenical poisoning. Could the arsenic have been swallowed by him accidentally? Impossible, I say. Was he murdered by some unknown person, not Madeleine Smith? That's improbable, to say the least. Who would want L'Angelier's death so much as to poison him? In spite of what has been said about him during the trial and later, he was liked by nearly all those who knew him.

One of the oddest explanations for L'Angelier's death, put forward by one of the men on Madeleine's side, is that, since she was accustomed to applying arsenic to her face, she sometimes put it on other parts of her body and, in the sort of ritual we see in some films nowadays, he licked it off and so poisoned himself!

If you agree that these solutions are not tenable, we have two others left. One is that Madeleine murdered L'Angelier, and the other is that L'Angelier committed suicide. Let us consider the suicide theory. First of all, the officers of the law searched all the chemists' books in Glasgow and the West of Scotland for the names of people who had bought poison in February and March, 1857. They did not only look for the name of Madeleine Smith (which they found three times) but also for the name of L'Angelier. They did not find it once. It's possible, I suppose, that he could have obtained arsenic by some subterfuge, but do you think that he would go about killing himself in such a painful way?

And why should he commit suicide? He returned from Bridge of Allan to Glasgow in response to a passionate note from Madeleine. What would he expect? If I read him aright, he would expect a wonderful reconciliation, maybe even the news that she was going to marry him after all. But Madeleine says that she wanted him there to tell him that she was going to marry Billy Minnoch. If she did, might not he be so overwhelmed with his personal tragedy that he would commit suicide? Then where did he get the arsenic, and did he swallow this huge quantity raw? As I've said, there was enough arsenic inside him to kill forty men.

There is yet another theory – that L'Angelier killed himself in the hope that his death would be attributed to Madeleine. In that case, why, when he was dying miserably in his lodgings, did he not mention the name of Madeleine

Smith to Mrs Jenkins or the doctor? He did not even say where he had been that night. Could it be that, after all, L'Angelier was so much in love with Madeleine that, even when he was so ill, he would not say anything that might bring her name into disrepute? Whatever way you look at this case, I think L'Angelier was a much traduced man.

So that leaves Madeleine. My own opinion is that she poisoned L'Angelier. Her defending counsel made the point that she must have known that, by killing her lover, her letters would be made public. I don't think a murderer's mind works that way. The first essential for Madeleine was to be rid of L'Angelier. Once he was dead, what could be simpler, she'd imagine, than to go round to his lodgings and his office and ask for her letters back.

No one can ever say the final word about this case of the 'prodigious damsel'. Madeleine herself behaved as if she were not only innocent, but even completely blameless of any sort of untoward conduct. Just after she had written to the matron of Edinburgh jail, she wrote to the chaplain of the same institution.

Of her trial she wrote:

'I trust that painful, unhappy affair may tend to do us all great good – I see a different feeling pervades our family circle already. I am so glad they all view it as an affliction sent from God for past errors and crimes, and if this be the means of drawing a family to the feet of Christ I shall not grumble at the pain that sad event cost me.

'I may live to hear my family exclaim that it was the most blessed day of their life – the day I was cast into prison.'

This pious hope was not realised. The trial had ruined the Smith family socially. The Smiths left Glasgow and went to Bridge of Allan and then to Polmont. James Smith continued his practice in a half-hearted sort of way. Mrs Smith kept to her bed. Bessie and Janet, the younger sisters, were destined never to marry and ended up as rich old maids in a house in Falkirk.

Although the *Glasgow Herald* said of Madeleine that 'her conscience was now her only tormentor', she does not seem to have suffered very much. Her brother Jack convoyed her to London, and from there she went to live in the home of a clergyman at Plymouth. She arrived in Plymouth about the end of 1857 and soon in the New Year she met a young drawing teacher named George J. Wardle. Madeleine had taken lessons in water-colour painting and drawing, and she had known the Glasgow coach-builder, Archibald McLellan, whose Old Masters became the nucleus of the great Glasgow Art Galleries collection. So she was interested in art and she soon became interested in the art teacher.

George Wardle was young, clever, intensely artistic and wore a beard, a broad-brimmed hat and a cloak. Soon Madeleine and he were close friends, although he knew her as Lena. The clergyman, seeing the way things were going, warned Wardle – indeed, he told the artist about Madeleine's past. But Wardle was a real romantic and this made him all the keener to marry the girl.

When he got a good job with William Morris's furnishing and decorating business in London, he proposed marriage and Madeleine Smith became Lena Wardle at St Paul's, the parish church of Knightsbridge, on July 4th, 1861. Her father travelled from Polmont to London to be at the wedding. So, in one sense, he gave her away. He seemed to the wedding guests to be a melancholy man, and he went back to Old Polmont and died two years later. Pierre Emile L'Angelier's mother died three years after that. Neither James Smith nor Melanie L'Angelier ever seemed to recover from Emile's death.

But for Madeleine all was sweetness and light. The Wardles settled down in Bloomsbury and Madeleine was introduced to William Morris and Socialist society. She became a renowned Bloomsbury hostess. It is said that it is to Madeleine that we owe the fashion of table mats on a bare dining table. She was the first to do away with the tablecloth at dinner time.

Here's something for the amateur psychiatrist to get hold of! The Victorians were so respectable that they chose to disregard legs – even table legs – completely. So they draped their tables with cloths which concealed the legs. And it was Madeleine, the girl who had been outspoken about sex in her letters, who revealed them.

The Wardles had two children, a son and a daughter. The son, Tom, is supposed to have been a real radical and to have been arrested for making political speeches in the Edgware Road. But Nigel Morland, in *That Nice Miss Smith*, denies that. There was a Tom Wardle arrested, but apparently he was a nephew of George Wardle's. The daughter, known as Kitten, is supposed to have believed in free love, smoked in public, and approved of Ibsen. But Mr Morland denies that too, and says that the children took after their father (who was not a Socialist) rather than their mother.

Madeleine was a Socialist all right. Some thirty years after she had been tried for murder, she became treasurer for a splinter group of the Socialist League, run by Karl Marx's son-in-law, Edward Aveling. In the Marx-Engels Museum in Moscow you can see a letter from J. L. Mahon to Frederick Engels mentioning a ten shilling subscription which 'I believe Mrs Wardle has already acknowledged'.

She also became manager of the Central Democratic Club in London, which had Cunninghame Graham as its president, Sidney Webb on its committee, and George Bernard Shaw as a member. Indeed, George Bernard Shaw received coffee at Madeleine's hands and had no ill effect.

Writing of the Central Democratic Club, G.B.S. said, 'It was managed and cooked for mainly by Mrs Wardle . . . . I met her once or twice. One day Belfort Bax rushed in to tell me that Mrs Wardle was Madeleine Smith and that we should all be poisoned . . . . She seemed an ordinary, good-humoured, capable woman with nothing sinister about her.'

All the same, in 1889 George Wardle left William Morris's

firm on health grounds and went to live in Italy – without his wife. The marriage had not been going smoothly and, according to one statement, George had seen 'a look that he did not like in Madeleine's eye'. They did not meet again, though George Wardle did not die until 1910.

It's difficult to trace Madeleine after her husband left her. She is supposed to have lived for some years at Leek in Staffordshire, in a house lent to her by her brother-in-law, Sir Thomas Wardle, and it's said that she wore 'aesthetic clothes' and a violent red wig. But we do know that, at the age of eighty, Madeleine decided to emigrate to the United States of America, where her son Tom was now living. Perhaps the Great War (the year was 1916) helped her decision. America had not entered it then.

Madeleine was very proud of the fact that most people took her for twenty years younger than she really was. One of them was an elderly and kind Roman Catholic named Sheehy. He proposed marriage and Madeleine accepted him. Now she was Lena Wardle Sheehy. The world seemed to have forgotten Madeleine Smith.

But, in 1919, Somerset Maugham was writing in his diary of an event which took place in 1907. He said:

'H.B. went down to stay in the country. His next-door neighbour was a very quiet prim old lady; becoming acquainted with her, he gradually connected her with the heroine of a celebrated murder case which had excited the world fifty years before. She had been tried and found not guilty but the evidence was so damning that, notwithstanding the verdict, the general opinion was that she had in point of fact committed the crime. She discovered that he had found out her identity, taxed him with it, and presently said to him: "I suppose you want to know whether I did it or not. I did, and what's more, if it were all to happen again I'd do it again." '

This appeared in Somerset Maugham's *Writer's Notebook* and, when he was asked about the details, Mr Maugham replied, 'H.B. was H. B. Irving and it was to Madeleine Smith that he was referring in the story he told me. I have no reason to suppose he was romancing.'

But this story did not appear in print until long after Madeleine's death. Her husband died in 1926, when they were living in New York. Some time after that she was approached by a Hollywood film company, who had discovered her identity. The film company proposed to make a picture about her case and wanted her to appear in it. Madeleine refused, and the Hollywood tycoons threatened to expose her identity and have her deported from America as an undesirable alien. But Madeleine remained as firm as ever. Nothing could shake the 'prodigious damsel'.

She died in the Bronx, New York, on April 12th, 1928, of kidney disease. She was ninety-two. On her simple tombstone is the name 'Lena Sheehy' and the date of death. According to Peter Hunt, in *The Madeleine Smith Affair*, she left £13 and an insurance policy worth £30. Madeleine was respectable to the end.

Amateurs of murder from many parts of the world come to Glasgow to this day to see what remains of the case of Madeleine Smith. If they go to the Ramshorn kirkyard in Ingram Street, they will not see a headstone marked 'Pierre Emile L'Angelier'. But they will see the Stevenson lair, and that is where sweet pet Emile is buried.

They can also go to Blythswood Square and view the famous No. 7. It looks much the same as it did in Madeleine's day. For many years it belonged to the West of Scotland Agricultural College. Madeleine fell in love with a seedsman and then, in my opinion, poisoned him. It's interesting to note that, if she'd come back in the Agricultural College days, she'd have found her old house full of seedsmen, and full of poison too!

But she would not have been allowed into her old bedroom, the boudoir where she made the cocoa and handed it out to Pierre Emile L'Angelier, shivering in the street outside the barred window. The College turned it into a gentleman's lavatory.

The future of the famous bedroom is uncertain. The building now belongs to the Glasgow School of Art, who may change the purpose of the room.

The other memory of Madeleine that is left is the collection of her famous letters. It is in the Court of Session in Edinburgh. Not long ago my friend Lionel Daiches, Q.C., told me that he had asked to see the letters of Madeleine Smith. A whole sack-full was produced. Lionel started to look through them and the custodian, who was watching him carefully, said, 'Ah, it's happened to you too.'

Lionel asked what had happened to him. 'I saw your nose twitch,' said the custodian. And then he explained that Madeleine had drenched her letters to L'Angelier with scent. One of the ingredients of scent in Victorian days was musk, and musk has the property of reviving its smell under heat. Apparently the heat of the human hand is strong enough to being out the musk scent.

And so, more than a hundred years after the trial of Madeleine Smith, something of her still lingers in the air.

The Man Who Did

The Case of Jessie McLachlan

A Footprint in Blood

In the Strathclyde Police Museum in Pitt Street in Glasgow
there are some interesting and remarkable exhibits. But one
outshines all the others. It is a footprint in blood.

Although it was made on that very wooden plank nearly
one hundred years ago, it is still quite clear in a good light.
Obviously a woman's, it is a rather delicate foot with a high
instep.

The footprint was made by a young married woman
named Jessie McLachlan in the basement of a house at 17
Sandyford Place, Glasgow. Once you leave Charing Cross,
the centre of our Square Mile of Murder, and go west along
Sauchiehall Street, you come to a series of terraces which,
although they are all part of the same thoroughfare, have
been given different names. One of them is Sandyford Place.

Today, like so many other West End terraces in Glasgow,
the Place is occupied by offices as well as residences, together
with the Glasgow Eye Infirmary and a nursery school. At
the moment of writing, Number 17 is still a residence. And,
apart from the fact that the imitation verandas have been
taken away from the upper floor windows, the house is much
the same from the outside as it was in July, 1862. Even yet
respectability seems to hang heavy in the air.

This is the scene of one of the most savage Glasgow
murders and one that remains, officially at any rate,
unsolved to this day. William Roughead, in his *Tales of the*

Criminous, says 'Every writer has a favourite child – Dickens has told us that his was David Copperfield – and of all my naughty progeny there is none I prefer to the much-wronged heroine of the Sandyford Mystery. Old Fleming, too, is another of my choicest characters . . . . With his piety, his cunning and his cleaver, to say nothing of his singular good luck, even the exclusive Lizzie Borden might have been proud to number him among her respected ancestors.'

Roughead's 'much-wronged' heroine is Jessie McLachlan. Old Fleming is the man that Jessie said committed the Sandyford Place murder. And Lizzie Borden is the subject of that famous verse:

> *Lizzie Borden took an axe*
> *And gave her mother forty whacks:*
> *When she saw what she had done,*
> *She gave her father forty-one.*

When Jess McPherson was found weltering in her gore in her basement room at 17 Sandyford Place she bore the marks of forty whacks, so Roughead's comparison between Lizzie Borden and Old Fleming is well chosen. And now we are going to see how Jessie McLachlan came to leave a footprint as famous, in its own way, as the one that Robinson Crusoe found.

About four o'clock in the morning of Saturday, July 5th, 1862, three girls were walking into Glasgow along what was then known as Sauchiehall Road. They were Margaret, Jessie and Peterina McLean, sisters whose ages ranged from twenty-four to nineteen. They had been to their brother's wedding in the burgh of Partick, and the celebrations had gone on far into the night. Indeed, they were not over when the McLean sisters decided to leave.

Sauchiehall Road was more like a country lane than a city thoroughfare, but there were respectable terraces on either side and between the road and the houses were shrubberies and trees. Dawn comes early in Glasgow in the summer and, as the girls walked along, they heard a great many small birds whistling in the trees – particularly in one tree. It was such a bonny, clear morning and the birds were so melodious that Margaret, Jessie and Peterina stood there enraptured.

Then something attracted them to the house behind the tree. They could see, through the cracks in the Venetian blinds on the ground floor, that one lamp of a four-lamp gasalier was blazing brightly. They wondered to each other why the people of the house should have a light on at that time in the morning, and decided that either someone there was sick, or else the inhabitants were having a party.

They all noticed, too, that the number of the house with the light was 17 Sandyford Place.

The McLean sisters were not the only people who thought there was something strange about 17 Sandyford Place that night. Mary McIntyre, a forty-year-old dressmaker, was doing some sewing for Mrs Service of 8 Sandyford Place. She was to spend the night there but, about ten o'clock on the night of Friday, July 4th, she walked to her home, not far away, to see whether her brother had succeeded in getting a passage to India. Miss McIntyre was returning to Sandyford Place about a quarter past eleven when she noticed two groups of people on the pavement in Sauchiehall Road, looking towards 17 Sandyford Place.

It was obvious to Mary McIntyre that something about 17 Sandyford Place had attracted their attention. One group was of two or three women and a man. The other was of two young men, and one said to the other as Mary approached, 'I heard—' and then said something she could not catch. The other man said, 'I think it came from that house where the light is.'

Then the two groups went off in opposite directions, just as Mary McIntyre drew abreast of the house at No. 17. She was passing the house when she heard a low, wailing noise, just like the moaning of a person in very great distress. She stood still for a moment and noticed that there was a light showing in a window in the area of the house. (That was a basement window below the window where the McLean sisters were to see the light).

Mary McIntyre debated with herself whether or not she should go up to the house and ask what was wrong. But she felt, she said later, 'sort of frightened', and hurried on to 8 Sandyford Place as fast as possible.

If Mary had only been brave enough, the Sandyford murder might never have taken place, or it could have been solved.

The house that was attracting all this attention on a lovely summer's night belonged to a respectable Glasgow accountant, John Fleming. He was passing rich as well as respectable and owned a house, Avondale, between Dunoon and Innellan on the Firth of Clyde. And, just as James Smith took his family down to Rhu for most of the summer, so John Fleming, a widower, took his sister and his family to Dunoon.

He had his business in St Vincent Place to attend to, and he and his son who worked with him could only manage week-ends until they went on holiday. So, on Friday, July 4th, he and young John left the office and went straight down to Dunoon. The only persons left in the house at 17 Sandyford Place were John Fleming's father, James (better known as 'Old Fleming'), and a well-trusted servant, Jess McPherson.

John Fleming paid his father £40 a year to collect the rents in some rather squalid properties. He also kept his father in the house, and John, Jr., shared a bedroom with the old man. The respectable accountant was ashamed of his father, for Old Fleming still spoke the Doric, got on better with the servants than with the family, and was given to the occasional dram. John would sometimes return from Dunoon and be surprised at how far down the level of the bottle of whisky in the dining-room sideboard had gone.

Yet he could hardly put his father out, for he owed what he was to the education that Old Fleming had given him. The old man – he was either seventy-eight or eighty-seven,

nobody ever discovered which – was a handloom weaver in
the village of Kilsyth. He made enough money to go to
Anderston and start as a manufacturer, employing other
weavers. He'd brought up his family in a most respectable
way and now, instead of enjoying his retirement, he was still
working.

Well, the filial accountant and his son went to Dunoon
for the week-end. They were sure that Jess McPherson,
would look after Old Fleming well. She was competent and
kind. Possibly the Flemings did not know that at the age of
thirty-five she had had two illegitimate children, one still-
born. And they may not have heard that she was so strong
and wiry that once, when the policeman on the beat said,
'I think I will have a kiss,' she said, 'Try me, Sam.' When
he did try her, she put his two shoulders on the ground. And
it's very unlikely indeed they would know that Jess
McPherson had been saying for months to her friends and
companions that Old Fleming was an 'auld deevil' and was
fair plaguing the life out of her, asking her to marry him.

So they had their pleasant week-end at Avondale and
came back much refreshed, doubtless, on Monday, July 7th.
They worked in their office in St Vincent Place until four
o'clock and then they took the horse-drawn omnibus out
west. Mr Fleming got off the bus at North Street, because
he had to go to the grocer's and the butcher's to get
something for dinner that evening. His son John went on to
Sandyford Place.

Son John ran up the six steps to the door of No. 17 and
rang the bell. To his surprise, the door was opened not by
the servant, but by his grandfather.

'Where's Jess?' asked the young man.

'Jess?' said Old Fleming. 'She's away. She's cut. I haven't
seen her since Friday.'

He added that Jess McPherson's door in the basement
was locked and when young John asked, 'Didn't you think
of opening her door?' he said no, he thought she was away
seeing friends, and would come back again.

Just then the butcher's boy arrived with the collops which Mr Fleming had ordered, and Mr Fleming himself was hard on his heels.

'There's no use sending anything for dinner here,' said young John to his father. 'There's nobody to cook it.' He nodded towards his grandfather. '*He* says he hasn't seen her since Friday, and her room door is locked.'

Mr Fleming led the way down into the basement and through the kitchen to the door of Jess McPherson's room. Sure enough, it was locked. There was a pantry next door and he found a key there and decided to try it. The key worked and the three Flemings looked into a darkened room, for the blinds were down, and the windows looked out into an area.

They saw Jess McPherson's bed, and a little later they saw Jess herself. She was lying alongside the bed. She was naked from the waist downwards, and some dark clothing was thrown over the upper part of her body and her head.

John Fleming was horrified at the sight. He led the way back upstairs, and rushed out into Sauchiehall Road to ask his neighbours to come and look at this. He rang several bells, but in each case the master of the house had not returned. When he did see one of his neighbours and explain what had happened, the neighbour declined the invitation to see the body. 'No, no,' he said to Mr Fleming, 'you have said enough to frighten me from my dinner.'

It was Mr Fleming's butcher who eventually called the police, although Mr Fleming did find a doctor, who put his finger on Jess McPherson's hip and said, 'Quite cold – has been dead for some time.'

Mr Fleming also persuaded his grocer to lend his moral support. And then he had another visitor, a Mrs Jessie Walker, who lived in Elderslie Street, round the corner from Sandyford Place, and whose delight it was to keep her eye on the passing show. She was a grocer's wife and lived above the shop, and she was much concerned with people who were no better than they should be. Behind Sandyford Place was a large tract of waste ground, and this was the resort of drunks, prostitutes and other undesirables.

Mrs Walker just happened to be looking out of her window on that Monday afternoon when she observed a policeman running into her husband's shop. A running policeman was a sight so unusual that Mrs Walker hurried out of her house and down to the shop. The policeman had gone, but the shop assistant told Mrs Walker that he wanted a candle because a servant had been found dead in a locked cellar.

'Did you give the policeman matches as well?' asked Mrs Walker and, when she was told no, she seized a box of lucifers and hurried round the corner to 17 Sandyford Place. So, in no time at all, there she was right in the middle of the stramash and making her presence felt too.

Old Fleming was saying that the last time he had seen Jess McPherson was about half-past nine on the Friday night, and he had found her door locked on the Saturday morning. Mrs Walker asked if he hadn't thought of enquiring about the girl, since she was so long away.

'No,' said Old Fleming.

'Did you not think of getting the door opened?' Mrs Walker asked. 'Did you not think of looking whether her chest was away or whether the house had been robbed?'

When Old Fleming did not answer, his son repeated Mrs Walker's questions, and he replied, 'No, I never thought.'

'Did you hear any noise?' persisted Mrs Walker, who had obviously missed her true vocation.

'Aye, I heard some moans,' said Old Fleming.

'When?' demanded Mrs Walker.

'It would be about four o'clock on Saturday morning,' he replied.

'Did you no' rise when you heard the moans?' asked Mrs Walker.

'No,' he said, 'I rose on my elbow and looked at my watch and it was just four.'

'Well,' said Mrs Walker, 'when you were up on your

elbow, could you no' have got up and cried down what was the matter?'

Again John Fleming had to repeat the question, and once more Old Fleming replied, 'No, I didna think.'

The police surgeon arrived and examined the body. He found that Jess McPherson had been severely assaulted about the head and arms, apparently with an axe or cleaver. The police discovered that parts of the kitchen, adjoining Jess's room, had been recently washed. So had a portion of the bedroom floor. But there were three footprints in blood, quite distinct, on one side of the bed. There were other traces of blood about the kitchen and the basement, and in a room where Old Fleming kept his clothes there were some shirts with spots of blood on them.

The police asked Mr Fleming to find out if any of his property was missing. He discovered that some silver-plated spoons and forks had disappeared, but nothing of any real value. But when the police made a search of Jess McPherson's room, they found that all her best dresses were missing and that a chest containing some clothes looked 'as if some bloody hand had been working among them'.

Now we cannot tell how the police investigations went, but it would be fair to say that they would ask some of the questions that the percipient Mrs Walker asked. Why did Old Fleming spend a whole week-end in the house, knowing that the servant should be there, and never have bothered to find out what had happened to her? He met a number of people over that week-end, including some of his son's staff in St Vincent Place, and never mentioned to a single soul that Jess McPherson was missing. He went to kirk twice on the Sabbath and said nothing about it.

When a post-mortem was held on Jess McPherson's body, the doctors decided, among other things, 'that the comparatively light degree of strength shown in the blows would point to a female or a weak man having inflicted them.'

Well, Old Fleming claimed to be eighty-seven years of age and might be termed 'a weak man'. But was there a woman in the case? The three footprints in blood were of the same naked foot. And that foot was smaller and more delicate than either the dead woman's or Old Fleming's. Then some marks of blood on the stairs just outside the kitchen looked as though they had been made by a woman's skirt brushing against them. Again, why should Jess McPherson's best clothes disappear?

Jessie Makes a Statement

Now the Glasgow newspapers, as soon as this was found to be a murder and not a suicide, came on to the scene. They published every detail they could get, including precise particulars of the missing plate and clothes. On Tuesday, July 28th, a Glasgow pawnbroker, Robert Lundie, returned from a week-end 'doon the watter' and read about the missing plate in his newspaper. This reminded him that a woman had been in his office on the previous Saturday about midday and pawned some plate. On Wednesday morning he returned to the pawn office, looked at the plate and saw that every piece bore the letter F. His books showed that it had been pawned by 'Mary McDonald, 5 St Vincent Street', and that she had received £6 15s. for it.

Immediately Robert Lundie went to the police, handed over the plate and described 'Mary McDonald'. It was a busy day for the Glasgow police. It did not take them long to discover that no Mary McDonald was living at 5 St Vincent Street. But they had to try to find this woman. And on the same day they arrested Old Fleming in connection with the murder of Jess McPherson. He was examined by the Sheriff for four hours and then committed to prison for further enquiry.

Now we have no idea what Old Fleming told the police or said in his examination by Sheriff Strathern. But we do know that, 'acting on information received', the police became interested in a married woman, twenty-eight years old, who lived at 182 Broomielaw. Her name was (in the Scottish style) Jessie McIntosh or McLachlan. She was known, of course, as Mrs Jessie McLachlan. Her husband was a mate on a cargo ship sailing between Scotland and Ireland. She had been a servant for two years in the Fleming household and was a close friend of the late Jess McPherson. She knew Old Fleming too, because she sometimes called to see Jess in the basement of 17 Sandyford Place and the old man was usually there as well. Indeed, Old Fleming had called at 182 Broomielaw on several occasions.

But Jessie McLachlan said she knew nothing of the crime or the pawning of the plate. The police took her twice to see the Procurator Fiscal that week. For my English readers I should explain that the Procurator Fiscal in Scotland is the man who collects evidence and reports to the Crown prosecutor, the Lord Advocate.

James McLachlan, Jessie's husband, came home from his Irish voyage on the Thursday after Old Fleming's arrest. That day the papers were full of the murder and had a description of the woman who had pawned the plate at Lundie's. When James read this, he said to his wife, 'That's unco like you.'

'Aye,' said Jessie, 'it's ower like me!'

On Sunday, July 13th, Superintendent McCall of the Glasgow Police, accompanied by four detectives, went to 182 Broomielaw and arrested James and Jessie McLachlan, despite James' explanation that he was at sea during the time of the murder, and Jessie's denial that she had anything to do with it.

James McLachlan spent only one night in the cells. Next day he was examined by Sheriff Strathern and liberated. Jessie McLachlan was not so fortunate. After an examination which lasted four and a half hours, she was committed to prison. Now we must understand the nature of this examination. Jessie McLachlan would not know what the police had discovered about her connection with the case. She would not know what Old Fleming had told them. As you can see, when you read her various official statements, she was, if I may say so, led up the garden path by the Fiscal and then confronted with the nigger in the woodshed.

Remember, as you read Jessie McLachlan's first statement, that it took four and a half hours to get it out of her.

'My name is Jessie McIntosh or McLachlan,' it goes. 'I am a native of Inverness, twenty-eight years of age, wife of James McLachlan, second mate on board the steamship *Pladda*, and I reside at No. 182 Broomielaw, Glasgow. I knew Jessie McPherson, who was a servant to Mr Fleming, Sandyford Place, Sauchiehall Road. I was a fellow servant of hers in Mr Fleming's employment in his house at Sandyford Place, and at his coast house near Dunoon, for two years prior to September, 1857. I left Mr Fleming's service then and got married, and since then I have kept intimacy with her, except for a period of about eighteen months prior to January, 1861, during which time she was at service in Manchester.

'I last saw Jessie McPherson in my own house at the Broomielaw, on Saturday evening, the 28th June last. I had also seen her the previous night at Mr Fleming's house at Sandyford Place, and I went there about ten o'clock. I rang the front door bell, but Jessie McPherson happened to be in the dining-room, and she told me to go round the lane behind the house and she would let me in by the back door. I went round and found the back door open, and Jessie McPherson speaking to a servant in the adjoining house, No. 16 Sandyford Place. McPherson and I left this girl in the lane and went inside the back door; we conversed there about McPherson going to New Zealand, which she had previously told me she intended to do. That night I went by appointment to see her on this subject; McPherson asked me to get a schedule from an emigration society in Jamaica Street that it might be filled up for her. I did not get the schedule when I applied for it, and it was to see if I had got it that McPherson came to my house, the last time I saw her on said Saturday night.

95

'I was not in or near Mr Fleming's house on the evening of Friday the 4th, or morning of Saturday the 5th of the current month of July, and did not see Jessie McPherson that night or morning, and I was in no way concerned in assaulting or murdering her, nor was I concerned in stealing any silver plate from McPherson's house on said night or morning.

'On said Friday the 4th July I was in my house the whole day till about seven o'clock at night, when I went to see Mr McFarlane, who had been factor for my house prior to Whitsunday, and whose place of business was at 112 West George Street, but he was not within, whereupon I returned home. I was not again out of my house till after ten o'clock, when I went out to convoy home a Mrs Fraser, a seaman's wife, who lives in Grace Street, Anderston. I walked with her as far as the Gushet House in Anderston, where I parted from her. I intended to go to the house of James McGregor, a foreman clothier, who lives in Main Street, Anderston, and who is a friend of my husband's, but I changed my mind and returned home by way of Argyle Street, James Watt Street, and Broomielaw. I reached home about a quarter past eleven o'clock; I let myself in by means of a check lock key, and which is in the house; this key I carried myself, and always let myself in by means of it; it is one of the keys of the press in the lobby of my house, and for which press there are two keys.

'On going upstairs I found John McDonald, a young man who lodged with Mrs Campbell, who occupied a part of my house. He was going upstairs before me, and went into the house along with me, he did not remain in the house above a minute, then went out again. I went straight to bed without speaking to Mrs Campbell, but in about half an hour I heard the door bell ring, and Mrs Campbell opened the door, and I heard from the voice that it was McDonald returning. I remained in bed until between seven and eight o'clock on Saturday morning, without ever having been up or out of the house. My son, a child of three years of age, slept in bed with me.

'When I rose I dressed, and went out without breakfast, leaving my child in bed. I went for coals to the house of an old woman in West College Street. I brought back the coals in a large basket, covered with a piece of old carpet, which I had taken out with me. I was not absent above a quarter of an hour. Mrs Campbell was not up and out of bed when I went out, but she was out of bed when I returned, because I rang the bell and she let me in. I had forgotten to take the check key with me. Mrs Campbell had taken my child out of my bed and dressed him while I was absent. I lighted my fire and made breakfast for myself and child.

'I remained in the house until about twelve o'clock on said Saturday, when I went out and went to the pawn office of Mr Lundie in East Clyde Street. I went there to pawn silver plate which I had received from Mr James Fleming, the father of Mr Fleming, my late master, on the previous evening, in my house. He came to my house about a quarter-past eight that evening, and I let him in, and took him into our parlour. He carried a parcel wrapped tightly up in a white cloth, and laid it down on the table. He asked me if I would go a message for him, and he would pay me well for it.

'I asked him what it was, and he said he wanted me to pawn some silver plate which was in the parcel. I said the pawnbroker would know the plate did not belong to me. He said I was to say it was rent I had to pay. I asked what name I would give as a pledger, and if I would give Mr Fleming's name, and he said no, not to put down Mr Fleming's name, as it would be in the directory. I then said, "What name will I give?" and he said I was to give the name of Mary McKay or McDonald, No. 5 or No. 35 St Vincent Street, and that I was to seek £3 10s. upon the plate, or as much more as I could get. Fleming said that he was short of money, and had to go to the Highlands, and did not like to lift the money out of the bank. I agreed to pawn the plate, and Fleming said he would come and see me next afternoon, and then he left the house. There was no one with Fleming and me in the parlour, and I do not know that anyone saw him in the house; but Mrs Campbell was in at the time he was there.

'I went, as I have already said, to Lundie's pawn office, and it was then between twelve and one o'clock on the Saturday. I laid down the parcel, rolled up, as old Mr Fleming had given it to me. The pawnbroker's young man who attended me opened down the parcel, and then it was I saw for the first time what the parcel contained. The young man asked me what I wanted on the articles, and I said £3 10s., and he said he would give me a little more than that, and I said I would take as much as he would give me, as the articles would not lie long in pawn. He said he would give me £6 10s. or £6 15s., I forget which. I told the young man that the money was wanted to pay rent, but I did not say who sent me. I gave as the pledger's name Mary McKay or McDonald, as Old Fleming had told me.

'I got the money and a pawn ticket, and left the silver plate in the same cover which Old Fleming had brought the articles in. I saw, when the parcel was opened down by the pawnbroker, that the articles consisted of a soup divider, a fish slice, some table spoons and forks, and toddy ladles. I knew the silver articles when I was a servant in the house, and saw them sufficiently well in the pawnbroker's hands to know them again.

'I returned straight home from the pawn office with the money and ticket, and reached home about a quarter past one. I remained in the house, and at about a quarter to three Fleming came there. I was at the moment cleaning the brasses of the door, and he and I turned into the parlour. He then asked me if I had got his message, and I told him I had got more than he thought, and then gave him the whole money I had got, together with the pawn ticket. He thereupon offered me £5 for having done the message, and not to mention it to any person. I told him that £5 was too much for me, and I took £4 from him. Fleming repeated that I was to tell no one of what I had done for him in case it would come to his son's ears, and that a pound or two would do him when he was away in the Highlands. On this Fleming left the house.

'I had promised Mr Caldwell, the present factor of my house, £4 on Friday, the previous day, and so, on getting the £4 from Fleming, I went and paid the whole of it to Caldwell about four o'clock on Saturday.

'I am shown a man who calls himself James Fleming, and I declare and identify that man as the person who gave me said silver plate to pawn on said Friday, and to whom I gave the money and pawn ticket on the Saturday.

'I had money of my own wherewith to pay the factor on the Friday, independent of the £4 which I got from Fleming on Saturday. I had £5 10s. of my own in the house, which was a balance of £11 10s. which I got from my brother in the end of May last. My brother's name is John McIntosh. He was a seaman on board the steamship *St George*, which plied between Glasgow and Quebec.

'On Friday night, the 4th July, when I went to convoy Mrs Fraser, I was dressed in a brown merino dress with three flounces, a large light grey cloth cloak, and a brown velvet bonnet. On Saturday, the 5th July, I took the grey cloak to Mr Murray, the dyer's shop in Argyle Street that it might be cleaned, where, at the same time, I left the brown merino dress to be dyed black. I gave my own name, Mrs McLachlan, to Mr Murray, as the owner.

'I took the velvet off the frame of the said bonnet because it was old, and I gave it to a salt and whiting girl at the door of my house on Tuesday last. I had a brown merino dress without flounces, but I gave the skirt of it to Mary Black or Adams, a washerwoman, last summer. I did not open down the brown merino dress left to be dyed.

'The washerwoman just mentioned has been in the habit of washing for me about three years past. She did not call for me at my house in the afternoon or evening of Friday,

4th July. I did not ask Mary Black or Adams to come to my house and take charge of my son James while I went and saw the late Jessie McPherson on said Friday night.

'Mary Black or Adams stays with Mrs Rainny in Holm Street. I called once there on Saturday, the 5th July. I wanted Adams to go a message, but she was not in, and Mrs Rainny said she would go the message. The message was to redeem from a pawnbroker a black and blue check poplin dress, and which I now have on as under dress, and Mrs Rainny relieved and brought me the dress. I wore the brown dress at this time, not having sent it to the dyeing. I left word for Mary Adams to be sent to my house that Saturday afternoon, and she came. I gave her two £1 notes to redeem other articles from the pawn. On the Monday following I gave her 11s. to redeem some other articles which were pledged. I gave her no more money.

'I had two crinolines on Friday and Saturday, the 4th and 5th July. I have now only one, the other having been burnt by accident on Saturday, 5th July. The wires of that crinoline I gave to Mary Adams. I purchased a new black straw bonnet on Wednesday last, the 9th, in a milliner's shop in Argyle Street. I paid 4s. 9d. for it.

'Mary Adams has a younger daughter named Sarah. I sent her with a box to the Hamilton railway on Saturday, the 5th July. I addressed it with the name, "Mrs Bain, Hamilton. To lie till called for". The box was empty. I intended to go up to Hamilton on said Saturday, and stay for a day or two with a Mrs Shaw there, but who I, through mistake, understood was called Mrs Bain. I did not go on Saturday, but went on Tuesday last, and called at Mrs Shaw's house, and found she was not within. I got said box at the Hamilton station on said day, and returned home with it, reaching Glasgow about six o'clock on Tuesday night. The box is now in the house. It is a leather box with a glazed cover. I meant the empty box to lie at the Glasgow station till I went myself to Hamilton, but through some mistake of the little girl Adams it had been sent on to

Hamilton. I meant to have put my clothes in the box at the station, because the little girl could not carry the box and clothes together. I carried my clothes across to the Glasgow station of the railway in a black leather bag, and which I took to Hamilton when I found the box had been sent forward.

'I am shown and identify as my property two sheets. My attention is called to the mark or impression of a key appearing on one of said sheets. I declare that the impression was made upwards of twelve months ago, and while I resided in a house at Stobcross Street. The impression is of the check key of the outer door of that house, and was made by my child making water on it as it lay on the sheet, which left an impression of the key in iron mould on the sheet. My sister, Ann McIntosh, who now resides at Garnethill in Edinburgh, knew of said occurrence.

'I am shown and identify as my property a chemise and flannel petticoat, both of which I was wearing when I was taken into custody yesterday. I put on said chemise and petticoat on the evening of Thursday, the 3rd July. I had two chemises, but one of which I have since put on. That now shown to me I have torn up, having been destroyed by my child. I had no flannel petticoat except that now shown me. I washed it on Wednesday, the day before I put it on.

'I was indebted to the late Jessie McPherson in the sum of £1 5s. for grocery goods, which I got from her when she kept a shop in Grace Street about two years ago. This sum I did not pay, because McPherson told me that she meant to have made a present to my child at its birth, and that I was to retain the money and expend it for the child.

'On being shown a black shawl or plaid, that is not my property, and I never had it in my possession, and I did not leave it at Murray's before mentioned, to be dipped in black dye, on Monday last, nor did I send it. Being also shown a grey cloth cloak in two pieces – I declare that is the cloak which I wore on Friday and Saturday, the 4th and 5th July, and which has now been cleaned, but it was not in pieces when I gave it to be cleaned. I am shown the bodice and skirt of a dress new dyed black. I declare that it is the brown dress which I wore on said Friday and Saturday, now dyed black, and which, as shown me, wants the flounces. I did not give the name of McDonald to Murray as owner of said cloth cloak and brown dress. I gave my own name, McLachlan. I got from the dyer a ticket on leaving said articles, which, I suppose, is now somewhere about the house. I dyed said dress black to get further use out of it, as, in its brown state, it was a good deal soiled and the colour faded.

'All which I declare to be truth.'

But is it True?

Well, now, most of Jessie McLachlan's statement was nonsense, and the police well knew it. Some students of this case consider that Jessie was a pathological liar. Others say that she was a panic-stricken woman in a desperate situation. I incline to the first verdict. I think Jessie enjoyed telling lies, though she'd have denied that strenuously. In all, she made five statements, and even in the penultimate and most famous one, she lied – although she also told the truth in it.

As far as her first statement was concerned, the police knew already that Jessie McLachlan had been out of her house all night of July 4th–5th. She had no key for the house door, so she couldn't have let herself in. From Mrs Campbell, who rented two rooms from Jessie's three and had the lodger McDonald in one of them, the police knew that Jessie had not returned to the Broomielaw until nine o'clock on the Saturday morning. They also knew that Jessie had gone out on the Friday night in her old brown dress with the flounces, but it had not been seen again, for when Mrs Campbell opened the door to Jessie on the Saturday morning, she was wearing a dress that Mrs Campbell had never seen before. But this new dress (new to Jessie, that is) was the one sent to Murray's the dyers. Finally, they had tracked her to Hamilton and found the empty black box there. What had it contained?

Superintendent McCall and his men did a lot of hard work on the day after Jessie McLachlan made her statement. They did not get very far, but next morning fortune favoured the bold once more. On Wednesday, July 16th, a man with a conscience arrived at police headquarters. It was James McLachlan, and he made a statement that sent the police hurrying to Bridge Street railway station. There they found another black box. And inside it were clothes that were missing from the chest in Jess McPherson's bedroom.

Now it was time to put Jessie McLachlan through the hoops again. She was brought from prison to be interviewed before Sheriff Strathern, and asked about her visit to Hamilton, about a pair of her boots that were missing, and about a bottle she had taken out of Mrs Campbell's cupboard. She did not know, of course, that the police had the black box and its contents in their possession. You can imagine the questioning and the sudden production of the murdered woman's clothes when you read the stilted language of this part of Jessie McLachlan's second statement:

'I know that the late Jessie McPherson had a black watered silk dress. She had another dress of silk, of a changing colour, with flounces, but with cotton cloth beneath. She had also a velvet cloak, the front of which was lined with blue silk; as also a drab cloth cloak. She had also a black dyed harness plaid. I do not know if she had a black silk polka, but she told me she had one. The other articles of dress I have seen. I have not seen any of these articles of dress lately, either in her possession or anywhere else.'

And then the Fiscal plays his trump card.

'Being shown two silk dresses having a sealed label attached, as also two cloaks having a sealed label attached, as also a black dyed plaid having a sealed label attached, as also a piece of twilled cotton cloth having a sealed label attached, I declare the said dresses, cloaks and plaid to be Jessie McPherson's and are the same that I have before mentioned. I do not know the twilled cloth.

'I am shown a japanned tin box with sealed label attached. I declare that box is mine. I despatched it to Ayr either on Tuesday or Wednesday, the 8th or 9th of this month, the said tin box containing the said dresses, cloaks and plaid wrapped in the said cotton cloth by the Ayr railway from Glasgow, and addressed to "Mrs Darnley, Ayr. To lie till called for".

'On Friday, the 4th July, the late Jessie McPherson sent down said dresses, cloaks and plaid to my house by a little girl whose name I do not know, but who was accustomed to clean knives for her. Along with these things there was a message that I was to take the watered silk dress to Anderson, in Buchanan Street, to get dressed. The changing-coloured silk dress was to be opened down and left with Anderson to be dyed brown. The cloth cloak was to be dyed black, because McPherson had spoiled it in the washing. The black velvet cloak was to have a puffing of silk round the bottom to lengthen it, and which puffing McPherson was afterwards to send down to me. The black plaid was to be re-dyed because it was not well done. The articles were sent to me by said girl about five o'clock on the afternoon of said Friday, wrapped up in the said twilled cotton cloth.

'I intended to have taken them to Anderson on Saturday, but was not very well, and unable to go to Buchanan Street. I was not out on Monday, and on Tuesday I could not take the articles, having charge of my child. I heard of the murder on Tuesday night, and next day I heard that some of Jessie McPherson's clothes were awanting, and, having them in my possession, I got frightened, and sent them off to Ayr, as before mentioned. I addressed the articles to Mrs Darnley, because I knew her and could speak to her on the subject, and sent them to Ayr to be out of the way till I should have seen Mrs Darnley.

'I told my husband about the clothes and where I sent them on Thursday night, and I asked him to bring them back from Ayr and take them to Greenock. He wanted me to go to the Fiscal's office, and tell about them, but I felt frightened. I bought the said japanned box on Saturday, the 5th July, in a shop in Argyle Street. I bought it for general use and paid 5s. 6d. for it.

'All of which I declare to be truth.'

On that same eventful day Jessie McLachlan had a visit from Dr George Macleod, who asked her to assist in an experiment he was making. He had with him several planks of wood, a piece of waxcloth, and a small phial of bullock's blood. He smeared the blood over the waxcloth and then asked Jessie to place her foot in it and then footprint herself on successive planks of wood. Jessie not only agreed but seemed almost to enjoy doing it. She may have felt it was a pleasant change from prison routine.

Dr Macleod carted off his paraphernalia. And, when he had compared the new prints made by Jessie McLachlan with the footprint on the piece of floor from Jess McPherson's bedroom, he was able to tell the Fiscal that they corresponded 'with a degree of accuracy which was quite marvellous'. The Fiscal, who knew the Fleming family personally, got in touch with the Crown authorities in Edinburgh, and on the next day, July 17th, old Fleming was liberated from prison.

The news was reported joyfully by *The Glasgow Herald*, which had been saddened by the fact that a member of a respectable Glasgow family was charged with murder. Under the heading – 'Liberation of Mr Fleming and Committal of Prisoner McLachlan' – the *Herald* said:

'On Wednesday afternoon, as mentioned in yesterday's paper, Mr Sheriff Strathern and Mr Gemmel, joint Procurator-fiscal, proceeded to Edinburgh and held a consultation with the Solicitor-General and Mr Gifford, Advocate-Depute, regarding this case. It was there resolved that old Mr Fleming should be liberated, as there was no ground whatever why he should be longer detained in connection with this unhappy case – the evidence bearing, we assume, that he was entirely guiltless of any knowledge of or any connection with the murder of Jessie McPherson. Mr Fleming was accordingly set at liberty yesterday morning. It was also resolved at the consultation above referred to that Jessie McIntosh or McLachlan should be fully committed on the charges of murder and theft.'

And next day the *Herald* announced:

'It is no small satisfaction to us, we must declare, that in spite of the strongest prejudice and gross perversion of facts, we struck in and took the side of the old innocent on Saturday last; and we believe we are the only paper in the city that did so without the least equivocation.'

As I have noted in the case of Madeleine Smith, newspapers lived a happy, carefree existence in those halcyon days. They could say what they liked. In the Sandyford murder case all the newspapers had been speculating and taking sides. The *Herald*'s principal opponent was the *Morning Journal*, and these two papers went at it hammer and tongs from the moment of the release of Old Fleming, throughout the trial of Jessie McLachlan, and far beyond. But in all fairness it should be said that *The Glasgow Herald* have changed their mind since 1862.

Jessie McLachlan certainly did not take the news of Old Fleming's liberation in the way the *Herald* did. She was sharing a cell with two young women of about her own age, Agnes Christie and Catherine Fairley. She didn't talk much to her fellow-prisoners and spent a good deal of her time writing. Neither Agnes nor Catherine could read, but they understood that Jessie was writing statements for her law agents. These statements were what Jessie remembered of her declarations before the Sheriff, and she did say to Agnes and Catherine that her agents had told her that, if only she had never made them, she would have been out of prison by now. Jessie added that she wished the County Buildings would go on fire, and all the declarations and books burned!

On July 17th Agnes Christie was taking her exercise on the prison green when she heard through the grapevine that Old Fleming had been liberated. As soon as she got back to the cell, she told Jessie the news. Jessie wouldn't believe it at first and called the warder, Mrs Broadley, to ask if it was true. When she was told it was, Jessie burst into tears and cried, 'He's an old murderer. He did the deed. The guilty has got out, and the innocent is kept in. If I had the money, I'd have got out as well as him.'

Just as Jessie was professing her innocence, three policemen from Hamilton were searching fields near the village of Low Waters, about a mile and a half from the town. They found portions of the skirt of a brown merino gown and also two petticoats torn into pieces and bloodstained heavily.

Hamilton police sent a telegram to Superintendent McCall, and that smart man ordered another search of Jessie McLachlan's house in the Broomielaw. This time the Glasgow police found something they had overlooked – the sleeve of a brown merino gown, and the sleeve matched the skirt found at Hamilton.

On July 21st Jessie McLachlan had the opportunity to make her third statement before Sheriff Strathern. When she was shown the pieces of skirt and petticoats and the torn sleeve, she just denied that they belonged to her and said she had never seen them before. And this satisfied the authorities because they had already taken the trouble to make certain that the gown and the petticoats were worn by Jessie McLachlan on the night of the murder at Sandyford Place.

The trial of Jessie McLachlan for the murder of Jess McPherson was fixed for the Glasgow Autumn Circuit. Judging by the intense interest in the case in Glasgow and the way the newspapers were already condemning Jessie

McLachlan or Old Fleming, according to the side they'd taken up, it would have been much better if the case had been heard at the High Court of Justiciary in Edinburgh. Then there would have been three judges instead of one and, as we shall see, that could have made a very considerable difference to the conduct of the case.

One newspaper discovered that there were marks on Jessie McLachlan's hands and announced that 'They had been inflicted by Jessie McPherson in her death struggle'. Jessie explained that these slight abrasions had been caused by her wee dog biting her, and the Crown doctors believed her.

Sir Archibald Alison, Sheriff of Lanarkshire, wrote later in his autobiography, 'Such was the public anxiety for intelligence that the newspapers for a month were daily filled with these details, accompanied by the most violent declamations against the woman, as each successive article of evidence was revealed. To such a pitch did the public excitement on the subject rise that the editors of some of the daily papers told my clerk, Mr Young, that their circulation since the precognitions began to be published had risen from 10,000 to 50,000 a day; and that if they could only secure a Mrs McLachlan a month, they would soon be in a situation to retire from business with handsome fortunes! I myself was obliged, when the trial of the prisoner was fixed, to write a circular to the editors requesting them to abstain from any further notice of the case, as, if the incessant discussion went on, the prisoner could never have a fair trial.'

As it turned out, she didn't anyway.

But, more than a month before the trial, long before she could know the nature of the evidence to be brought against her, Jessie McLachlan had a meeting with W. M. Wilson, one of her law agents, and made yet another of her statements. This time her statement electrified the listener. He got one of his partners, J. A. Dixon, to call on Jessie, the following day, and Mr Dixon took a note of what Jessie had to say about the events of July 4th and 5th. Mr Dixon was just as electrified as Mr Wilson, and they brought in the third partner, John Strachan, to discuss this new statement. At this time, you must remember, neither the agents nor Jessie had the slightest idea of who the witnesses against her might be, nor, indeed were they aware of the nature of the indictment, which was not served until August 30th.

The law agents went into consultation with counsel. One outstanding point about Jessie's new statement was that she admitted she was in 17 Sandyford Place on the night of the murder. Counsel advised against using this statement and its admission. They were certain that the Crown could not prove that Jessie was in the house on that night. As they said, 'In an issue of life or death, no admission, especially one of such vital importance, should be volunteered by the defence.'

So Jessie stayed in her prison cell until Wednesday, September 17th, when she was to appear before Lord Deas in the High Court of Glasgow. One of her cell mates, Agnes Christie, told a story later of how Jessie said that her agents had told her that, when Old Fleming was being examined against her in court, she was to rise up and confront him, saying, 'Mr Fleming, was it me that did the deed?' Then there was no doubt that he would shudder at it, and it would be seen that he had done it. Jessie also told Agnes that she was to keep herself very calm.

Jessie kept writing on a slate, and she explained to her fellow prisoners that this was a chapter from the Bible. She kept writing it so that she could commit it to memory, and she would repeat it in court at her trial. When Agnes Christie was liberated from prison on September 5th, Jessie said she was sure that she would be acquitted at her trial, for her agents had told her so. 'So when I am free,' she said to Agnes, 'I want you to call at my house and have tea with me.'

Fanfare for Lord Death

At ten o'clock on the morning of September 17th, the trumpeters marched into the High Court of Glasgow and blew their fanfare. Everyone in court rose and Lord Deas took his seat. Judging by a contemporary photograph, he was an impressive figure, with deep-set suspicious eyes, a noble nose, luxurious side-whiskers, and a mouth that turned down very decidedly at the corners. He was so inclined towards capital punishment that he was known in the Court of Session in Edinburgh as 'Lord Death'. William Roughead records the remark that a fellow judge, Lord Young, made when the clergyman appointed to say the prayer at the opening of the High Court in Glasgow gave an unusually long one. Lord Young's companion judge on this occasion was Lord Deas, and later that day Lord Young said to a friend, 'Very long prayer that fellow gave us. I suppose when Deas goes on circuit, they think it right to call the Almighty's attention to the fact.'

The Old Court in Jail Square (now Jocelyn Square) was packed when the panel, as the accused is called in Scotland, was placed at the bar. Beauty, we learn early in life, is in the eye of the beholder. Jessie McLachlan's appearance seemed to lie in the opinion of the newspaper. According to *The Glasgow Herald*, the accused 'entered the dock with a quick step, but she was very pale, and evidently slightly agitated'. But the *Morning Journal* described her as 'presenting not the slightest appearance of agitation' and added that she had 'a slight flush on her cheek'.

At the opening of the trial John Fleming and his son told their stories of how the body of Jess McPherson was found. And then there was a sensation in court when the usher called the name 'James Fleming'. According to the *Morning Journal*, Old Fleming 'entered the dock nimbly'. But it was really the witness-box he was entering. The dock was reserved for the accused.

Old Fleming looked calm and collected and much younger

than the age he gave of eighty-seven. It's interesting to see in the contemporary newspapers that he was reported as he spoke, in what was then called the Doric. Nowadays the court reporters 'translate' the dialect that is used into English, so that the reader doesn't always get the full flavour of what is said.

In addition to a fine flow of the Doric, Old Fleming spoke in a loud voice, as many slightly deaf people do. The whole thing must have been torture to his respectable relatives. He agreed with Mr Adam Gifford, Advocate-depute conducting the prosecution, that he had breakfasted at Sandyford Place on the morning of Friday, July 4th.

Mr Gifford – Did Jessie McPherson serve you that morning?

Old Fleming – Yes.

Mr Gifford – Where did you go upon that Friday?

Old Fleming – She had been thrang for three days wi' a washin', and she was finishin' the shirts and dressin' them that day.

Mr Gifford – What o'clock?

Old Fleming – And her maister's were laid by, and mines were finishin', an' they were hangin' on the screens, ye ken, at the side o' the fire, an' I cam' hame to my dinner at the usual time, aboot four o'clock, an' took my dinner. An' after I took my dinner I had a custom of going up to the West End Park an' takin' a walk after dinner. This was Friday, an' I went away the fecht o' couple of hours.

Mr Gifford – Stop a moment.

Old Fleming – It was very wat thae days. I was verra much fasht wi' cauld feet, and there was no fire in the room, and I went doun to the kitchen fire to get my feet warmed, and Jessie McPherson made my tea.

Mr Gifford – What o'clock?

Old Fleming – I reckon it wad be weel on eight o'clock. She made my tea, and she poored it oot, and took a cup alang wi' me. And after the tea was by—

Lord Deas – Was it in the kitchen you got the tea?

Old Fleming – Yes. Then after I got my tea by, I yoked

to the readin'. I had always the papers in my pouch. And then I stopped till half-past nine o'clock.

Mr Gifford – In the kitchen?

Old Fleming – At the kitchen fire. At that hour I said I would go and mak' ready for bed, and I went away to my bed up the stair. I left Jess McPherson working away in the kitchen, ye ken. And in the mornin' I wauken't wi' a loud squeal.

Mr Gifford – Where is your bedroom? What flat of the house is your bedroom on?

Old Fleming – It is a flat above the kitchen ye ken. Weel, I was sayin' I was wauken't i' the mornin' wi' a loud squeal, and after that followed ither two, not so lood as the first ane. But it was an odd kind o' squeal I heard, and I jumped oot o' bed, and I heard no noise. A' was by in the coorse o' a minute's time. In a minute a' was quate, and I heard naething nor saw naething. I took oot my watch – I kept the time beside my pillow – and looked what o'clock it was. It was exactly four o'clock, a bonny, clear mornin'. I gaed awa' to my bed again. A' was quate. I thocht she had got somebody to stay with her. There was a woman she ca'd a sister o' hers. She booed to be in her room. So when I heard a' was quate and no noise, I gaed away to my bed again, and wisna lang in it till I fell asleep again. I lay till about six o'clock o' the morning, and she always used to come up. I lay wauken after that. She always used to come up with a little porridge about eight o'clock. She did not come up that morning, and I was surprised she did not come. I wearied very much for her. I lay still till nine o'clock. Then I raise and put on my claes. I forget whether I washed myself before I went down, but I gaed down to her door and gied three chaps that way. (And here Old Fleming tapped the front of the witness-box three times.) I got no answer. I tried the sneck of the door and fan' that the door was locked – no key in the door. Sae I gaed up till the storeroom. The storeroom and her bedroom was just adjoining ane anither maistly. I gaed into the storeroom, and then I found what was a bit window in the area standing open. It did not use to be that way. I drew it to, and returned to the kitchen again. The fire was wake. I put on some coals on the fire. It was still burning. This was Saturday morning, ye ken. And after that the main-door bell was rung. I went to the door. It was Mr Stewart, the next door neighbour's servant. I dinna mind her name. She wanted the len' o' a spade to clean the back door. She said their people were all away to the coast the nicht before. So I gaed doun to get the bit spade to the washing-house, and when I got to the washing-house there was nae key in it. I could not get the key, and the girl did not get the spade. At the same time, ye ken, when I got out to give the girl the spade, the back door was locked, and the key was in the inside o' the door, ye ken. That was the way I gaed down to look for the spade.

Mr Gifford (getting a chance at last) – What o'clock was it?

Old Fleming – About eleven o'clock, sir, I think. After that Mr Watson, the baker's man, cam' wi' his van, and the bell was rung, and I gaed up. But did I tell you first about the main door being not locked?

Mr Gifford – No, tell us that.

Old Fleming – It was not locked. The key was in the inside o' the door, and the door was on the latch – just snecked, ye ken, not locked. Sae whaever had been in, they had got out by the door. There is nae doubt o' that. An' so Mr Watson, the baker's man, cam' wi' his van shortly after that the servant girl was seeking for the spade, and I took a half-quarter loaf. The man was sitting upon the cart, but he had a little boy that handed me in the loaf at the door. So, always looking and wearying, wondering what was become of Jessie that she did not make her appearance, I stopped in till about twelve o'clock, when I thought I would go to the office. I looked for the check key, and got it on a shelf in the pantry, and I locked the door and went away to the office, then I gaed awa' down to the Briggate to see a property that I had a charge of. A water-pipe had burst there two or three days before, and I went down to see if it was all right – it had to be plaistered up wi' lime, ye ken. All was right, and I came awa' up again to the office, and stopped till about two o'clock. I then took the bus and gaed up to Sandyford, thinking, maybe, that Jess would be waiting till I gaed up. When I got up, all was quiet and no appearance o' Jess. I did not go out after that night, and made myself some bit dinner. About seven o'clock at night the bell was rung, and a young man came to the door. He said he was from Falkirk, and his name was Darnley. He said he promised to call on Jess when in the town. I said she was not in, and he went away. My shirts were on the screens in the kitchen. I laid them, one by one, off the screens which were laid against the pantry door. They had been laid or driven down. There was a pantry door they keep their things in, and the screens were either laid or driven ower upon it. So I took my shirts off the screens. There was a room off the kitchen that my drawers and kit stood in. I laid by my shirts. There were two marked with blood on them. I laid them all by, and laid these two on the tap.

Mr Gifford – Did you get any supper that night?

Old Fleming – I made myself a cup of tea. This would be eight o'clock. I thought if Jess had gone away with any of her acquaintances that she would make her appearance, but she did not. On Sabbath morning the bell was rung by the milkman, but I did not answer.

Mr Gifford – You supposed that it would be the milkman?

Old Fleming – Yes. Well, I made my breakfast again. A cup of tea and a boiled herring to it, and that was my breakfast. I made ready for the church. I went to the church in the forenoon, Mr Aikman's, in Anderston. After the church skailed I went straight hame. When I was going to the church, Mr John McAllister, who was coming out of his house door to go to the church, spoke to me. In the afternoon, after I had had a bit of bread and cheese, I went to the church again. After I was home the lad Darnley, who had ca'ed before ca'ed again, and asked if Jessie McPherson was in. He asked, 'Is she at church?' I said, 'I don't know.' Says he, 'If she comes out the town, will she come this way?' I said, 'I suppose she will.' He went away. I had no more calls that night I recollect, and at half-past nine I went to bed. On Monday morning I rose at eight o'clock, as was usual, to go through the properties on that day. Some tenants paid weekly, and others monthly, but we had to go through every Monday morning to collect the rents. I went to the office and got my books, and gaed awa' to collect and to lift what I could. I afterwards went to the office and gied in what cash I had gotten. I then gaed awa' hame to Sandyford. This would be about one or two o'clock. All was quiet, and I heard nothing. I kent that Mr Fleming (for so this father referred to his son) would be hame after he came up frae doun the water in the morning, and that he would be out for dinner. About four o'clock young John came in, and his father followed him. I told them what had taken place and said I had not seen Jess McPherson since Friday nicht. My son, astonished, ran away downstairs, and his son and me followed him. He found her bedroom locked, but had the recollection of trying the storeroom key, and it open the door. When he open it he saw the murdered woman lying near the empty bed. Her head was covered either with a skirt or white sheet, which was all blood, and her body was naked as she was born, downwards. She was lying on her face.'

Old Fleming added a little more but, in essence, that was his story and he stuck to it. There was a bit of stir in the court when he said he knew Jessie McLachlan and had visited her house a year ago, but had not seen her again until they met face to face before the Sheriff in the County Buildings. This didn't quite fit in with what the spectators had read in their newspapers at the time of the examination, when it was reported of Old Fleming that 'he denied that he even knew her, and being reminded that she had once been his servant, affirmed that he would not have taken her at all for the same person.'

Now he denied also that he had taken the silver plate to Jessie McLachlan's house and asked her to pawn it. He didn't need any money, because he had £150 in the Glasgow Savings Bank (the maximum allowed by that Bank at that time) and £30 in the Royal Bank of Scotland.

Then came the cross-examination by Mr Andrew Rutherford Clark, Sheriff of Inverness, who was Jessie McLachlan's chief counsel. He gave Old Fleming a tough time, but it might have been even tougher had not Lord Deas kept intervening on the 'old innocent's' behalf. Lord Deas, in fact, hardly ever stopped intervening throughout the trial, except that he had very few questions to ask Old Fleming.

The most important facets of this case are linked with questions of time, and it was very significant that Mr Clark's first question to Old Fleming was, 'Was your watch right that Saturday morning?' 'Aye,' was the answer, 'it gangs very reg'lar.' Mr Clark's point soon came out. It was whether or not Old Fleming admitted that the milk came on the Saturday morning. Now later in the trial the milk boy was to swear that he went to 17 Sandyford Place as usual about 7.40 on that Saturday morning, that the door was opened by Old Fleming fully dressed, and that Old Fleming said 'he was for nae milk'.

Mr Clark and Old Fleming fenced for a while and then Mr Clark said, 'Why did you not let Jessie open the door when the milk boy came?'

'On Saturday morning, you mean?' asked Old Fleming.

'Yes, on Saturday morning.'

Old Fleming's answer produced the legendary sensation in court. Unfortunately we can't be absolutely certain what he said. According to the *Morning Journal*, he said, 'Jessie, ye ken – it was a' ower wi' Jessie afore that.' But, according to the *North British Daily Mail*, Old Fleming said, 'Jessie? We ken't it was a' ower wi' Jessie afore that.' Either answer was a remarkable one, but those who thought he said 'we' must have wondered who else was with him in the house.

This did not seem to worry Lord Deas. He merely asked Mr Clark to put the question in another way. Mr Clark, though harried by Lord Deas, continued to harry Old Fleming and got three replies – 'There was nae Jessie to open the door that mornin' '; 'She was deid before that'; 'On Saturday morning, ye ken, Jessie was deid – she couldna open the door when she was deid'. When Mr Clark asked him if he knew, when he answered the bell to the milk boy, that Jessie was dead, he replied very quickly and loudly that he did not.

As Mr Clark kept pressing him, Old Fleming made a plea for pity. 'I can say no more than I have,' he said. 'I have told you everything in my heart. The memory of a man of seventy-eight years of age is not so fresh as a young man's. Be as easy as ye can. I am willing to answer every question.'

At this point a member of the jury stood up and pointed out to Lord Deas that Mr Fleming had just said he was seventy-eight, whereas he had already given his age as eighty-seven. Old Fleming, questioned on this point, said he was eighty-seven.

Mr Gifford, for the Crown, must have felt a lot happier when Lord Deas said kindly to Old Fleming, 'You may go now.' He was then able to get on with the case against Jessie McLachlan. He had no trouble at all with the various witnesses who could prove that Jessie's statements were full of lies, that she had been out of her house from Friday night until Saturday morning, that she had sent her own blood-stained clothes to Hamilton, and Jess McPherson's clothes to Ayr.

All was going well, indeed, until John McAllister, who had met Old Fleming on his way to the kirk on the Sunday, was asked by Mr Clark if he had ever heard anything against Old Fleming's character. Mr McAllister said he hadn't until the murder and he did not know, until he read it in the papers, that Old Fleming had been up before his own kirk session.

'Now, Mr Clark,' said Lord Deas at this point, 'this need not be opened up just now with the witness.'

Mr Clark sat down. As William Roughead says, 'It is hard to see why Mr Clark submitted thus to be put down; the proof available of Old Fleming's amorous activities throws the strongest light on the darkness of the case, and was, one would think, of vital moment to the defence.'

Mr Gifford now produced proof that Jessie McLachlan was so poor that she was continually pawning things. Some forty-one pawn-tickets were found in her house. He had also proved that Old Fleming had £180 behind him, so it was not likely that he'd steal his son's plate to get money to go to the Highlands.

After the medical evidence, the declarations of the prisoner were read, not without a spirited protest by Mr Clark, who said they were unfairly taken.

The evidence for the defence did not take long. Donald McQuarrie, the milk boy, could not be shaken about his evidence that it was Old Fleming who opened the door on the Saturday morning about 7.40, and that he was fully dressed at the time.

Mrs Mary Smith knew Jess McPherson well and, when out walking with her husband on Sunday, 29th June, had met her in Sauchiehall Street. When Mrs Smith told Jess that she was looking ill, Jess replied, very seriously, 'I don't feel very happy or comfortable with old Mr Fleming, for he's actually an old wretch and an old devil.' Jess said she'd call on Mrs Smith on that day fortnight to tell her something that she didn't like to tell before Mr Smith. 'I can't tell you what is the cause, because Sandy is with you,' she said.

Mrs McKinnon, a sister of Jess McPherson's, had asked Jess a month before the murder why she never came to see her. Jess replied that she had too much to do, and her heart was broken by the old man, who was so inquisitive that the door bell never rang but he must see who was there and know all about them. Martha McIntyre, a servant along with Jess McPherson, said the same, but added that Old

Fleming always enquired particularly about Jess, more than about the other servants.

The addresses to the jury followed. Mr Gifford presented the case for the Crown fairly, and found it necessary to remind the jury that they were trying Jessie McLachlan, and not Old Fleming.

Mr Clark did not do so well for the defence. He had to start his address at 7.30 in the evening of the third day of a strenuous trial and, when he finished his speech at 9 o'clock, the spectators burst into applause. But where Mr Clark was hampered was that he was following the same line of defence that was followed in the case of Madeleine Smith. You'll recall that the prosecutor could not prove that Madeleine and L'Angelier met on the fatal night. Mr Clark hoped that here the prosecution would not be able to prove that Jessie McLachlan met Jess McPherson on her fatal night. Yet all the time he had in his pocket the accused's statement that she *was* in the house that night.

Lord Deas summed up on the following morning, and it was remarked that, when he entered the court room, he carried the black cap ostentatiously in his hand and laid it down on the bench before him. He started his address to the jury at 10.30 a.m., and did not finish until 2.25 p.m. It was a very one-sided address indeed, and many people remarked that it was more like the address for the prosecution than the address for the prosecution had been.

The jury were out for a mere fifteen minutes. Possibly they had taken a hint from Lord Deas's entrance with the black cap, but they brought back a unanimous verdict of Guilty. Or maybe they wanted their lunch. At any rate, it was later revealed that the foreman had gone into a corner of the jury room and asked each juryman to write his verdict on a slip of paper and hand it to him.

Jessie Keeps Talking

When the verdict was announced Jessie McLachlan remained calm, except for a slight twitching of her mouth. She signed to Mr Clark and her counsel had an earnest conversation with her.

Lord Deas asked whether the prisoner had anything to say why judgement should not be pronounced against her, and Mr Clark replied, 'My Lord, I understand that the prisoner desires to make a statement before sentence is pronounced, either by her own lips or to be read by someone for her.'

'She is quite at liberty to do so any way she prefers,' said Lord Deas.

Jessie McLachlan threw her veil back, stood up in the dock and said loudly, 'I desire to have it read, my Lord. I am as innocent as my child, who is only three years of age at this date.'

She sat down, and Mr Clark read what is surely one of the most remarkable statements read in any court.

Jessie McLachlan's statement said:

'On Friday night, the 4th July last, I went up to Fleming's to see Jessie McPherson. I had been up seeing her that night fortnight, and had promised to come up again that night. We generally arranged a Friday night for my coming, as she had then most time, none of the family but the old man being at home, and I usually went late to let the old man away to bed, because, being of a jealous and inquisitive turn, he prevented us from talking freely. The old man was always very glad to see me, and very civil any time he happened to be in the kitchen when I went to see Jessie.

'I had put my child to bed about half-past nine. I told Mary Black in the morning I was going to see Jessie, and asked her to come and take charge of him till I returned, but she did not come. As I did not expect to be long out and he was sleeping, I did not give Mrs Campbell any charge, but I knew she would attend to him if he wakened. I had put on my things to go out when Mrs Fraser came in. Mrs Campbell opened the door for her. Mrs Fraser had her two children with her.

'I told her that my sister Ann intended to go to Australia, and I wanted her to write a certificate of character for her. She began to do so. I went into the kitchen to the press, and took Mrs Campbell's bottle. Mrs Campbell was in bed, but her clothes were not off. I took a little black basket with me, and Mrs Fraser's boy, Tommy Fraser, and went up to Monteith's shop in Argyle Street and purchased a gill and a half of rum, and paid 7½d. for it. I meant to give Mrs Fraser a dram, and have a dram for Jessie, and enough to taste with them.

'I came down, and Mrs Fraser opened the door and let me in. I gave Mrs Fraser a glass out of the bottle, and took about half a glass myself. I also bought some biscuits when I was out and offered them to her. After that I put the bottle and biscuits into my basket. I told her I had been intending to go to James McGregor's to get the certificate written, but she would do as well. She had stopped writing when I was out, as she could not please herself with it that night, and I said I would call on her next night and get the certificate written. I said McGregor's child had been ill, and that I had not been there for some time, and that I ought to have gone to see them before this. We also spoke about Mrs Fraser's husband being expected home.

'It was ringing ten as we went down our stair. I took the basket and bottle with me. We parted at the Gushet House about ten minutes past ten. I went up North Street to the house of Mr Fleming in Sandyford Place. I went to the front door and Jessie answered the door. She told me the old man was in the kitchen, but took me downstairs. The old man was sitting in the big chair in the kitchen when I went in. He said, 'Oh, is that you Jessie? How are you?' There was bread and cheese and a tumbler and glass and two plates on the kitchen table. I sat down on a chair at the end of the table next the door.

'Soon after the old man, without saying anything, rose and went upstairs. I gave Jessie the bottle I had brought. She filled out a glass of rum for me, part of which I took, and then poured out a glassful for herself, and took it, and she put the bottle away into the press. Soon after the old man returned with a bottle and glass in his hands. He filled scarcely a glass of spirits and gave it to me. I tasted it, and he told me to take it up, but I did not, and he poured the rest back into the bottle.

'Jessie, in a displeased way, said to him that wasn't a way to treat any person – that he ought to put it round. He said, "You ken, Jess, we've had twa three since the afternoon" – and that he wouldna mind, but that Mr Fleming had said before when they were left in the house that they had done well in drink, and spoke about their using so much, although the old man said it had been used by young John.

'He added: "However, if ye'll haud your ill tongue, I'll gi'e ye half a mutchkin if ye'll sen' for't." She said, "Aye, I've a tongue that would frighten somebody if it were breaking loose on them." The old man said something as if to himself, but I did not hear what. He poured the whisky into a tumbler on the table, and handed the bottle to me, and at the same time gave me 1s. 2d., and bade me go out for a half-mutchkin. The bottle was one with a long neck and round, flat bottom.

'Jessie gave me the key of the back door into the lane, and I went out by the kitchen back door, leaving it open, and locked the lane door after me, and went down Elderslie Street, and along the first street that crosses it as you come out from the lane, and along to North Street, to a whisky shop in North Street, very near right across from the end of the first street where it leads into North Street. It is a shop near the top of North Street, on the right hand side coming up from St Vincent Street, and not far from Mr McGaw, the flesher's.

'It would be a minute or two after eleven o'clock when I got to the shop. It was shut, but I knocked twice or thrice,

as there was a light inside visible at the top of the shutters,
but I did not get admittance; so I came back along
Sauchiehall Street and down Elderslie Street, and round the
corner into the lane behind Sandyford Place. I saw Mrs
Walker, the grocer's wife, standing at her own close mouth,
with her bonnet and shawl on, and another person, whom
I did not know, speaking with her. When I got to the back
of No. 17 Sandyford Place I opened the lane door and went
in, and locked the door behind me.

'I found the kitchen back door shut, which I had left open.
I knocked, but received no answer. I then went to the
kitchen window and looked in. The gas was burning, but I
saw nobody in the kitchen. I rapped at the door with the
lane door key, and after a little old Mr Fleming opened the
door. He told me he had shut the door on "them brutes o'
cats". I went into the kitchen, and put the money and the
bottle on the table. The old man locked the door and came
in after me. I told him the place was shut, and I could get
nothing. I then said, "Where's Jessie? It's time I was going
away home." He went out of the kitchen, I supposed to look
for her, and I went out with him.

'When in the passage, near the laundry door, I heard her
moaning in the laundry (Jess McPherson's bedroom), and
turned and went in past the old man, who seemed at first
inclined to stop me. I found Jessie lying on the floor, with
her elbow below her, and her head down. The old man came
in close after me. I went forward, saying, "God bless us,
what is the matter?" She was stupid or insensible. She had
a large wound across her brow and her nose was cut, and
she was bleeding a great deal. There was a large quantity of
blood on the floor. She was lying between her chest and the
fireplace.

'I threw off my bonnet and cloak, and stooped down to
raise her head, and asked the old man what he had done
this to the girl for. He said he had not intended to hurt her
– it was an accident. I saw her hair all down, and she had
nothing on but a polka and her shift. I took hold of her and

123

supported her head and shoulder, and I bade him fetch me some lukewarm water. He went out into the kitchen. I spoke to her and said, "Jessie, Jessie, how did this happen?" and she said something I could not make out. I thought he had been attempting something wrong with her, and that she had been cut by falling. He did not appear to be in a passion; and I was not afraid of him.

'He came in again, bringing lukewarm water in a corner dish. I asked him for a handkerchief and some cold water, as the other was too hot. He brought them in from the kitchen, and I put back her hair and bathed away the blood from her face, and saw she was sore cut. I said to the old man, "However did he do such a thing as that to the girl?" and he said he did not know, and seemed to be vexed and put about by what had happened. I asked him to go for a doctor, but he said she would be better soon, and he would go after we got her sorted.

'The old man then went ben the house again, and I supported her, kneeling on one knee beside her. In a little she began to open her eyes, and come to herself, but she was confused. She understood when I spoke to her, and gave me a word of answer now and then, but I could get no explanation of things from her, so I just continued bathing her head. I bathed it for a long time till she got out of that dazed state and could understand better. I asked her whether I would not go for a doctor, and she said, "No, stay here beside me." I said I would. I did not trouble her much with speaking to her at that time.

'While I was sorting at her head, the old man came into the room with a large tin basin and water and soap in it, and commenced washing up where the blood was all round about me, drying it up with a cloth and wringing it into a basin. I had raised Jessie to sit up, and was sitting on the floor beside her. As he was near us he went down on his elbow, and spilt the basin with a splash when he was lifting it. He spilled the water all over my feet and the lower part of my dress, and my boots were wet through.

'After Jessie had quite come to herself, I tied a handkerchief, which the old man brought me at my request, round
the cut on the brow. I assisted her to rise off the floor, and
took her over to a chair near beside the bedside. She was
very weak and unsteady on her feet, and she asked me to
put her into bed. I was not able to do it, and I asked the old
man to help me, and we put her into bed, just as she was.
After she was put into bed I continued bathing away the
blood from the nose, which continued bleeding a little.
When put to bed I took a crotchet night-cap, which was
hanging on the looking glass, and put it on the top of the
handkerchief.

'The old man was drying and redding up the blood and
the water that had been spilt over where Jessie had been
lying. When she was put to bed she appeared to be getting
weaker, and lay with her eyes shut, and I said to the old
man that the doctor should be got now. He came and looked
at her, and said, "No, there was no fears, and that he would
go for the doctor himself in the morning." I thought she was
asleep, but she had heard what was said, and, turning her
eyes to me, she said "No". I understood her to mean that
she did not wish a doctor brought at present.

'She lay in bed till the morning was beginning to break,
or till, as I supposed, it would be well on to three o'clock.
She had been sleeping, and gradually came to herself again,
and I thought there was no danger. Latterly she spoke a
good deal to me as I sat by the bedside when the old man
was out. He sat a while by the bedside after redding up the
floor, but he rose and went ben to the kitchen, and was
going about both ben the house and upstairs. I heard him
chapping up the fire and moving about; and when I went
ben to get her a drink of water I observed he had put the
teapot to the fire, I supposed for her. He was but and ben
several times, but afterwards came and sat down at the
bedside, and remained there till she rose. I was twice in the
kitchen during this period; once when I went in for water
for her, and once when I took ben my boots and stockings

(which I took off after the water was spilt on them) to the kitchen fire to dry.

'She told me that on a Friday night some weeks before there was a gentleman in the house, who had remained all Thursday night in it, and until the Friday afternoon, when he left, and that old Mr Fleming convoyed him to the station. She said he was a brewer, and she mentioned his name; but I can't remember it; and that the old man left with him at four o'clock in the afternoon of the Friday she spoke of, and that he did not return till eleven o'clock, when he was gie an' tipsy. He asked her to help him off with his coat, which she did, and then she went downstairs, and to bed.

'She said that between one and two in the morning he came down to her room, and in alongside her into bed, and tried to use liberties with her; that she made an outcry about it, and was angry then, and spoke to him next morning about it, and said she would tell his son, her master; that he begged her to say nothing about his having done so, or that he had come home the worse of drink; that unless for the drink he would never have done it; that there had been words between them ever since; that the old man was in terror in case it would ever come out about what she had told me, and that he had offered her money, but that for her own character she never meant to tell Mr Fleming upon him. But she said she was going to Australia at any rate, and that she was determined to make the old rascal pay well before she left, and she would make him pay for this too.

'She said that after I went out for the half-mutchkin they had a great quarrel, and he was very angry because he had thought when she said that about her tongue breaking loose she was hinting a threat to tell me. She said they had words on the same subject during the day, and when it began again on my going out she left the kitchen to take off her stays, which were uneasy, and that she took them off, and had her petticoats untied after that, when she was struck by him. She had given him some word on leaving the kitchen, and he was flyting and using bold language to her in the lobby after she was in the room, and she was giving him it back while loosing her stays; and that when he was there and going to take them off she went and shut the door to in his face, and that he came back immediately after and struck her in the face with something and felled her.

'What I have stated was told me by Jessie during the time I sat with her. It was not told me all at once, but it is the substance of what she said. We did not speak on any other subject. She also asked me if she was badly cut, and I said she was, and she said when the doctor came in the morning she would need to tell some story or other how she got it.

'I asked the old man once, when he came into the room, how he had ever allowed himself to be provoked to strike the girl after his own doings with her. He did not give me a direct answer, but just said it couldna be helped now, although he was very sorry, but he would make everything right to Jess, and make up for it as Jess very well knew, and if I would never mention what I had seen, he would not forget it to me. I said it was a great pity I had anything to do with it, and that I did not know what to do, as I had left my child without anybody in charge of it. Jessie said the lodger would take care of him; that I must go away before the doctor came, but that if she must tell about this in the morning, or when Mr Fleming came home, she was afraid she would just have to tell who did it and why.

'This was before the old man, who said, "No, no, Jess, ye'll no need to do that"; and he begged me never to say anything about this matter, and he would put everything to rights. I said I had no occasion to speak of it; and I promised never to mention it, and Jessie and he could take their own way. He would not rest content till I would swear it, and he went upstairs and brought down the big Bible with a black cover on it, and in the presence of Jessie he made me swear on the Bible, by the Almighty God, that I would never tell to man, woman or child anything I had seen or heard that night between him and Jess, and he said he would swear

Captions

1. *Daguerrotype of the Smith family taken at Bridge of Allan in 1852. Madeleine, then fifteen, is the tallest child. (Baillie's Library, University of Glasgow)*

2. *Caption as on picture (Baillie's Library, University of Glasgow)*

3. *The cleaver used to kill Jess McPherson (Strathclyde Regional Police Headquarters)*

4. *One of the many portraits made of Jessie McLachlan during the trial. (William Hodge & Co. Ltd)*

5., 6., 7., and 8. *The Pritchard menage at Sauchiehall Street – the doctor and his wife, his mother-in-law Mrs Taylor, and Mary McLeod with one of the children. (Baillie's Library, University of Glasgow)*

9. *Detective Lieutenant John Thomson Trench who investigated Oscar Slater's case. (The Glasgow Herald)*

10. *Oscar Slater (Glasgow Herald)*

never to forget it to either her or me. He said that he would make her comfortable all her life. After this he sat at the bedside.

'About three o'clock, I would suppose it was, Jessie told him to go away ben the house. He said he was very weel where he was. She told me she wanted to rise and make water, and she got up in bed. I told the old man to go away for a little, which he did, and I helped her out and assisted her. She said after she rose that she felt stiff and cold, and if she could get ben to the fire. I put a blanket round her, and I called to the old man, and he and I took her ben to the kitchen. She walked ben, assisted by us, but I think she could have gone herself.

'She sat down at the kitchen fire on the floor, on a small piece of carpet. The old man, at my bidding, went ben to the bedroom and brought ben the pillow and bedclothes; and I put the pillow under her head, and the blankets on her, and tucked them in below her. Some time after that she fell asleep for a while, but wakened and complained that she was too near the fire, and moved herself, with our help, without rising from the floor to her feet, away from the front of the fire, and turned herself, so that she lay with her feet in towards the fire and her head further from it, and between the table and the press, or in that direction. She lay in this position for a good while. The old man was sometimes about the kitchen, where I remained, and sometimes going about the house. He was ben in the bedroom more than once.

'After lying there in the kitchen a considerable time, Jessie got restless and uneasy, and complained of feeling worse. I thought she was getting sick, and I brought her water. In a very short time (I would suppose at this time it would be between four and five) she got worse very rapidly, and she said to me to go for a doctor. With that I drew on my boots, and went into the bedroom, and threw on the French merino dress which was hanging there over my own, as it was all wet and draggled, and I put on my cloak and bonnet.

'As I came out of the bedroom the old man was coming

down the stairs, and I said to him that Jessie was very ill
and I was going for a doctor; where would I go to? He said
he didna ken where any doctor lived near, but wait a minute
till I see how she is. I knew there was a doctor in the
neighbourhood, and, without waiting for him, because I
thought he did not want a doctor, and I wished one brought
at once, I went upstairs to the front door, but found it
locked, and the key was not in it.

'I went down into the kitchen again, and he was leaning
over Jessie with his hands on his knees, looking at her. I
went forward and asked him for the key, and saw that Jessie
had become far worse than when I left her. I thought she
was dying. She appeared to be insensible, but not dead, as
she was moving. It was the first time I thought she was
going to die, and I said the girl was dying, and I insisted on
him letting me out for a doctor. He said he would not. He
would do it in his own time.

'I went upstairs again and into the parlour, and opened
the shutters, and put up the back window to see if I could
see anyone stirring about the back of No. 16, or the other
houses, but saw no one.

'I was leaving the parlour to go into the dining-room to
look out in front, when I heard a noise in the kitchen, and
I turned downstairs as fast as I could, and as I came in sight
of the kitchen door I saw the old man striking her with
something which I saw afterwards was the meat chopper.
She was lying on the floor with her head off the pillow, a
good piece along the floor, and he was striking her on the
side of the head.

'When I saw him I skirled out, and ran forward to the
door, crying to him, and then I got afraid when he looked
up, and I went back up the lobby and part of the stair,
where I could go no further, as I got very ill with fright and
palpitation of the heart, to which I am subject.

'My fright was caused by hearing him coming out of the
kitchen, and I thought he meant to murder me, and I
stopped and leaned or held to the wall on the stair without

the power of moving, and began to cry, "Help, help." He came to the stair-foot, and cried to me to come down, he was not going to meddle me.

'I saw he had not the cleaver in his hands as he came; and I cried out, "Oh, let me away, let me go; for the love of God, let me go away!" He said he would do me no harm. I said the girl's killed, and what was I going to do, and entreated him to let me away.

'He came up and took me by the cloak, and said, "I kent frae the first she cou'dna live; and if any doctor had come in he would have to answer for her death, for she would have told." I was crying and said, "Oh, what am I to do, out of my house all night, and Jessie killed?"

'He said, "Don't be feart, only if you tell you know about her death you will be taken in for it as well as I; come down and it can never be found out."

'I went down to the kitchen in great agitation. I did not know what to do. I was terrified, because I was in the house and saw the body lying there, and myself connected with her death. He said, "My life's in your power, and yours is in my power," but if both of us would keep the secret it never could be found out who did it, and that if I would inform on him he would deny it, and charge that I did it. He said it was as much as our lives were worth if either of us would say a word about it.

'So he bade me help him, and to wash up the blood from the floor, but I said I could not do it if I should never move. He took the body by the oxters and dragged it ben into the laundry, and took the sheet and wiped up the blood with it off the floor. The sheet and blankets he had thrown up off the floor on to the end of the table; and when he took off the sheet to wipe up the blood I saw the chopper all covered with blood lying beneath it, or else it rolled out of it on to the table.

'I beseeched and begged him to let me go away, and I would swear never to reveal what I had seen, in case of being taken up for it myself as well as him. He said that the best way would be for him to say that he found the house robbed in the morning, and to leave the larder window open. He brought the dresses from Jessie's room into the kitchen, and said that if I would taken them away, and buy a box, and take them by some railway out of the way to some place, or to send the box to some address by the railway to lie till called for, that it never could be found out what had become of the clothes.

'He said I knew very well that he liked Jess, but he was sure from the first that she was not able to recover from what he had done to her at first; and when I asked him what tempted him to strike her, he said I knew Jess had a most provoking tongue, and that she had been casting things up to him, and he was mad at her; that he had no power of speaking whiles when she was at him, and that he had just struck her in a passion; and that even on the Sunday night before he had been just on the brink of doing the same thing to her.

'He "dichted" up the floor and lobby with a clout, and took ben the blankets and the sheets, and the hacking knife, and the bit carpet into the bedroom. He came back and burned some things, I don't know what – clothes of the girl's. He got some water at the sink in a tin basin and washed himself. He had taken off his coat, and was in his shirt sleeves since after the time he killed the girl. His shirt was all blood when he took it off to wash himself, so he put it into the fire. He put on a clean one off the screen, and went ben to his own room and changed his trousers and vest, I think. He went down to the cellar for coals, brought them up, and put them on the fire.

'The bell rang; he bade me open, but I said, "No, I'll not go to the door, go you." It was the milk boy. The old man took no jug up with him. He was in his shirt sleeves when he went up, but in a coat when he came down again. He brought no milk with him.

'After that he brought the plate, and said I had better take this too, and take it and pawn it in Lundie's pawn, in the name of Mary McDonald or McKay, No. 5 St Vincent Street, and nobody could trace it. He afterwards said I had better not pawn it, but put it away in some place with the dresses. He told me that I would get a tin box in any ironmonger's for 5s., and to take the things through to Edinburgh, where I was not known, and find some water where they could be sunk and never heard of.

'He took out his purse and gave me £1 7s. I consented to take the things, and promised never to breathe a syllable of what had passed. He said if I did it would be my life as well as his, and that he would set me up in a shop, and never see me want.

'I went out from the house after eight o'clock, it might be half-past eight, taking the things in a bundle. He opened the back door for me, and came down and opened the lane door with the key. I went along the lane westward, and home down by Kelvingrove Street, along the Broomielaw, where I met the people coming from their work, and I went up Washington Street to avoid them, and down James Watt Street again, and in by the back court into my own close by the court door and up the stair, where Campbell let me in.

'I never had any quarrel with Jessie. On every occasion we were most affectionate and friendly. I was not pressed for money. I paid my rent on Saturday, 5th July, before I pawned the plate. I paid £4.'

Jessie is Sentenced

Mr Clark took forty minutes to read Jessie McLachlan's statement, and, as he reached the end of it, the hitherto silent spectators buzzed with excitement. The only person who seemed unaffected was Lord Deas, who proceeded to pass sentence. I know of no other convicted person who was sentenced in so cruel and vindictive a manner as Lord Deas used towards Jessie McLachlan.

In the course of his speech he said:

'You left your own house on Friday night and you went to the house in which Jessie was residing, and would, of course, have no difficulty in getting admission there. You would have no difficulty in getting her permission, if you had any plausible excuse for it, to stay with her and sleep with her all night. It is now stated, upon your own confession, you did remain there all night.

'In the course of that night, at what precise time and in what precise manner we do not know . . . . probably when she was asleep, you did attack her with that cleaver we saw here, or some other deadly instrument . . . . Upon that night you did most barbarously and most cruelly murder that unsuspecting woman, who believed you were up to that hour the best friend she had in the world. Of that crime you have been convicted by the unanimous verdict of as attentive and intelligent a jury as I ever saw in the box.'

That last sentence, by the way, did not exactly match with the way Lord Deas slapped down the jury during the trial.

'You chose to put in a defence,' continued Lord Deas, 'to the effect that a gentleman, whose character up to this time has been quite unstained, was the murderer; you have chosen to repeat that statement now with all the details to which we have just listened.'

'Well, my Lord,' began Jessie McLachlan, but the court officials motioned her to silence. Lord Deas went on:

'I sit here, no doubt, primarily to do my duty in the trial and the conviction – if there is evidence for a conviction – of those who are guilty. But I sit here, and the jury also sit here, to protect the innocent, especially the innocent who are absent and cannot defend themselves; and it is my imperative duty, after what has now been stated deliberately in writing for you, to say that there is not upon my mind a shadow of suspicion that the old gentleman had anything whatever to do with the murder.'

As he went on, he added for good measure, 'I am bound to say that I never knew an instance in which the statements made by prisoners after conviction were anything else than in their substance falsehoods; and that the result of all the experience I have had in these matters is to lead me to the conviction that the person who would commit such a crime as you have committed is quite capable of saying anything . . . . Your statement conveys to my mind the impression of a tissue of as wicked falsehoods as to any to which I have ever listend; and, in place of tending to rest suspicion against the man whom you wish to implicate, I think if anything were awanting to satisfy the public mind of that man's innocence, it would be that most incredible statement which you have now made.'

Lord Deas put the black cap on his head and ordered that Jessie McLachlan be returned to prison and kept on a diet of bread and water only, until October 11th, when she would be hanged: 'And may God Almighty have mercy on your soul.'

'Mercy!' cried Jessie McLachlan. 'Aye, He'll ha'e mercy, for I'm innocent!'

And despite what Lord Deas had said, a great many people in Scotland and England agreed that, though Jessie was certainly implicated in the case, she was innocent of murder.

Jessie McLachlan was sentenced on a Saturday and *The Glasgow Herald* leader on the following Monday said, 'Lord Deas's summing up was remarkable for all that could distinguish a judge's charity – dignity, calmness, lucidity, and a searching analysis of every part of the evidence, without a single expression of feeling by which the minds of the jury might have been unduly influenced.'

Among the many letters which poured into the *Herald* after that statement was one which, addressing the editor, said:

135

'You, sir are a partisan, and view everything in a false light – very much in the manner of the poor Anderston donkey on whom some person had very wickedly put green spectacles, when the animal quite innocently commenced to eat shavings, thinking them grass. This, sir, is what you are doing – you see everything through the medium of these celebrated spectacles introduced into court on the nose of "the old gentleman", Fleming.'

The *Morning Journal* which *The Glasgow Herald* was now describing as 'the woman's organ', was furious with Lord Deas, the jury, and the *Herald*. Describing the way its office had been besieged for copies on the Saturday night, the *North British Daily Mail* said, 'The gentleman who, in the scramble in the crowd in front of our office, shortly after eight o'clock on Saturday evening, lost one of the skirts of his coat can have the lost skirt returned to him on applying at our office.'

It was necessary to go across the Border to find newspaper comment which was sound and reasonable. A leader in the *Daily Telegraph* said:

'No tittle of evidence, strange to say, was brought forward to show the previous relations between Mr Fleming, senior, his family, the servants, the deceased woman, or the prisoner. The one circumstance clearly established in his favour was that at the time of the murder he stood in no obvious want of money. The single fact indisputably proved against the prisoner was that she was in possession of some of Jessie McPherson's property immediately after the commission of the crime; but there was nothing further to connect her with it. On this fact, or rather presumption, the Glasgow jury have found her guilty.

'Upon her conviction she made a fresh statement through her counsel, to the effect that it was true she had been in the house on the night of the murder, that during her absence to purchase drink the deed had been committed by Old Fleming, and that afterwards she had been bribed to silence.

This statement the judge characterised as a tissue of falsehoods. Now, we have no wish to impugn the justice of either the Scotch jury or of Lord Deas. It is certain that Jessie McLachlan was in some form or other an accomplice, whether after or before the fact we do not say. It is impossible, however, to believe, on the evidence before us, that the prisoner left her home with the deliberate action of killing Jessie McPherson, and almost as difficult to credit that the crime was committed by her, alone and unassisted.

'An awful mystery still hangs over this strange tragedy – a mystery which the present trial has failed to clear up. It has been proved, indeed, that the prisoner is guilty of some participation; but till it is proved to what degree her guilt extends, and whether she is the sole or principal criminal, we cannot think the sentence of the law can be justly carried into effect. There must be more inquiry before Jessie McLachlan should be sent to her last account as the murderess of Jessie McPherson.'

And that was also the conclusion of the Sheriff of Lanarkshire, Sir Archibald Alison, who wrote in his autobiography years later: 'She had not a fair trial; the minds of the jury were made up before they entered the box. This was proved by their bringing a verdict in fifteen minutes, in a case where the evidence had occupied three days. There was a miscarriage of justice; but it arose from the publicity of their proceedings, not their secrecy.'

Now a petition to delay the execution of Jessie McLachlan until more enquiries could be made was started in Glasgow, and soon spread to every principal town in Scotland, and to a large number of towns in England. At a mass meeting in the City Hall, Glasgow, on September 29th it was announced that 50,000 Glaswegians had signed the petition. In Edinburgh the Rev Dr Guthrie recommended every man and woman in the Capital to sign.

Meanwhile Old Fleming had not been forgotten. Since the day he had left the High Court, when Lord Deas said

'You may go', Old Fleming had been pursued by the mob. As he left the court the crowd thronged round him, groaning and hissing, and he only escaped by jumping into a cab. He went, or was sent, to his son's house between Dunoon and Innellan, and there were constant demonstrations. When he went to his barber in Dunoon, he was recognised and chased by a stone-throwing mob through the streets. He escaped, and the mob turned their attention to the barber, who was forced to throw Old Fleming's shaving tackle into the Firth of Clyde.

Every day the postman arrived at Avondale with a budget of mail for Old Fleming. Some letters praised him, some condemned him, and some asked for his autograph! At any rate, his piety and his principles must have upheld the "old innocent" because, one afternoon, he was looking over the Avondale hedge when a friend passed by with a newspaper. 'Hey!' cried Old Fleming to him. 'Hiv' they no' hangit that wumman yet?'

On September 30th, on the instructions of the Lord Advocate, Sir Archibald Alison started a private investigation into the case. And a week before the execution, the Lord Provost of Glasgow received a letter from the Home Office respiting the sentence of death on Jessie McLachlan until November 1st.

An official enquiry was opened by the Sheriff of Haddington and, four days after the result had been sent to the Home Secretary, the Lord Provost received a second letter. This time Jessie McLachlan was reprieved. The Lord Provost took the good news to Jessie in the condemned cell. 'Will there be naething done on Saturday, then?' she asked, and she was assured that there would be no execution on November 1st.

This reprieve was treated by the *Morning Journal* as a resounding, but typical, success of that newspaper's. *The Glasgow Herald* was horrified.

'Trial by jury,' said their leader, 'the palladium of British liberty, has been subverted. The unreasoning public have been taught that, if they only cry loud enough, they can snatch a convicted murderess out of the hands both of the High Court of Justiciary and of the British Executive. They, or their organs, have denounced the judge as a hard-hearted wretch and blood-thirsty officer of the law; they have stigmatised the jury as idiots or savages; they have yelled execrations into the places of business of these gentlemen; and they have cursed them on the streets and spat upon them in public omnibuses.'

Obviously the jury should have followed the example of Old Fleming and taken a cab!

The *Herald*'s horror was merely intensified when the Crown Agent wrote to the Governor of the North Prison, Glasgow, saying:

'I beg to inform you that I have received Her Majesty's conditional pardon in favour of Jessie McIntosh or McLachlan, who was at a Justiciary Court holden at Glasgow in September 1862, convicted of murder, and sentenced to death for the same, pardoning the said Jessie McIntosh or McLachlan of the said crime, and sentence passed upon her for the same, upon condition of her being kept in penal servitude for the terms of her natural life.'

By this time the 'wumman' realised she was not to be 'hangit', and all she said to the Governor was, 'And I'm tae be kept in jail a' my days!' She was taken to Perth Prison and, for the fifteen years she remained there, she was a model prisoner. She kept insisting on her innocence and refused to have anything to do with the other prisoners. Even when she went to the prison chapel on Sundays, she asked that a screen should be put up to keep her from the rest. Jessie had her respectability too. She also had her disposition for lying. Even though it had proved almost fatal to her, she could not resist it.

First, though, it must be said that the respectable John

Fleming treated Jessie McLachlan's pardon as a loss of face for the Flemings. What he wanted was an admission from the Crown that 'the alteration upon the sentence was not intended to lead to the inference that . . . . Mr Fleming was otherwise than innocent of the murder'. He got no satisfaction, and the matter was brought up in Parliament several times, with the same result.

Jessie's Confession

What would the Flemingites (that was the popular term for the supporters of Old Fleming) have said if they had known that, before the Sheriff of Haddington's enquiry which led to the pardon, Jessie McLachlan had 'confessed' to the murder? This last strange story of Jessie's did not come out until a year after the crime. *The Glasgow Herald* had made several references to a 'confession', and on the first anniversary of the murder, Mr J. A. Dixon, Jessie McLachlan's law agent, wrote to the editor and said that, rather than a hearsay version should be published, he enclosed a correct statement. And this is the fifth and last of Jessie's famous statements.

'When the trial of Mrs McLachlan was concluded, and after the Home Secretary had ordered the enquiry by Mr Young, but before it began, Mrs McLachlan's agents applied to the Prison Board for permission to confer with the prisoner, the objects of the agents being to ascertain whether she could give any information which would assist them in dealing with the numerous reports current after the publication of the "Statement", and particularly a report which was persistently made, and which came to them through many different channels, that old Mr Fleming had been seen on the door steps in front of the house between four and five on the morning of the murder.

'Mr Dixon asked her whether she was aware that the old man had been out in front of the house, mentioning at the same time that they had hitherto been unable to discover any ground for the rumour. Mrs McLachlan answered that she did not think there was any truth in it, and they need not trouble themselves in hunting after the rumour further, as she did not think it was possible it could be true.

'Mr Dixon then proceeded to ask her a number of questions as to details of the old man's movements, with a view of ascertaining whether she had any particular reason for saying that the rumour could not possibly be true. She showed some little hesitation in answering these questions, preferring to turn aside to talk about the incidents of the trial, particularly criticising the portraits in the pamphlet account of the trial, and trifling with other irrelevant topics of that kind.

'She appeared to Mr Dixon to be hysterical; sometimes crying and sometimes laughing or giggling. There was nothing, however, about the peculiarities of her behaviour to indicate that she was insane, or that she did not know perfectly well what she was speaking about.

'On resuming the questions, as he could get her to attend to him, he put some questions such as "Where was the old man at this time?'

'After a little hesitation she looked in his face laughing, and said "I may just as weel tell ye that the auld man wasna there at a' ". And on the question being repeated, she explained that she meant to say that she had not seen the old man at all that night.

'Mr Dixon then asked her, "Do you mean to say that you did not see the old man sitting in the armchair when you went down to the kitchen?'

'She said, "No, I did not go down to the kitchen; I did not go in at the front door at all."

' "Then how did you enter?"

'She said, "By the back door," and that "she had not been upstairs at all that night."

' "Do you mean to say that the old man did not send you out for whisky?"

'She answered, "No – and I was not out for whisky at all."

' "But," said Mr Dixon, "Mrs Walker and Miss Dykes saw you out. What were you doing out?" She answered that when these two people saw her she had not been in the house at all, and was then going to it for the first time.

'On being asked if she had been anywhere else after leaving Mrs Fraser near the Gushet House a little after ten o'clock, she said she had been nowhere but on the road to Sandyford Place. On its being pointed out to her that from the time she left Mrs Fraser till she was seen by Mrs Walker and Miss Dykes, about an hour had elapsed, she still adhered to her statement, and apparently could give no other account of what she had been doing in the interval.

'In answer to the question, "Who had opened the door to the milkboy?" if she had not seen the old man at all, she stated that she herself had opened the door to the milkboy, and that "the old man was in bed at the time", she supposed. On being then asked whether she therefore meant to say that it was she who had committed the murder, she said she could not tell – that she knew nothing about it.

'On being requested to explain what she meant by this, as, if the old man did not do it, she must have done it, she went on to say that Jessie and she had been drinking; that there had been a good deal of drink going; that Jessie got sick with the drink, and was lying on the kitchen floor vomiting; that she, Mrs McLachlan, washed the vomit from Jessie's face, and brought in blankets and put them over her; that Jessie vomited on the blankets, and she (Mrs McLachlan) afterwards washed part of them; that the blankets were not washed to remove blood stains; and that she then washed up the floor after Jessie began to get better.

'She then said that from drink and nausea she herself became sick and retched violently and Jessie (who, she said, was always in the habit of working with laudanum when anything was wrong with her) made her take a large dose of laudanum to stop the vomiting.

'She then said that the effect of the laudanum upon her had always been to take her head and make her delirious; that her husband and her sister could tell that when the doctor gave her a sleeping draught during one of her illnesses, it had the effect of making her start to get out of bed and rush about the room, and that they had to hold her (a statement which the husband and sister afterwards contradicted to Mr Dixon); that the laudanum given her by Jessie had the same effect, and took her head; that she had no remembrance of any quarrel, or of anything except a confused recollection of Jessie crying, "Jessie! Jessie! What are you doing?' And that she (Mrs McLachlan) was creeping about in the dark on her hands and knees, somewhere, she did not know where.

'After that she had no recollection of anything whatever till she found the body in the morning; that the old man was not down the stairs that night or morning at all, a statement which she reiterated again and again; that she could not tell whether any person had been in the house or not.

'She repeated that she had opened the door to the milkboy, and on being reminded that the old man himself and the milkboy had sworn it was the old man who had opened the door, she said that she was aware of that, but that it was she that did it notwithstanding.

'She said that she remained in the house till near nine o'clock, and that she was so dazed by the drink and the laudanum that she never thought of escaping sooner, and that she left by the back door. No questions were put to her regarding the clothing or the silver plate, and she said nothing about them. Nor did she make any other statement regarding the night's proceedings.

'On receiving this communication from Mrs McLachlan, Mr Dixon told her that he did not know what to make of it, and it placed him in a very awkward position, and that it suggested some doubts as to his continuing to act as her agent.

'Upon hearing this, the prisoner said that it was all

nonsense, that he need not believe a word of it, and that there was not a word of truth in it, and that she only said so to see how he would look.

'As this statement immediately followed Mr Dixon's expressed doubt about acting as her agent, he told her that he was afraid there was some truth in it, and that he would take time to consider how he would act. She then said that she hoped he was not going to mention what she had now told him, repeating that it was all lies, and that the statement read at the trial was the truth; upon which Mr Dixon explained to her that from his position as her agent he was bound to secrecy, and that she might rest satisfied upon that point.'

Mr Dixon continues his account at some length, but I'd just like to interpose here and mention that he was not as tightly bound to secrecy as he mentioned. He talked to a couple of friends about Jessie McLachlan's 'Confession', and he also mentioned it to two detectives, though he denied this afterwards.

Indeed, Mr Dixon was such a respectable man that even *The Glasgow Herald* took him to their heart later – especially after he had communicated the 'Confession' to Mr Fleming's agents. And now the Dean of Faculty in Edinburgh was brought in, and he suggested that Mr Dixon should go to Perth Prison and interview Jessie McLachlan, 'representing to her the injustice done to the Fleming family if the old man was innocent'.

On June 19th, 1863, the agent did interview his client, but I prefer the Prison Governor's version of what happened to that written by Mr Dixon.

'At the interview,' reported the Governor, 'Mr Dixon commenced by assuring the prisoner that anything she might say would have no effect upon her sentence, and that she could not now be hanged for the offence – a fact of which she appeared to be fully aware.

'He then asked her if she remembered having said anything to him about laudanum, when she at once, without the least hesitation, positively denied that she had ever spoken about laudanum to him, and, moreover, that she had only once seen him after the trial, and then but a very short time.

'Mr Dixon put the question relative to the laudanum to her in different forms at least three or four times, and she as repeatedly denied that she had spoken of laudanum at all; she also asserted that she was as innocent as Mr Dixon himself; and when he then asked her if Mr Fleming was the guilty person, she replied that "he did the act"; and again, on Mr Dixon making the observation that Mr Fleming's friends all declared he was innocent, she exclaimed, "How could his friends know whether he was innocent or not; they were not there."

'She also said that it was a great hardship that she should be kept here so long, apart from her delicate child. He said, "Your child is with your relatives, and will be well taken care of; but the Flemings are ruined, every one of them, and are about to leave the country," and he then added, "the case has lately been before Parliament." The prisoner's persistency in denial being obvious, the interview was not very protracted.'

Jessie must have wondered whose side her agent was on! The fact is that, when this hysterical 'Confession' was published, it caused no excitement at all. The *Morning Journal* said it was worthless, and all *The Glasgow Herald* could say was, 'According to the laws of evidence and the rule of universal experience, a liar is entitled to belief, and is only to be believed when he makes a revelation which incriminates himself, and we are not going to deny this time-honoured privilege to the heroine of the cleaver.'

This charming remark can only have been made by one who had no experience whatever of the world of crime. Time after time, in the history of murder, people have come forward to 'confess' crimes of which they were innocent.

But, talking of charming remarks, the Governor of Perth Prison forwarded, with his report on Dixon *v*. McLachlan, this 'Note by Miss Hislop, Scripture Reader in the General Prison, of a conversation held by her with the convict Jessie McLachlan.'

'I had visited the prisoner several times in my official capacity,' reported the ineffable Miss Hislop, 'but had never once alluded her to crime, but had spoken to her as I do other prisoners, as being a lost sinner in the sight of God. On this occasion she referred to the crime with which she was charged, and said her case was a very sad one.

'I said to her, "You will have noticed that in all my dealings with you I have carefully avoided speaking to you of your crime; but since you have mentioned it yourself I shall let you know my mind on the subject. I believe you to be the guilty person, and to me you seem to have acted as a guilty person throughout. You have been guilty of a deed for which you ought to have been hanged, as God has never repealed that law He gave, that blood should answer for blood, but by a very mysterious providence your life has been spared, and I would beseech you to make early and earnest application to Him whose blood cleanseth from all sin."

'She looked at me and said, "Well, Miss Hislop, I am obliged to you for this honesty." She sat silent for a minute or so after this, and then she said, "I had as little thought of it half an hour before I left my own house as you have at this moment." I said I believed it was not a premeditated thing, but that one sin had led to another till the deed was committed.

'She said, "I feel sometimes as if I could go through these prison walls. I often think my mind will give way." She began to tell me about going out for some spirits that night at the request of Fleming. I stopped her, and said it was no use going over it, as nothing she could say would alter my opinion about it. She immediately added, "But Fleming is not a good man." I said, "I don't say he is a good man, but I believe him to be innocent of that crime." '

When this was published, the *Daily Telegraph* had an acid comment:

'Even in a Scotch gaol, we can scarce believe that Scripture-readers are allowed to act as private inquisitors, and to report their investigation to the authorities of the gaol . . . . Really this is too bad. Let gaolers, lawyers and policemen try, if they like, to extort some statements to her own detriment from the lips of the unhappy woman who has fallen to their tender mercies; but, for Heaven's sake, let us have no more of a lady Scripture-reader acting as an amateur detective. Our law does not admit of moral torture.

'Surely there are other ways by which the partisans of Mr Fleming may establish his innocence, if that be possible, than by torturing this poor creature into some garbled admission in his favour. Let them show, as they have never done yet, what his character was – what his relations were with his family, his servants, and the murdered woman – and they will do more to clear his repute than by recording every doubtful expression twisted, none knows how, from a woman half-crazed with misery.'

This was at least the second time that the *Telegraph* had suggested an investigation into Old Fleming's background. I wonder how much they knew? For Old Fleming had a rather unsavoury past, including an appearance before his own kirk session at the age of seventy-seven to confess that he had just had an illegitimate child by a domestic servant. The kirk session were so impressed that they entered his name as William Fleming, instead of James, in the record book.

No enquiry seems ever to have been made by the police into the extent of Old Fleming's wardrobe. He had, by his own admission, a fire going for the whole week-end of the murder. He had plenty of opportunities to burn any clothing of his that was bloodstained.

Then there was the gaslight seen by the three McLean sisters at 17 Sandyford Place at four o'clock in the morning.

The Crown theory was that Jessie McLachlan slept with Jess McPherson until four o'clock, then rose and murdered her. In that case, who lit the gas upstairs?

And then there is the business of Old Fleming and the milkboy. He never did explain why he was fully dressed when he opened the door to Donald McQuarrie at twenty to eight on that Saturday morning.

There was a score of reasons why we suspect that Old Fleming had, at least, something to hide over that weekend. And finally, there's the washing of the kitchen floor so recently that it was still wet when the murder was discovered on the Monday afternoon.

If, on the other hand, you look at Jessie McLachlan's famous statement, the one read out by Mr Clark after she had been found guilty, you find you can test its truth in a number of different ways. Most of it fits into known facts and no less a personage than Professor (later Lord) Lister expressed his opinion 'that the medical features of the tragedy are in remarkable accordance with the prisoner's statement'.

The best proof of Jessie McLachlan's innocence came nearly a hundred years after the murder. It is brought out by Christianna Brand in her reconstruction of the case, *Heaven Knows Who*. She pointed out that there were three witnesses (Mrs Walker, Miss Dykes and Miss McIntyre) who saw Jessie McLachlan going along the lane behind Sandyford Place after eleven o'clock on the night of Friday, July 4th. Miss McIntyre went up Elderslie Street and into Sandyford Place and saw a group of people listening to something at 17 Sandyford Place. They left as she approached, but it was obvious they had been listening to something. Just as she was passing she heard a low moaning coming, apparently, from the basement of the house.

Now Mary McIntyre would reach the front of 17 Sandyford Place just about the time that Jessie McLachlan, according to her statement, was letting herself in by the lane door. Then Jessie had to cross a green and she discovered that the back door, which she had left unlocked, was now locked. Eventually Old Fleming opened the door and, soon afterwards, she heard moaning and found Jess McPherson lying bleeding from wounds across the face.

It's obvious, from outside witnesses, that there was an attack on Jess McPherson before Jessie McLachlan got into the house. Who made the attack? There was only one other person there, and that was Old Fleming.

According to Jessie McLachlan, he made another attack on Jess about four o'clock in the morning. I suppose it might be said that it is possible that the second attack was made by Jessie McLachlan. But why should *she* attack her friend Jess? What surprised the police and the doctors when they saw the body was that the head and neck of the murdered woman had been washed. That, again, fits in with Jessie McLachlan's statement.

Then there is the story that Jess told Jessie McLachlan of the attack on her virtue, two weeks before, by Old Fleming. The defence found the man who had spent the night at Sandyford Place with Old Fleming, and the cabby who brought him back tipsy. Jessie McLachlan, when she made her statement, could not possibly have known about this affair except from the mouth of Jess McPherson.

No one can say with absolute certainty what happened in the basement of 17 Sandyford Place on that night. But all the evidence points to Jessie McLachlan's statement as being correct, in the main, and to Old Fleming as the murderer. A flyting woman can cause a man to lose his reason for the moment, as I know well from several murder cases I have investigated. I know of three murders committed by quiet, respectable Scotsmen who could not stand a woman's tongue a moment longer. And so I think it likely that Old Fleming lost his reason altogether when Jess McPherson was flaying him, and he seized the nearest weapon and attacked her.

Jessie McLachlan was released on ticket-of-leave from Perth Prison on October 5th, 1877. By that time Old

Fleming was dead, and buried in the kirkyard in Anderston – a place which disappeared when Glasgow Town Council transformed that area into a series of motorways. In that year Lord Deas died, doubtless believing to the end that he was right.

James McLachlan, her husband, had disappeared. He had emigrated to Australia soon after Jessie was sent to Perth. Jessie was now forty-four years old, and she met her son, who was now eighteen. She had earned £30 in prison. From Perth she went to Greenock, for she thought she might be recognised in Glasgow. But a smart representative of the *Greenock Advertiser* found her out, and that paper published an 'interview', which was denounced by the *Greenock Telegraph* as a fabrication and a 'performance that would be disowned by any schoolboy'. (I'm glad to say that, while the *Advertiser* is no more, the *Greenock Telegraph* goes from success to success!)

The *Evening News* of Glasgow, a very fine newspaper for which I had the honour to write, said of the *Advertiser* interview, 'We can conceive of nothing more cruel than this retransfixion of the unfortunate woman upon the spear of notoriety. A disgraceful attempt has been made to achieve popularity and profit by harassing an unfortunate woman, and hawking the result about for a halfpenny.'

Jessie McLachlan escaped to America and, like Madeleine Smith, married again. She died at Port Huron, Michigan, of a heart attack on New Year's Day, 1899.

Gradually the notoriety of 17 Sandyford Place faded away, even in Glasgow. Some years ago the address came into the news again. It was discovered that it was the birthplace of the well-known actor Derek Bond, who is appearing – at the time of writing – in a London stage production of *Murder at the Vicarage* by Agatha Christie.

The Human Crocodile

The Case of Dr Edward William Pritchard

Murder for Pleasure

In the whole portrait gallery of crime there is not one murderer quite so loathsome as Dr Edward William Pritchard, of Sauchiehall Street, Glasgow. He will go down in criminal history as the man who had a coffin lid unscrewed so that he could kiss the dead lips of the wife he had tortured by slow poisoning.

He was the last man to be hanged in public in the city of Glasgow and, though I disagree with capital punishment, I cannot feel it in my heart to be sorry about Dr Pritchard's turning off. Miss F. Tennyson Jesse classified six reasons for murder. In her opinion there was:

1. Murder for gain.
2. Murder from revenge.
3. Murder for elimination.
4. Murder from jealousy.
5. Murder from lust of killing.
6. Murder from conviction.

To these William Roughead adds his No. 7 – Murder for fun. He gives a list of people who he thinks murdered for fun. These fun lovers included Jack the Ripper, John Watson Laurie (the Arran murderer), Madeleine Smith and Dr Pritchard. I think a better term is – Murder for pleasure. Dr

Pritchard committed at least three murders, and I think he got pleasure out of each of them. Certainly there was no other motive worth the naming.

It was this aspect of Dr Pritchard which, I think, made James Bridie choose him as the model for the eponymous hero of his play *Dr Angelus*. That piece is, in the main, the story of Dr Pritchard, and the character of Dr Angelus was perfectly played by Alistair Sim, a very smiling villain who enjoyed every moment of his perfidy and poison.

Respectability was rampant, once again, in the Pritchard case, but it was not merely the respectability of the ordinary citizen. It was also medical respectability or, as some would say, medical etiquette.

Dr Pritchard, eminent murderer though he was, was not a Scotsman. But he spent the five years of his life in Glasgow in our square mile of murder. He committed his first murder just round the corner from 17 Sandyford Place, and his second and third just round the corner from Blythswood Square. To be fair, though, I should say that his first murder was never proved. But, in the light of his later actions, I have not the slightest doubt that it was murder.

We go to *The Glasgow Herald* of 6th May, 1863, for a report on 'Lamentable Occurrence – Young Woman Burned to Death'. This, as far as we know, was Dr Pritchard's first brush with the Glasgow Police.

'Yesterday morning,' says the *Herald*, 'a melancholy accident occurred in the residence of Dr E. W. Pritchard, situated No. 11 Berkeley Terrace, Berkeley Street. The house, which is on the north side of the street, consists of two flats and attics, the servants' sleeping apartments being in the top flat fronting the street.

'About three o'clock one of the constables stationed in the vicinity of the dwelling observed the glare of fire through the attic window, and immediately proceeded to the front door and rang the bell.

'The door was opened by Dr Pritchard, who slept in a

bedroom on the second floor, and who had been wakened a few minutes before the bell rung by his two sons, who slept in an adjoining apartment, calling out 'Papa, papa'.

'The doctor rose, and, on opening the room door, he was alarmed to find smoke in the lobby; and on proceeding to the room in which his sons slept, he learned they had been awakened by smoke and the cracking of glass. It was quite apparent that the house was on fire; and, after leaving his boys in the lobby leading from the street door, he rushed up to the attic flat, pushed open the door of the servants' sleeping-room, and called out "Elizabeth", but received no answer.

'The apartment was so completely filled with smoke that he could not enter; and on proceeding downstairs for the purpose of raising an alarm, the bell rang, and he admitted the constable. Dr Pritchard told him that the servant slept on the attic flat, and on proceeding thither, and reaching the door of the apartment, they were unable to proceed further in consequence of the smoke and flames. The alarm was immediately conveyed to the Anderston Police Office, and then to the central engine station by telegraph, and the brigade was speedily in attendance, and extinguished the flames.

'On entering the sleeping apartment on the top flat, a sad spectacle presented itself. The poor woman, whose name was Elizabeth McGirn, was found in bed, dead, her body being a charred mass. The bed was placed at the north-west corner of the room, and the body lay at the front of the bed, the head towards the west.

'The body was lying on its back, the left arm being close by the side, and the right arm appeared to have been in a bent position; but the fire at this part had been so strong that the arm, from the hand to the elbow, was entirely consumed; the head was a charred mass, and the flesh was burned off the breast, the ribs being visible. The limbs of the deceased were comparatively uninjured, in consequence of being protected by stockings and blankets, but the toes, which had not been protected by the blankets, were charred.

'The fire had evidently broken out at the head of the bed,

because at this part of the apartment the floor was burned through, and the joists forming the roof of the drawing-room were considerably charred. The roof of the house, with the exception of a portion at the back, was entirely destroyed.

'Dr Pritchard, on returning home about eleven o'clock on Monday evening, observed that the servants' apartment was lighted. He entered the house and, contrary to his usual custom, he did not call her to ascertain whether or not he had been wanted. After visiting the apartment in which his boys slept for the purpose of ascertaining if they were comfortable in bed, he retired to rest about twelve o'clock.

'It is said that the poor girl, who has met such an untimely death, was in the habit of reading in bed; and the supposition is that, after she had fallen asleep, the gas-jet, which was close to the head of the bed, had ignited the bed-hangings, and that the deceased had been suffocated by smoke. This is the more apparent from the position in which the body lay, because if the deceased had not been suffocated while asleep, she would have made some attempt to escape, and been found in a different position. The neighbour servant of deceased happened to be out of town with her mistress, and possibly, in her absence, the girl McGirn had read longer than usual, and fallen asleep without extinguishing the gas.

'The damage to the dwelling is, we understand, covered by insurance.'

It was the insurance, though, which caused a bit of bother to Dr. Pritchard. The good doctor included in his claim a number of articles of jewellery, but no trace of any jewels could be found in the debris. The insurance company were not at all satisfied, and eventually Dr Pritchard accepted just a small portion of his original claim.

The police were not too happy about the fire either. They questioned Dr Pritchard closely, and they had a post-mortem examination carried out on the body of Elizabeth McGirn. Dr Pritchard had been in Glasgow for not much more than two years, but already he had his detractors. Some of them hinted that the servant girl was pregnant, and talked of stories of Dr Pritchard's sexual prowess in the south. But the police took no action after they had made their investigations.

All the same, there were some odd points about this fire. First, that Dr Pritchard opened the door to the constable fully dressed – yet he said he had been wakened by his sons' cries only a few moments before. It was interesting too, that Mrs Pritchard and the other servant were away from home that night. Also this was the one night when Dr Pritchard had not asked Elizabeth McGirn whether he had been wanted or not.

After he had been sentenced for his two other crimes, an observer wrote of the Berkeley Street fire:

'It requires a large amount of very easy credulity to believe that the girl, under the circumstances stated, would either not have escaped by the door (only a few feet from the bed), or made an attempt in that direction, or at the very worst would not in the lie of the body, and in the contraction of contortion of the muscles, have exhibited some of the ordinary indications of pain.

'We can easily conceive a case where, by the sudden influx from another quarter of a great body of smoke, a person in a deep sleep may be so suddenly caught by asphyxia as to be choked as she lay, yet even in that case there will always be some contraction or contortion; but in the case we are examining the smoke had its beginning in the room; it was therefore under the law of progress, it was close by the sleeper, and it is scarcely possible to conceive that a young, active woman would not have been quickened by the first touch of asphyxia either to an attempt at escape, or a voluntary or involuntary action of the muscles. Such absolute quiescence as set forth would seem to amount to a physical impossibility.

'The only presumption which can make the story quadrate with natural laws, is that the girl was dead, or under the influence of a soporific, before the fire was kindled. As to the means of death, or the hand that applied the flame, these must be left to the judgement or imagination of the reader.'

*

But, whatever was whispered by his enemies, Dr Pritchard walked the streets of Glasgow a free man – particularly Sauchiehall Street, where he was in the habit of handing out picture-postcards of himself to any passer-by he thought deserved the honour.

Naturally the family did not live much longer at Berkeley Street. Less than a month after the fire, the Pritchards flitted to 22 Royal Crescent, on the opposite side of Sauchiehall Street from the nearby Sandyford Place. There they engaged a new servant to take the place of the unfortunate Elizabeth McGirn. The new girl's name was Mary McLeod, she was good-looking and she was fifteen years of age. When Mrs Pritchard took the family down to Kilmun, near Dunoon, for the holidays, Dr Pritchard improved the happy hours at home by seducing his servant girl. Mary McLeod did not meet a violent death, however. What happened to her was that she was accused of killing the two women poisoned by Pritchard.

However, let's look at this remarkable man, who was determined to leave his mark on Glasgow – and succeeded too! He was nearly six feet tall, but had a slight stoop. He was partly bald but brushed some of his hair across the bald patch in an attempt to conceal it. He had a very luxurious beard, but no moustache. Some people regarded his expression as effeminate and were all the surer about that when he spoke, for a South of England accent was regarded as somewhat suspect in the Glasgow of those days.

Edward William Pritchard came from a naval family. He was born in 1825 at Southsea in Hampshire. His father was a captain in the Royal Navy, two of his uncles are said to have been admirals, one of his brothers was secretary to the Naval Commander-in-chief at Plymouth, and another was a surgeon in the Navy. Edward was evidently going to follow in his brother's footsteps. At the age of fifteen, he was apprenticed to surgeons in Portsmouth. Then, he said himself, he went to King's College, London, for his hospital studies. But King's College, London, later denied that any such person as Edward William Pritchard attended there in 1843.

Actually, the information about attending King's College comes from the *Medical Directory*, and it was Dr Pritchard who furnished the editor of that work with the details about his qualifications. There's no doubt that a great many Glasgow doctors thought very little of his abilities as a doctor. On the other hand, it is true that he appeared before the Court of Examiners of the College of Surgeons on May 29th, 1846, and was, after examination, admitted a member of the College. He was also examined by the Navy Board and gazetted as an assistant surgeon.

That same year he went to sea in H.M.S. *Victory*, and later did service in H.M.S. *Collingwood*, H.M.S. *Calypso*, H.M.S. *Asia*, and H.M.S. *Hecate*. While it couldn't be said that he had sailed the Seven Seas, he did visit the Pacific, the Mediterranean, the Atlantic and the Baltic. In 1850 H.M.S. *Hecate* came into Portsmouth. The Officers were invited to a ball in the town, and there Assistant Surgeon Pritchard was introduced to a Miss Mary Jane Taylor, a young lady from Edinburgh, who was staying with her uncle in Portsmouth. Her uncle was Dr David Cowan, a retired naval surgeon.

It seemed to be love at first sight. Mary Jane's uncle approved of young Pritchard, and when he met her father, Mr Michael Taylor, a well-to-do silk merchant, and her mother, they were quite delighted with him. Mary Jane and her Edward got married in the autumn of the same year they met. Unfortunately, Edward did not have enough money to buy himself out of the Navy, so he had to continue serving in H.M.S. *Hecate* and going wherever she took him. Mary Jane was with him whenever possible, but for long periods she stayed with her parents in Edinburgh.

Mr and Mrs Taylor were determined to have him ashore, however, and they fixed him up with a practice in Hunmanby in Yorkshire. Edward and Mary Jane set up house there in March, 1851, and started to rear a family. By the time they reached Glasgow in 1860 they had two boys and three girls. This must have taken up a lot of Mary Jane's time, but Edward was able to do other things. He extended his practice to Filey, a seaside resort near Hunmanby which was becoming fashionable. He wrote several books on the district, including a *Guide to Filey*. He was appointed medical officer of the No. 3 District of the Bridlington Union. And he managed to conduct quite a number of affairs with his lady patients.

After Dr Pritchard's trial, the *Sheffield Telegraph* wrote:

'Dr Pritchard, the poisoner, is well known at Hunmanby and Filey, where he practised before his removal to Glasgow. He left those places with a very different reputation. He was fluent, plausible, amorous, politely impudent, and singularly untruthful. One who knew him well at Filey describes him as the "prettiest liar" he ever met with.

'He pushed his way into publicity as a prominent member of the body of Freemasons, and made that body a means of advertising himself. In the *carte-de-visite* we have seen of him, he is taken in the insignia of the order.

'His amativeness led him into some amours that did not increase the public confidence in him as a professional man; and his unveracity became so notorious that, in his attempts to deceive others, he succeeded only in deceiving himself. Hunmanby and Filey were much too small for a man of that kind. He was soon found out. His imagination overran the limits of probability as much as his expenditure overran his means; and, if we are rightly informed, he left Yorkshire in discredit and in debt. It was said of him, after he had gone, that he spoke the truth only by accident, and seemed to be an improvisor of fiction by mental constitution and by habit.'

We don't know how much his wife was aware of Dr Pritchard's peccadillos, but it was obvious that her father and mother thought the world of dear Edward. Indeed, to his mother-in-law, Dr Pritchard was 'an idol'.

In 1857 the idol became a Doctor of Medicine by the simple means of buying the diplomas *in absentia* from the University of Erlangen. And on the appropriate date of the first of April, 1858, he became a Licentiate of the Society of Apothecaries of London. He was now well enough equipped with letters after his name to go anywhere. He sold his practice at Hunmanby and Filey for £400 and joined his wife at her parent's home in Edinburgh. She had gone there because she wasn't feeling well. Soon after Dr Pritchard fell ill too, and Mr Taylor, Mary Jane's father, thought it would be a good idea for Edward to go out to Egypt and the Holy Land as medical attendant to a gentleman who was travelling there. Edward returned so refreshed that he was glad when the Taylors suggested that he should take up practice in booming Glasgow. And that was how he came to be in his house in Berkeley Street when the fire took place.

Garibaldi's Friend

Now, though Dr Pritchard had brought letters of introduction to various eminent medical men in Glasgow, he was regarded by his fellow doctors in this city with suspicion. He tried to get into the Faculty of Physicians and Surgeons, but couldn't find a single Fellow who would propose him. He was just as unlucky when he wanted to join various medical societies in Glasgow. In this case all that was wanted was a decent diploma and a fair character, but, apparently, these jealous Glasgow doctors thought he had neither.

When the Chair of Surgery became vacant at the Andersonian College in October, 1860. Dr Pritchard applied for it. 'I have had many opportunities in almost every part of the world,' he wrote, 'of gaining practical experience, and promulgating the principles of modern surgery.' And with his application he enclosed a sheaf of testimonials from well-known English doctors. Would you believe it, some of the Glaswegians who saw these glowing testimonials suggested that they were forgeries! The Chair of Surgery went to the Dr McLeod who was later to get Jessie McLachlan to make her footprint in blood.

Possibly it was the way that Dr Pritchard talked that annoyed his fellow doctors. He kept mentioning the admirals in his family – not just the two uncles, but also his grandfather.

When Ceylon was mentioned in his company, he remarked casually that one of his brothers was Governor-General there.

The Italian liberator, Garibaldi, was much in the news at that time, and Dr Pritchard, when he arrived in Glasgow, said he'd been taken for Garibaldi, arrested and imprisoned for three months on the Continent. Later he took to carrying a walking stick with a silver band round it and the inscription, 'Presented by General Garibaldi to Edward William Pritchard.' The effect of this was slightly reduced because of the number of people who recollected seeing the doctor carrying this walking stick for months without any inscription on it at all. And at a dinner given in connection with the Glasgow Athenaeum, the literary and scientific club which Charles Dickens had addressed. Dr Pritchard arranged to have his health proposed as 'a distinguished physiologist, and a friend of Garibaldi.'

As far as we know, Dr Pritchard never even saw Garibaldi, far less met him.

But, if Dr Pritchard was getting nowhere fast in his own profession, he certainly made his presence felt when he plunged into the public life of Glasgow. He became a member of the Glasgow Athenaeum and was so assiduous an attender that he was made a director. He was appointed an examiner in physiology under the Society of Arts. He was constantly giving lectures on his experiences in various parts of the world. One of his favourite subjects was his visit to the Fiji Islands, but regular lecturegoers discovered that, every time Dr Pritchard spoke of Fiji, it seemed an entirely different place from the one described on the last occasion.

One fine sentence from a Pritchard lecture will give you the style of the man.

'I have,' he said, 'plucked the eaglets from their eyries in the deserts of Arabia, and hunted the Nubian lion in the prairies of North America.'

When a member of a platform party said, after one lecture, that Pritchard had been talking nonsense, the doctor replied, 'What of that? it goes down!'

Just as Dr Pritchard had cultivated Freemasonry in Yorkshire for his own ends, he followed the same path in Glasgow. He was appointed to Lodge St Mark in March, 1861, and was elected Master in the following year. He became a member of the Glasgow Royal Arch Chapter in December, 1861, and completed the hat-trick for that month by becoming a Knight Templar in the Glasgow Priory and joining the Grand Lodge of the Royal Order in Edinburgh. But the Freemasons found him out, just as the doctors had.

Dr Pritchard also cultivated the ladies, just as he had in Yorkshire. Little Mary McLeod, his servant, he had turned into a concubine. But he also exercised what the *Sheffield Telegraph* called his 'amativeness' on his lady patients, married or single.

One prosecution against Pritchard was actually started by an indignant husband, but then dropped owing to 'adverse circumstances overtaking the gentleman whose wife had been grossly insulted'.

At Whitsunday, 1864, Dr Pritchard moved house again. He went from 22 Royal Crescent to 131 Sauchiehall Street, which no longer exists. Of the £2000 price for this house, dear Edward did not pay a penny. Mrs Taylor provided her idol with £500 (she said as a loan, but he said as a gift), and £1600 was borrowed on security of the property. The exact reader will note that that's £100 too much, and Mrs Taylor explained it to Mary Jane in these words:

'I have told the law agent to get the order drawn for the money in two sums, one for four hundred pounds and one for one hundred pounds, so as Edward may hold the hundred in his own hand and pay the other £400 as part of the purchase-money. I have done it in this way so as these lawyers may not get hold of the whole £500, and keep it under some pretence or other.

'Now, my dear Mary, you must take care that this money is well spent. We have all felt the trouble in getting it; and I have no doubt it would be a source of satisfaction to us all if it is the means of getting Edward forward in life, and much depends on his going on quietly and perseveringly – he is now in a better position, and with his industrious and steady attention to his practice, all will be well. Give him my kind·love and earnest wishes for success.'

But all was not rosy in dear Edward's world. Though he had a big practice, he seemed to spend all his money. He was overdrawn at both his banks. Then Mrs Pritchard discovered the doctor kissing Mary McLeod, and there were scenes and rows. Not only that, but Mary McLeod was going to have a baby, and the good doctor had to see that there was a miscarriage. Dr Pritchard told his servant that, if his wife died before he did, he would marry her.

All this happened in the summer and autumn of 1864, and in October of that year Mrs Pritchard became ill. She was constantly harassed by attacks of sickness, and Dr Pritchard said he thought it might be gastric fever. On November 16th, by the way, he bought an ounce of tartarised antimony – a very large amount of a deadly poison. And on November 24th he bought an ounce of tincture of aconite, another deadly poison. He bought these poisons, incidentally, from Murdoch's and Currie's in Sauchiehall Street, the two shops which had supplied Madeleine Smith with arsenic seven years before.

Also in November the doctor took in two young medical students as pupils and boarders. This meant that the house was fairly crowded, because, besides Dr and Mrs Pritchard, there were four of their five children (the eldest, a girl, lived with the Taylors in Edinburgh), the two medical students, Catherine Lattimer, the cook, and Mary McLeod.

On November 26th, when she was feeling a little better, Mrs Pritchard went to stay with her father and mother in Edinburgh, until Christmas. She improved in health immediately she got to Edinburgh, and, only ten days after she had arrived there, her daughter Fanny was writing to her father, 'Ma is very well, all fat and blooming. She has gained three pounds of flesh since she came. We can't keep her any longer for she eats too much . . . . Ma has been very gay; she has been out twice, once at dinner to Mr Bain's and once out to tea.'

Dr Pritchard received this good news on December 6th. Two days later he bought another ounce of tincture of aconite. He was evidently stocking up, especially as this time he bought Fleming's Tincture of Aconite, which is six times stronger than the stuff he had bought before.

The Pritchard family had a merry Christmas, and Mrs Pritchard was a new woman – until about a week after the New Year, when her sickness returned. She was at her worst just after meals, especially if she had had liquid food. She felt so ill that she seldom had a meal with the family. She stayed in her room and her husband either took up or sent up food and drink.

On February 1st, 1865, she had her first serious attack of illness. Catherine Lattimer, the cook, was in her kitchen, having, as she thought, a last look at it. She was due to leave Dr Pritchard's employment next day. According to the doctor, he had detected her giving away Pritchard food to a washerwoman, so he gave Catherine her notice.

Catherine was worried about her mistress. Mrs Pritchard had managed to get down to the dining-room and had dinner with the doctor about three o'clock in the afternoon. But later Catherine heard Mrs Pritchard retching in the pantry, and knew her sickness had returned.

Then Mrs Pritchard's bedroom bell rang, and Catherine hurried upstairs. She found her mistress in bed, but with all her clothes on. 'Catherine,' said the poor woman, 'I have lost my senses. I never was so bad as this before.' Then she took cramp in her hands and in her stomach, and Catherine ran to get the doctor.

Next day she was very exhausted and Dr Pritchard wrote to a cousin of his wife's in Edinburgh, a Dr James Cowan, who had retired from the practice of medicine. He asked Dr Cowan to come through to Glasgow to see her, and to stay the night.

When Dr Cowan arrived, Dr Pritchard told him that his wife's illness arose from irritation of the stomach. Dr Cowan had found his cousin looking much better than he expected, and he didn't think her illness was at all serious. He prescribed a mustard poultice and small quantities of champagne and ice. Doubtless Dr Pritchard bought a bottle of champagne. But he also bought yet another ounce of tartarised antimony and one of tincture of aconite.

Dr Cowan had a look at the patient again next day, was quite satisfied, but suggested to Mrs Pritchard that it would be a good idea if her mother came through from Edinburgh for a while, to look after her and keep her company. Mrs Pritchard agreed and Dr Cowan told Dr Pritchard of his plan for Mrs Taylor to travel to Glasgow next day.

But, before Mrs Taylor could arrive, Mary Jane had another violent attack. At midnight on the day that Dr Cowan departed, Catherine Lattimer heard Mrs Pritchard screaming with pain. Once again she hurried up the stairs. She should have left Dr Pritchard's service on February 2nd, but there was no replacement for her, and she had agreed, because her mistress was so ill, to stay on until the new cook arrived.

Catherine Lattimer found Mrs Pritchard in bed, with her husband standing beside her. Mrs Pritchard told Catherine she had taken chloroform. She was very excited and Dr Pritchard was trying to soothe her. 'I want to see another doctor,' she cried. 'I want to see Dr Gairdner. Fetch Dr Gairdner.'

Mary McLeod had heard Mrs Pritchard screaming too, and she came into the bedroom. Mrs Pritchard sent Mary off for Dr Gairdner.

Fortunately Dr Gairdner, who was Professor of Medicine in Glasgow University, was still up. He was preparing for a lecture that same morning. He went round to Sauchiehall Street right away and was met by Dr Pritchard, who said his wife had been sick for some weeks, and that she was having spasms due to catalepsy. He added that Dr Cowan had already seen her and had ordered stimulants. So his wife had had champagne and also chloroform.

When Dr Gairdner saw Mrs Pritchard, he decided right away that she was drunk. But he was also struck by the way that she lay with her hands outside the bedclothes, above her head, with the wrists and fingers so turned in that they looked like claws. Drunk or not, she was able to apologise for not sending for him sooner and to remind him that her brother, Dr Michael Taylor, of Penrith, and he had been classmates.

Then, all of a sudden, she looked at her husband and shouted, 'Don't cry. If you cry, you are a hypocrite. You are all hypocrites!'

Dr Gairdner decided to examine her and went over to the fire to warm his hands. 'Oh, you cruel, cruel man!' screamed Mrs Pritchard. 'You unfeeling man! Don't leave me!' Dr Gairdner went back to the bedside and assured Mrs Pritchard that he wasn't going to leave her. But as soon as he moved away again, she became hysterial. Dr Gairdner decided she was in such a state that there was little he could do. He arranged to call later in the day, and he read Dr Pritchard a lecture on not giving his wife stimulants of any kind, as it was very bad treatment.

Dr Pritchard put the blame on Dr Cowan once more, and asked about chloroform. 'No,' said Dr Gairdner. 'No stimulants and no medicine till I see her again.'

Well, apparently tincture of aconite is not a stimulant, so doubtless it was perfectly all right for Dr Pritchard to buy another ounce of it before Dr Gairdner paid his second visit. Dr Gairdner called in about one o'clock and found Mrs Pritchard quiet and considerably better, although she was still having spasms in her hands. He told her she was to take no more stimulants and no more medicine, and go on a diet of bread and milk with an occasional boiled egg. He repeated this to her husband, and left the house. He never saw Mrs Pritchard again.

But Dr Gairdner was rather puzzled about this illness of Mrs Pritchard's and he wrote to his old friend, her brother, in

165

Penrith. He said in his letter that he did not approve of the treatment she was receiving and thought she should visit Dr Taylor's house for a time. Dr Taylor acted on this suggestion but, when he wrote to Dr Pritchard, and suggested that Mrs Pritchard should come south for a while, the good doctor replied that, while he was delighted with the idea, he was afraid that she was not in a fit state to travel.

Arrival (and Departure) of a Mother-in-law

The day after Dr Gairdner's visit, Mrs Taylor arrived from Edinburgh. Mary Jane's mother was seventy, but she was a strong, healthy woman, and the managing type. She soon had the household under control, even though she spent much of her time sitting by her sick daughter's bedside. Mrs Pritchard was improving, but she was still far from well.

Soon after she arrived, Mrs Taylor gave Mary McLeod a bottle and told her to go to a chemist's and have it filled with Battley's Sedative Solution. Now Mrs Taylor was a most respectable inhabitant of that most respectable city, Edinburgh. And Battley's Sedative Solution was a most respectable medicine, even though it was actually a preparation of opium.

Mrs Taylor had started taking Battley's to combat her neuralgic headaches, and gradually she had acquired a liking for the stuff. She had taken so much for so long that she was now able to swallow a dose that would have laid the average woman low. At one time a bottle of Battley's lasted Mrs Taylor for two or three months. Now it lasted her only two or three weeks. She always had the same bottle filled and, probably at her son-in-law's suggestion, gave the name of Dr Pritchard when she had it filled in Edinburgh. This meant that she got a bottle of Battley's for seven-and-six instead of ten shillings.

Equipped with her Battley's, Mrs Taylor sailed serenely along at 131 Sauchiehall Street. That is, until Monday, February 13th. On that day her daughter felt she would like some tapioca. Mrs Pritchard's little boy Kenny went for the tapioca and it was left for about half an hour on a table in the hall, just beside Dr Pritchard's consulting room, where, naturally, the doctor kept a cupboard locked because it contained poisonous substances. Indeed, Dr Pritchard had more poison on the premises than all the other Glasgow doctors put together.

Catherine Lattimer, the cook, made a little tapioca, and Mary McLeod carried it up to Mrs Pritchard's bedroom. Apparently Mrs Pritchard, as unwell people do, changed her mind, so Mrs Taylor decided to eat the tapioca. Almost as soon as she'd finished, she was violently sick. When she recovered, she said she thought she must have got the same complaint as her daughter. She didn't know it, but how right she was!

The new cook, Mary Patterson, arrived on February 16th, and Catherine Lattimer left the Pritchard household. She did not leave Glasgow, however, and she was so interested in her former mistress that she called at 131 Sauchiehall Street every now and then to see how she was getting on, and to take the youngest children for a walk. In his 'Lett's Medical Diary' for 1865 Dr Pritchard wrote on February 15th:

'Pd. Cath. Lattimer £11.00 – left my service – too old.'

On February 18th he bought another ounce of the really strong stuff, Fleming's Tincture of Aconite.

Catherine Lattimer called at the Pritchard's on the morning of Friday, February 24th, to take the youngest child out. She met Mrs Taylor and thought she was looking rather wearied and not so well, but Catherine put this down to the strain of nursing Mrs Pritchard. Mrs Taylor said to her, 'Well, Catherine, I don't understand her illness. She is one day better and two worse.'

Mrs Taylor spent a normal day (or as near normal as was possible in that house), had tea with the family about seven o'clock, and sent Mary MacLeod for sausages for her supper. About nine o'clock she went up to join her daughter, and soon after that the bell sounded in the kitchen. Mary McLeod went up and found Mrs Taylor trying to vomit. She asked Mary to get her some hot water. Mary brought hot water twice, and she also told Dr Pritchard about his mother-in-law's illness. But Dr Pritchard was seeing a patient at the time, and said he would be up as soon as possible.

When Mary McLeod went up a third time, she found Mrs Taylor sitting unconscious in a chair, with her head lolling on her breast. She seemed very ill indeed. Dr Pritchard arrived, and Mary Patterson was hard on his heels. She waited outside the bedroom door and heard Mrs Pritchard say, 'Mother, dear mother, can you not speak to me?'

Then Dr Pritchard emerged and told one of his pupils, Connell, to go for Dr Paterson, who lived only two hundred yards or so along Sauchiehall Street. Mary Patterson went into the room and found that Mrs Taylor had been put, fully dressed, into Mrs Pritchard's bed. She felt Mrs Taylor's forehead and found it getting cold. Mrs Pritchard looked imploringly at her husband and asked, 'Edward, can you do nothing yourself?'

'No,' replied Mrs Taylor's idol, 'what can I do for a dead woman? Can I recall life?'

And now Dr James Paterson the second most remarkable medical figure in this case, arrived. He knew Dr Pritchard slightly, but this was his first visit to the house. He had been told that this was a case of apoplexy, and Dr Pritchard took him into his consulting room and explained that his mother-in-law had been writing a letter when she had been suddenly taken ill. She had fallen from her chair to the floor and had been carried upstairs to Mrs Pritchard's bedroom.

This was so much nonsense, and Dr Pritchard added to it by telling Dr Paterson that Mrs Taylor and Mrs Pritchard had been drinking some beer during supper and were sick afterwards. He also led Dr Paterson to believe that Mrs Taylor was in the habit of 'taking a drop' occasionally. Then he took Dr Paterson upstairs to see the patient.

As he entered the fatal bedroom, Dr Paterson looked on

a macabre scene. Old Mrs Taylor lay unconscious on the bed, fully dressed and with a cap with a small artificial flower on her head. Behind her, sitting up in bed, was the haggard figure of her daughter. Mrs Pritchard's hair was dishevelled and her face was thin and white, except for a hectic spot on either cheek. Her voice was weak and peculiar, and Dr Paterson thought she looked a semi-imbecile.

He examined Mrs Taylor and came to the conclusion that she was under the influence of opium, or some other powerful narcotic, and was dying. When she was roused a little, her pulse became perceptible at the wrist and Dr Paterson pointed this out to Dr Pritchard. The idol clapped his mother-in-law on the shoulder and said, 'You are getting better, darling.' But Dr Paterson looked at him and shook his head ominously, as if to say, 'Never in this world.'

The two doctors went downstairs to Pritchard's consulting room and Dr Paterson told Dr Pritchard that the old lady was suffering from narcoticism. Immediately Dr Pritchard explained that his mother-in-law was addicted to Battley's Sedative Solution, that she had bought a half-pound bottle of the mixture only a few days before, and that he had no doubts she might have taken a good swig of it.

As to Mrs Pritchard's case, her husband had told Dr Paterson that Mrs Pritchard was suffering from gastric fever, but his conviction, which he kept to himself, was that she was suffering from the depressing effects of antimony.

Feeling there was nothing more he could do, Dr Paterson went home about eleven o'clock. He went to bed, but was roused at one o'clock by Mary McLeod, who asked him to come at once and see Mrs Taylor. Dr Paterson said no, he could be of no service, but, if Dr Pritchard really wanted him, he was to send back word. No other message came, and Dr Paterson slept the sleep of the just.

At 131 Sauchiehall Street Mary Patterson, the cook, was still standing by. She had left Dr Pritchard in the bedroom with his wife and mother-in-law, but in the early hours of that morning Dr Pritchard came out and said that Mrs

Taylor was gone. Mary Patterson went into the bedroom and saw Mrs Pritchard kneeling in bed, frantically rubbing her mother's right hand. Dr Pritchard asked her to go down to a spare bedroom on the ground floor, but she insisted that she should be left a little longer with her mother, because she thought her mother was not quite dead.

Mary Patterson went down to get the spare bedroom ready, and soon afterwards Dr Pritchard led his wife in. Then Mrs Nabb, the family washerwoman, arrived on a summons from Mary MacLeod, and Mary Patterson and Mrs Nabb proceeded to 'dress' the dead body. As they took off her dress, they heard the sound of a bottle clinking against a key. They took it out and it was the half empty bottle of Battley's. Mary Patterson thought it was laudanum and hid it under the chest of drawers.

But in came Dr Pritchard and asked for the bottle. When Mary retrieved it and showed it to the doctor, he raised his eyes and hands and said 'Good heavens, has she taken this much since Tuesday?' He asked Mary Patterson to say nothing about this bottle, as it would not do for a man in his position to be talked about.

In his *Blackwood's Shilling Scribbling Diary, 1865* (he kept two), Dr Pritchard noted for Friday, February 24th:

'About 9 p.m. (Jane Cowan) Mrs Taylor was seized with vertigo and rigors, quickly becoming comatose, with paralysis of the left side – moribund in three hours – dying.'

And for Saturday, February 25th:

'About 1 a.m. this morning passing away calmly – peacefully – and the features retaining a lifelike character – so finely drawn was the transition that it would be impossible to determine with decision the moment when life may be said to have departed.'

It's probable that these entries were for other eyes to see, in case any questions were asked about Mrs Taylor's death.

There was, for example, the watchful Dr Paterson to consider.

At ten o'clock that Saturday morning Dr Paterson had a visit from Mr Michael Taylor, husband of the lady who had just died. He said he had come for the death certificate. Dr Paterson told Mr Taylor he was surprised that Dr Pritchard did not know that the death certificate was never given to friends, but to the district registrar.

On the following Wednesday Dr Paterson met Dr Pritchard accidentally in Sauchiehall Street. Dr Pritchard asked Paterson if he would look in to see his wife next morning as he was going to Edinburgh to attend Mrs Taylor's funeral. Dr Paterson said he would, and called about eleven o'clock on Thursday morning. Mrs Pritchard looked very ill indeed. In a weak voice she asked the doctor if he really thought her mother was dying when he first saw her.

'Most decidedly I did,' he replied, 'and I told your husband so.'

Mrs Pritchard clasped her hands, looked up, and moaned, 'Good God, is it possible?' And she burst into a flood of tears.

Dr Paterson asked Mrs Pritchard a great many questions about her mother and about herself. Then he prescribed for her soothing drinks, easily digested foods and a powder.

At this time Dr Pritchard was attending the funeral of his mother-in-law. Later he attended the reading of Mrs Taylor's will, and noted that the old lady had left two-thirds of her estate of £2500 to Mrs Pritchard, and one-third to her doctor son in Penrith.

The day after he had seen Mrs Pritchard, Dr Paterson received a form from the registrar in which he had to give the cause of Mrs Taylor's death and the duration of her disease. He sent it back in its virgin state, with a note, as he said, 'explaining the circumstances'. Maybe the registrar thought this note was going a bit too far. At all events, he destroyed it.

However, Dr Pritchard filled up the death certificate

himself. After all, he was a doctor too. He described the primary cause of death as: 'Paralysis, duration twelve hours; secondary cause, apoplexy, duration one hour.' Dr Pritchard does not seem to have known that apoplexy always precedes and produces paralysis. Still, he probably wasn't quite himself when he made up that death certificate.

Things seemed to go quietly in the Pritchard household after that. Dr Pritchard called on Dr Paterson and gave him the happy information that his wife was better. He was so pleased that on March 7th he spent five shillings and three-pence on an anchor brooch for Mary McLeod. And, in view of what he told Dr Paterson, it's little surprising that, on March 9th, he wrote to his widowed father-in-law in Edinburgh:

'I am very much fatigued with being up at night with dear Mary Jane, who was very much worse yesterday and passed a wretched night. Wednesday has been a periodic day with her during this illness and she always dreads it – Her prostration is extreme and appetite quite failed – Dr Paterson has recommended Dublin Stout and some very simple medicine. I am glad she seems to like it and tho' very depressed bears up with good heart.'

But Dr Paterson had recommended sips of champagne and brandy, and never mentioned Dublin Stout.

Death of a Wife

On the morning of March 13th Dr Pritchard made a modest purchase – for him. It was a mere half an ounce of Fleming's Tincture of Aconite. Still, that was the equivalent of three ounces of the ordinary tincture. On the same day he wrote to his eldest daughter in Edinburgh:

'I am sorry to tell you dearest mama is too weak to write today and did not like you should have no letter. I therefore drop a few lines in a great hurry – Misses Kennedy seemed to me very kind and nice homely sort of creatures – They will do all they can to make you happy and I will take care to mention their names amongst my patients and get them pupils.

'I hope to be over again soon when we will pop in and see you. I liked all your companions on a single glance.

'One had very bonny eyes and looked as if she would like to clip off my little beard just for the mischief in doing it.

'Learn all you can, darling, and remember poor dear departed Grandma is watching over you.'

This strange sickness which affected Mrs Pritchard sometimes seemed to communicate itself to the rest of the household. That very evening the doctor sent Mary McLeod up to his wife's room with a piece of cheese for her supper. Mrs Pritchard asked Mary to taste the cheese, and when Mary did, she felt a burning sensation in her throat. Mary Patterson, the cook, ate a little of the cheese next morning and became so ill that she had to take to her bed.

Next night Dr Pritchard asked Mary Patterson to make some egg-flip for Mrs Pritchard. He said he'd get the sugar for it, and she heard him going into the dining-room, where the sugar was kept, then into his consulting room, and then saw him come into the kitchen and drop two lumps of sugar (or what looked like sugar) into the egg-flip. The cook tasted the egg-flip and remarked to Mary McLeod on its horrible taste.

Mary McLeod took the mixture up to Mrs Pritchard, who drank it and immediately became violently ill. Downstairs in the kitchen the cook was sick too, and spent the whole night in pain.

Fortunately Mary Patterson had recovered by midday on Friday, March 17th. At that time Mrs Pritchard's bell rang violently once and then again. The cook knew Mary McLeod was in the house and it was her duty to answer the bell, so paid no attention. But when the bell rang a third·time, she decided she had better go up herself. As she wasn't absolutely sure which bell had rung, she went to the consulting room first. The door was partly open but, when

Mary Patterson tried to open it further, she found that something was holding it.

So she went up the stairs to Mrs Pritchard's room, and almost immediately Dr Pritchard emerged from the consulting room, followed by Mary McLeod. It turned out, however, that Mrs Pritchard had rung her bell because she was lonely. Dr Pritchard then made up a drink for her.

About five o'clock the bell rang again, and this time Mary McLeod went up. She found Mrs Pritchard out of her bedroom, on the landing. Mrs Pritchard pointed to the floor and cried, 'There is my poor mother dead again.'

Mary McLeod realised that Mrs Pritchard was raving, and got Mary Patterson to help her to get the patient back into bed. As they did, Mrs Pritchard said, 'Never mind me. Attend to my mother. Rub her, and give her breath.' She asked for one of the pillows and started to rub it with one hand imagining that it was her mother.

Dr Pritchard himself went along the street for Dr Paterson about eight o'clock. Dr Paterson found Mrs Pritchard sitting up in bed and looking dreadful. She muttered something about vomiting, and her husband kindly explained to Dr Paterson that she was only raving. She complained of thirst, and he poured out some water into a tumbler and said, 'Here is some nice, cold water, darling.'

Mrs Pritchard began to grasp with her hand, as if to catch at some imaginary object on the bedclothes. She muttered something about the clock, but there was no clock in the room.

Dr Paterson went downstairs with Dr Pritchard to the consulting room. He prescribed a sleeping draught of thirty drops of solution of morphia, thirty drops of ipecacuanha wine, five or ten drops of chlorodyne, and an ounce of cinnamon water.

To his surprise, Dr Pritchard asked him to repeat the prescription so that he could write it down. Dr Paterson had made it so simple that he expected that Dr Pritchard would have these ingredients in stock, but Pritchard said he kept no medicines in the house except chloroform and Battley's Sedative Solution. So Dr Paterson dictated the prescription and Dr Pritchard wrote it down. But it never reached a chemist.

Dr Paterson left the house and Dr Pritchard returned to his wife's bedroom. As it grew late he half-undressed and got into bed beside her, and Mary McLeod lay on a sofa in the bedroom, so that they would be ready for any emergency. About one o'clock in the morning Mrs Pritchard moaned, 'Edward, don't sleep. I feel very faint.'

Dr Pritchard asked Mary MacLeod to get a mustard poultice. It was applied to Mrs Pritchard but she felt no better, and he asked the girl to get another poultice. Mary Patterson had been awakened and had made the poultices, and now the bell rang and she went up to the bedroom. She saw immediately that Mrs Pritchard was dead, but the second mustard poultice was lying on the bed and Dr Pritchard pulled up his wife's nightdress and told Mary Patterson to put on the poultice.

'There's no use putting mustard on a dead body,' said Mary Patterson.

'Is she dead, Patterson?' asked the doctor.

'Doctor,' replied the cook, 'you should know that better than I.'

But Dr Pritchard said his wife could not be dead, she had only fainted. He told Mary McLeod to get hot water. Once again Mary Patterson pointed out that it was no use applying heat to a dead body.

At that Dr Pritchard burst into tears and cried, 'Come back, come back, my darling Mary Jane. Do not leave your dear Edward.' He collected himself and then said, 'What a brute! What a heathen! To be so gentle – so mild. Kill me, Patterson. Get Mr King's rifle and shoot me!'

The cook knew that King, one of the medical students in the house, had a rifle, but she said, 'Doctor, don't provoke the Almighty with such expressions. If God were to shut your mouth and mine, I don't know how we would be prepared to stand before a righteous God.'

'True, Patterson,' said Dr Pritchard. 'You are the wisest and kindest woman I ever saw.'

He then went downstairs and wrote one or two letters. One particular letter was to the Clydesdale Bank. Its secretary had written to him that very day about his account being overdrawn by £131 12s. 4d. Dr Pritchard had recovered sufficiently from his wife's sudden death to write:

'I am fully aware of the overdraft, and nothing short of the heavy affliction I have been visited with since the year commenced – in the loss of my mother, and this day of my wife, after long and severe illness – would have made me break my promise. If you will kindly tell Mr Readman, to whom I am well known, that immediately I can attend to business I will see him on the matter, please ask him if he can wait till after my dear wife's funeral on Thursday.'

Then he noted in his *Blackwood's Shilling Scribbling Diary* under March 18th, 1865:

'Died here at 1 a.m. Mary Jane, my own beloved wife, aged 38 years – no torment surrounded her bedside – but, like a calm, peaceful lamb of God – passed Minnie away.

'May God and Jesus, Holy Gh., one in three – welcome Minnie. Prayer on prayer till mine be o'er, everlasting love. Save us, Lord, for they dear Son.'

Can you wonder that, after his trial, Dr Edward William Pritchard was known as the Human Crocodile?

He went out to post his letters and, when he came back, he called Mary Patterson from the kitchen to tell her that his wife had walked down the street with him, and said to him to take care of Ailie and Fanny (his daughters), but that she never spoke about the boys, and that she kissed him on the cheek and went away.

On Monday, March 20th, Dr Pritchard wrote a death certificate saying that Mrs Pritchard had died from gastric fever, duration two months. Then he arranged to take his wife's body through to Edinburgh that afternoon.

That same morning the Procurator-Fiscal in Glasgow received an anonymous letter. It was dated 'Glasgow, 18th March, 1865', and said:

> Sir
>
> Dr Pritchards' Mother in law died suddenly and unexpectedly about three weeks ago in his house Sun chichall Street Glasgow under circumstances at least very suspicion. His wife died to-day also suddenly and unexpectedly and under circumstances Equally suspicious. We think it right to draw your attention to the above as the proper person to take action in the matter and see justice done.
>
> So Hurt Egs
>
> Your &
> Amor Justitia

Afterwards most people thought that this letter was written by Dr Paterson. And, while that gentleman denied it, there is no proof that anybody else connected with this case had any suspicions of foul play. It was an effectual letter anyway. The Procurator-Fiscal told the police and the police started enquiries right away.

Knowing nothing of this, Dr Pritchard was on top of his form. He met a lady friend in Sauchiehall Street that morning and told her his wife had died, even though he had had three doctors in to attend to her. 'It's a case of too many cooks spoiling the broth,' he said.

He also had the time to sign a requisition in favour of an organ for Park Church, which was very decent of him as he was an Episcopalian.

But his finest moment came when he took the coffin containing the body of his wife to her father's home in Edinburgh and asked that the coffin should be opened so that relatives present could look their last upon their darling Mary Jane. When the coffin lid was opened, Dr Pritchard went forward and 'with great feeling' kissed his dead victim on the lips. The funeral was arranged for Thursday of that week, and Dr Pritchard took the train back to Glasgow.

On the way back he fell into conversation with a carriage companion and insisted on giving the rather astonished man a photograph of himself. He stepped out of the train at Queen Street Station, Glasgow, and there, waiting on the platform, was Superintendent McCall. The Superintendent gave Dr Pritchard the customary warning and arrested him on suspicion of having caused the death of his wife.

When the news of his arrest became known, most people thought that the police were acting very stupidly indeed. His wife's relatives said right away that they did not believe for one moment in his guilt. While he was in prison, his friends made a point of calling there and leaving their cards. Pritchard himself was calm and made a declaration affirming his entire innocence.

The police arrested Mary McLeod on suspicion of having been concerned in Mrs Pritchard's death, but soon released her.

On March 28th it became known that Mrs Pritchard's body had been examined and that it was full of the dangerous poison antimony. It was then decided to exhume Mrs Taylor's body, and antimony was found there too. Dr

Pritchard was asked to make a second declaration. It was the same as his first, that he was entirely innocent.

The Glasgow Herald for April 24th remarks:

'The prisoner looked somewhat pale, but he still retains the same amount of self possession that he has exhibited since the night of his apprehension. It may be mentioned that, on that occasion, after having been conveyed from the railway station to Mr Superintendent McCall's apartment, the doctor, previous to retiring to rest, and before the room was vacated by the officers, engaged in prayer.

'His subsequent behaviour, we have reason to believe, has been of the calmest possible description. A day or so after his incarceration in the North Prison he seemed to feel a little annoyed that he could not be favoured with a supply of pomatum for the trimming of his beard and hair. The prison regimen has not at all suited his taste.'

But, right up to the end, Dr Pritchard's calmness deserted him only once. That was when, having been convicted, he had to take off his black mourning clothes and put on prison garb. It was stated then that 'he became quite faint'.

His law agent was not at all happy about the case but, when they travelled through to Edinburgh together for the High Court trial, Dr Pritchard said to him, 'Keep up your heart. We will return to Glasgow together.'

He took with him a photograph of a family group, including his wife, his mother-in-law, and his children, and he showed this photograph to his warders and anyone else who cared to look at it.

Like Madeleine Smith, and unlike Jessie McLachlan, Dr Pritchard was tried before three judges in Edinburgh. The Lord Justice-Clerk, Lord Inglis, was the senior judge. He was the man who had defended Madeleine Smith, and undoubtedly he would know something about poison! Among the prosecuting counsel was Mr Adam Gifford, who had represented the Crown against Jessie McLachlan. And Dr Pritchard's chief defender was Mr Rutherfurd Clark, who had defended Jessie McLachlan. One unusual feature of the trial was that the accused's brother, Charles Augustus Pritchard, was permitted to sit by him in the dock and did so until the second last day of the trial.

The trial started on July 3rd and lasted five days. It is summed up very well indeed by a newspaper reporter of the time. He wrote of Pritchard:

'His naturally handsome countenance, and a certain plausibility of manner which characterised him, favourably impressed spectators. This was strikingly illustrated by his bearing in court, particuarly in the earlier stages of the trial. None who saw the intelligent, thoughtful, and mild-looking individual seated in the dock on the first morning of the eventful trial, could be prepared for anything like the refined and consummate villainy and diabolic cruelty which each day brought to light, until, when the whole murderous plot was laid bare, the assembled auditors saw before them a perfect fiend in human shape.

'It was only when his unfortunate victim, Mary McLeod, reluctantly confessed the relations which subsisted between them, that the real nature of the man was made known, and that a change might be seen stealing over his features. Before this, the attention which he paid to the evidence was only what might be expected from one interested in the proceedings, but whose fate could in no way be affected by them. With the anxiety which had now evidently taken hold of him, a certain vulpine look might be detected, as he keenly fixed his eyes upon the girl's countenance, when – under the skilful but gentle questioning of the counsel for the crown, and of the presiding judge – she rent aside the curtain which had hitherto veiled the inner life of that apparently happy home.

'Throughout the greater part of her protracted examination a change came over the seducer's features. The mild, gentlemanly expression which these had hitherto worn had now in some degree disappeared; and at times one could almost fancy that traces of malignity could be seen blended with his keen and steady gaze. This was, however, but momentary, as the sinister look speedily gave place to the usual self-complacent, but thoughtful and somewhat benign expression.

'Viewed in the light of the evidence, his demeanour throughout was studied, and designed to deceive spectators. The only piece of real humanity which peeped out during the five days of the trial was when two of his children, the one girl of fourteen and the other a boy of eleven, were placed in the box by his counsel to speak to the kindly feelings which subsisted between him and his wife and mother-in-law. Even his hardened nature was overcome, and what had all the appearance of genuine tears trickled down his cheek. This was the one vulnerable spot in the villain's breast, and the scene altogether was such as none who witnessed it will soon forget it.'

I need not go over the case for the Crown. The only thing they could not prove was the actual administration of the poisons to Mrs Pritchard and Mrs Taylor. But the circumstantial evidence and the medical evidence were overwhelming. The best that Rutherfurd Clark could do for the defence was to try to throw the blame on seventeen-year-old Mary McLeod.

The one witness who got a real roasting was Dr Paterson. Why, he was constantly asked, did he not communicate his suspicions that Mrs Pritchard was being poisoned to the authorities? He said that medical etiquette made this impossible. Lord Inglis, in his summing-up, said on this point: 'He (Dr Paterson) said, in answer to a question I put to him, that his meaning was – what he intended to state in the box was – that he was under the decided impression, when he saw Mrs Pritchard, that somebody was practising upon her with poison. He thought it consistent with his professional duty, and I must also add, with his duty as a citizen, to keep that opinion to himself.

'In that I cannot say that I concur, and I should be very sorry to lead you to think so. I care not for professional etiquette or professional rule. There is a rule of life and a consideration that is far higher than these – and that is, the duty that every right-minded man owes to his neighbour, to prevent the destruction of human life in this world, and in that duty I cannot but say Dr Paterson failed.'

The jury were out for an hour and, when they came back into court, it was seen that some of them were weeping. The foreman announced that, unanimously, they found the prisoner guilty of both charges.

Lord Inglis addressed and sentenced to death Dr Pritchard, who kept bowing to him as if assenting with all he said. And, when a great crowd gathered outside the High Court to see Pritchard taken to Calton Jail, he came out, took off his hat, and bowed to them also.

Two police officers took him back to prison in Glasgow. He was handcuffed to them, but this did not seem to worry Pritchard at all. He mentioned to them how fine the crops were looking, and eventually presented them with the family picture which he had been carrying about with him.

In the twenty-one days between his sentence and the execution, Dr Pritchard became more and more religious. He was always reading the Bible and quoting texts. He was glad to see not only his own minister, the Rev. R. S. Oldham, of St Mary's Episcopal Church, Renfield Street, but also ministers of other denominations. It was to Mr Oldham, however, that he made his first 'confession'. He said he had murdered his wife by an overdose of chloroform, and that Mary McLeod was present and knew all about it.

Mr Oldham and the prison authorities regarded this 'confession' as nonsense – at least, as far as Mary McLeod was concerned – and decided that it should not be revealed to the public. When Pritchard heard this, he said, 'I can understand now how the Founder of Christianity was so little believed.'

Some days later, on July 11th, he made a second confession. In it he said:

'It was when my wife was at Kilmun, in the summer of 1863, that I first became intimate with the girl Mary McLeod, sleeping with her in my house, 22 Royal Crescent. This continued at intervals up to the time of our removal to 131 Sauchiehall Street. She became pregnant in May last, and with her own consent I produced a miscarriage. I have reason to believe that Mrs Pritchard was quite aware of this, and rather sought to cover my wickedness and folly.

'My mother-in-law, Mrs Taylor, came last February to our house, and caught Mary McLeod and myself in the consulting-room; and the day before her death, having apparently watched us, she said to me in the same room – "You have locked her into a cupboard", which was true, but nothing more passed. I declare Mrs Taylor to have died in the manner I have before stated, and I now believe her death to have been caused by an overdose of Battley's Solution of Opium. The aconite found in that bottle was put in by me *after her death*, and designedly left there, in order to prove death by misadventure in case any inquiry should take place.

'Mrs Pritchard was much better immediately after her mother's death, but subsequently became exhausted for want of sleep. I accounted for this by the shock produced by her mother's death; and, hardly knowing how to act, at her own request I gave her chloroform. It was about midnight, Mary McLeod was in the room, and in an evil moment

183

(besides being somewhat excited by whisky) I yielded to the temptation to give her sufficient to cause death, *which I did*.

'I therefore declare, before God, as a dying man, and in the presence of my spiritual adviser, that I am innocent of the crime of murder so far as Mrs Taylor is concerned, but acknowledge myself guilty of the adultery with Mary McLeod and the murder of my wife.

'I feel now as though I had been living in a species of madness since my connection with Mary McLeod, and I declare the solemn repentance of my crime, earnestly praying that I may obtain Divine forgiveness before I suffer the penalty of the law.'

The same day that this 'confession' was made, Dr James Paterson had a very long letter in *The Glasgow Herald*. He had irked under the criticism of Lord Inglis ever since it was made, and most of the newspapers had followed it up. Dr Paterson's name, to coin a phrase, was mud. His reply now was that the fault lay with the registrar who had destroyed his letter refusing to certify the cause of Mrs Taylor's death. This letter, according to Dr Paterson, read, 'I am surprised that I am called on to certify *the cause of death* in this case. I only saw the person for a few minutes a very short period before her death. She seemed to be under some narcotic, but Dr Pritchard, who was present from the first moment of the illness until death occurred, and which happened in his own house, may certify the cause. The death was certainly sudden, unexpected, and to me mysterious.'

To the *Herald* Dr Paterson wrote now, 'I wrote that letter to the registrar after the mysterious death of Mrs Taylor with the express view of scaring the prisoner, and thus arresting him in his diabolical and cursed career of slow poisoning of his unsuspecting and confiding wife.'

Supposing, Dr Paterson went on, he had denounced Pritchard to his face, what would have been his position?

Pritchard could have brought forward no less than three medical friends, all *Edinburgh* graduates, namely, Professor Gairdner, Drs Cowan and Taylor – not one of whom suspected that Mrs Pritchard was being poisoned by antimony! Would the diagnosis of a *Glasgow* graduate have been believed for one moment when opposed by such a galaxy of professional talent and experience in consultation?'

Later in his letter he says, 'It is abundantly evident that there was a most decided bias against everything professional connected with Glasgow, and an apparent feeling that it would never do to promulgate to the world that a Glasgow medical man knew his profession better than the three Edinburgh graduates.' And so he goes on, poor soul, doing his best to justify himself in any way he can from the condemnation of Lord Inglis, the newspapers, and the world at large.

Dr Pritchard, in the condemned cell, was not in the least concerned with Dr Paterson. He was now coming up to his third confession. He made it a week before he was due to be hanged. And this time he said:

'I, Edward William Pritchard, in the full possession of all my senses, and understanding the awful position in which I am placed, do make a free and full confession that the sentence pronounced upon me is just; that I am guilty of the death of my mother-in-law, Mrs Taylor, and of my wife, Mary Jane Pritchard; and that I can assign no motive for the conduct which actuated me, beyond a species of "terrible madness" and the use of "ardent spirits".

'I hereby freely and fully state that the confession made to the Rev. R. S. Oldham, on the 11th of this month, was not true; and I hereby confess that I alone, not Mary McLeod, poisoned my wife in the way brought out in the evidence at my trial. Mrs Taylor's death was caused according to the wording of the indictment.'

He went on to make various religious comments and then to thank almost everybody he had met in court and in jail. The only names left out of his list were his defence counsel.

Dr Edward William Pritchard was hanged in Jail Square on July 28th, 1865. There is an old Glasgow saying: 'You'll die facing the Monument!' This was an insult, because it meant that you'd be hanged. The scaffold was erected in front of the South Prison and about the last thing that anyone who was about to be hanged would see would be Nelson's Monument on Glasgow Green, directly in front of him.

A crowd estimated at between 80,000 and 100,000 turned out for the hanging. They started to gather on the night before the execution. After five o'clock on the morning of the 28th six ministers addressed them at various points. One had come all the way from Dublin.

About half-past seven Calcraft, the executioner, had a look at the scaffold, to make sure that everything was in working order. The crowd recognised him and greeted him with cheers and hisses. 'But there is no doubt,' says the *Edinburgh Evening Courant*, 'that the cheers were more general than the hisses.'

The procession appeared from the South Prison. Dr Pritchard was wearing the same suit of mourning that he had been arrested in. He wore one white glove and carried the other in his hand. He had suggested that he should be allowed to address the crowd, but had been dissuaded.

Again I quote the Edinburgh *Courant*:

'When he appeared on the scaffold great commotion prevailed amongst the crowd. Exclamations were heard to proceed from every quarter, among which were such expressions as, "How well he looks!" "He's very pale!" "That's him!" and "Hats off!" &c. Mr Oldham read a short written prayer, while Calcraft adjusted the cap, put aside the long hair and beard to allow the rope to be rightly placed, and tied the legs.

'Calcraft, after putting the rope around the prisoner's neck, and drawing the cap over his face, steadied the wretched man by placing his hands on his back and breast. On a signal being given by the culprit, the bolt was drawn, and at ten minutes past eight o'clock he was launched into eternity.

'As soon as he was seen dangling from the rope a loud shriek arose from the crowd, and many turned their heads away from the horrid spectacle.'

Among the crowd were men selling the penny poems which, in those good old days, always accompanied a public occasion. One of them was entitled *Dr E. W. Pritchard turned into a Pillar of Salt.* The author was Alexander Allan, and he did so well that he published a sequel entitled *An Hour with the Ghost of Pritchard, the Prince of Poisoners! A Full Confession with the Murderer's Motive, A Dialogue in verse, Interrupted occasionally by Voices from the Lost! and a Demoniac Song!* Mr Allan wrote on a high moral and religious note, and here is a sample of his work:

> *When one, enkindled by unholy rage,*
> *Drives some poor fellow-mortal from life's stage,*
> *The deed draws down the vengeance of the sky,*
> *And men condemn the murderer to die.*
> *But when a wretch, in secret hate and guile,*
> *A foul, cold-blooded human-crocodile!*
> *Plots calmly on for months, from day to day,*
> *To take his fellow-creature's life away —*
> *(And that the wife that in his bosom lay);*
> *Counts out the grains of poison it requires*
> *To do the deed his hellish heart desires;*
> *Sees that the deadly drug works grief and pain,*
> *And yet administers the same again;*
> *Deals out the poisoned cheese, egg-flip and wine,*
> *And, smiling, says, 'My darling, it is fine!'*
> *And, when at last he has deprived his wife*
> *Of precious health and all the joys of life,*
> *And thinks that now the fitting time has come,*
> *He sends her to her everlasting home;*
> *And then declares, his murd'rous deed to hide,*
> *It was of gastric fever that she died!*

> *Compared with this, the other crime is light —*
> *This is a mighty mountain — that a mite.*

There is a macabre footnote to this macabre story. Many years after Dr Pritchard was hanged, the authorities replaced the South Prison with a High Court. A firm of Glasgow plumbers were called in to lay new pipes, and they found that some of these pipes were to be laid in what had been the murderer's graveyard alongside the South Prison. The murderers were marked only with an initial.

Under a stone marked 'P' they found the skeleton of Dr Pritchard. But, by some chemical freak, the patent leather boots which he wore to the scaffold were still in a perfectly preserved state. Somebody took these boots and sold them to an unsuspecting member of the public.

Fancy being in Dr Pritchard's boots!

The Man Who Didn't

The Case of Oscar Slater

The Man in the Lobby

Of these four respectable murder cases the one in which respectability was rampant is that of Oscar Slater. He was a German Jew who ventured into Glasgow's square mile of murder and paid for it with nearly nineteen years in prison. It could have been worse. He might have been hanged. Instead he outlived, as a free man, the judge who had sentenced him to death, the counsel who prosecuted and the one who defended him, and practically everyone closely connected with the case. True, he did not outlive the man who was suspected for years of being the actual murderer, nor the one woman who could have told the truth that might have released him. The suspect has since died, and so has the woman. I wonder if her conscience ever troubled her.

This respectable story has a respectable beginning in a respectable family's flat in a respectable Glasgow street. It was about seven o'clock on a wet night in West Princes Street, which runs off St George's Road, and is less than half a mile from Charing Cross, the centre of our square mile. There were only three shopping days to Christmas, 1908, and in the dining-room of the Adams' flat at 51 West Princes Street, Arthur Montague Adams was tying up a Christmas parcel.

Mr Adams was a flautist in the Scottish Orchestra, and he lived with his mother and sisters in a house on the ground floor with its own door. Next to this private door was what

we call in Glasgow a 'close door'. When you opened it, a
flight of stairs led up to the first floor, where there was a flat
occupied by a Miss Marion Gilchrist. the stairway continued
up to the second floor and an unoccupied flat. Miss
Gilchrist's dining-room was directly above the Adams'
dining-room, and in those days in middle-class Glasgow,
the dining-room was the family's living-room. The parlour
was kept for best.

Arthur Adams and his sisters, Laura and Rowena, were
in their dining-room when they heard a thud above them,
then three distinct knocks. Was this the signal? Miss
Gilchrist, who was eighty-three years old and very afraid of
burglars, had made an arrangement with the Adams family
that if she ever needed help she would knock down to them.
Laura Adams, a determined woman, decided it was the
signal and told Arthur to go straight up to Miss Gilchrist's
and see if anything was wrong.

Arthur left his Christmas parcel, and also his spectacles,
and went out his front door and stepped across to the close
door. He was rather surprised to find it open. It was usually
kept locked. However, up the flight of stairs he went and
rang Miss Gilchrist's bell. There was no reply and no sound
inside, so he rang again – a 'rude' ring, in his own phrase.
On either side of the solid door were glass panels. When
Arthur looked through, he could see that the gas was lit in
the lobby. He rang a third time.

Then he heard a sound he thought was somebody
chopping sticks. He knew Miss Gilchrist had a young
servant, Nellie Lambie, and he decided that the servant
must be chopping sticks in the kitchen so Arthur turned and
went back to his own dining-room. But when he explained
the situation to his sisters, Laura told him to go back at
once. She was certain something was wrong upstairs. Arthur
went up a second time, and rang the bell again. The
chopping noise had stopped and he stood there in silence,
until he heard the sound of someone coming up the stairs

behind him. He turned round and saw that it was Nellie Lambie.

Arthur Adams explained why he was there, and Nellie Lambie said it would be the pulleys in the kitchen. they needed oiling, and were making an awful noise. Arthur said he'd wait and see that everything was all right. Nellie Lambie unlocked the door with two keys (there were three locks altogether, but the third was only locked when the occupants of the house were safely in for the night) and Arthur Adams saw the lobby. It was a broad hall, with two doors on the right and two on the left, and it was dimly lit by a gas mantle inside a stained glass shade.

Then a queer thing happened. Nellie Lambie was going to the kitchen door on the left, to see the pulleys, when a man appeared from the bedroom entrance on the right. This man wore a light overcoat and appeared to Arthur Adams to be a gentleman. He walked up to Arthur as if he was going to speak to him, then stepped past and disappeared down the stairs 'like greased lightning', to quote Arthur's own words. Nellie Lambie didn't look in the least surprised, and Arthur Adams decided she must know this queer customer.

The servant went into the kitchen and came back to report that there was nothing wrong with the pulleys. 'But where is your mistress?' asked Arthur.

She went into the dining-room and screamed, 'Oh, come here!' When Arthur Adams followed her, he saw Miss Gilchrist lying in front of the fireplace, with a rug thrown over her head. There was blood all round her.

The flautist was a brave man. He decided he must follow the strange man who had walked through the lobby. He told Nellie Lambie to go down to the close-mouth and wait there till he came back. Then he dashed down the stairs and into West Princes Street. First he ran east, towards St George's Road. But there wasn't a soul in sight. He looked back west and in the light of the gas lamps he could see figures some distance away. He ran after them, but soon realised it was useless.

When he got back there, he found that Nellie Lambie had got a policeman. They went into the dining-room and uncovered the body of Miss Gilchrist. They saw that the old woman had been terribly battered about the head, but seemed to be still breathing. Arthur Adams ran across the street to the nearest doctor, also an Adams, but no relation. This Dr Adams came across, found that Miss Gilchrist was dead, and came to the conclusion that a bloodstained chair by her side was the murder weapon. And then Dr Adams disappears completely from this case.

When it came to the trial of Oscar Slater for the murder of Miss Gilchrist, Dr Adams was not called as a witness. It was the only case that murder experts for the last hundred years knew of where the first medical man on the scene of the murder was not called to give evidence.

Some time on that sad night, Nellie Lambie left the house to go along West Princes Street to Blythswood Drive (now Woodlands Drive) to let Miss Gilchrist's niece, Miss Margaret Birrell, know about the murder.

The C.I.D. arrived and examined the flat. They found, in a spare bedroom, a gas lamp lit which Nellie Lambie swore was not lit when she left the house just before seven o'clock. She had gone to collect the *Evening News* for her mistress, and had been out of the house for just over ten minutes. On a table below the gas lamp was a spent match and a box of *Runaway* matches. They were not used in the house, and Nellie Lambie had never seen them before.

On this table was a wooden casket, a gold watch and chain, and a tray with some jewellery in it. The casket had been smashed open and there were papers strewn over the floor. Nellie Lambie was asked if there was anything missing. She said that a diamond crescent brooch, about the size of half-a-crown, was gone.

The detectives questioned Nellie Lambie and Arthur Adams about the man who walked through the lobby, but

Nellie said she had hardly seen him, and Arthur explained that his view was rather indistinct because he didn't have his spectacles on.

However, the police put out a note to all pawn offices to watch out for a diamond crescent brooch, and they also issued a description of the wanted man: 'A man between twenty-five and thirty years of age, 5 feet 8 or 9 inches in height, slim build, dark hair, clean shaven; dressed in light grey overcoat and dark cloth cap. Cannot be further described.'

Will you please put a book-marker in this page? As this strange case unfolds, it would be a good idea if you now and then turned to this original description of the man in the lobby.

The murder of Miss Gilchrist cast a pall over Glasgow. The city had advanced beyond the good old Victorian days when to have three *causes célèbres* in one small district in eight years was hardly worth remarking. Respectable people were horrified that an old lady of eighty-three, living in a West End flat, should be murdered in the ten minutes while her maid went for the evening newspaper.

The newspapers went at it with a will, and there was a great deal of criticism of the Glasgow police. The public wanted an arrest right away. Now the police were working on a theory that the murderer was someone known to Miss Gilchrist. It would be almost impossible for anyone unknown to her to get into her house. They were suspicious of Nellie Lambie and were enquiring about any boy friends she had whom she might have told about the jewellery in the flat.

One of the odd things about the late Miss Gilchrist was that she had over three thousand pounds' worth of jewellery hidden in various parts of her flat – pinned behind curtains, wrapped in bed linen, stuffed in dress pockets in wardrobes, and so on. Indeed, the rumour was already going around Glasgow that Miss Gilchrist was a resetter (or receiver, in English law) and that she might have been done to death by an unsatisfied client. Like most rumours, this was completely untrue. All Miss Gilchrist's jewellery transactions were perfectly open. She was elderly and eccentric, that was all.

The police were, as they say in these modern days, getting nowhere fast when they got a nice little present on Christmas Eve. It was in the shape of a fourteen-year-old message girl named Mary Barrowman, who confessed, at the prompting of her mother, that she had been walking along West Princes Street about ten minutes past seven on the night of December 21st and had seen a man rush from Miss Gilchrist's close, pause a moment on the steps, then dash west along the street.

She was under a lamp-post as he rushed past her and he knocked against her. Then he turned south down West Cumberland Street (now Ashley Street) and disappeared. She thought he was running for a tram-car and followed him for a few steps, maybe to see whether he caught it or not. At any event, from this lightning glimpse under the lamp-post, Mary Barrowman was able to give a much fuller description than Nellie Lambie and Arthur Adams had provided.

Her description differed so much from the Lambie-Adams one that the police decided that there were two wanted men. On Christmas Day, 1908, Chief Constable Stevenson issued a Murder notice which said, 'On her return with the paper the servant met the man *first* described leaving the house, and about the same time another man, *second* described, was seen descending the steps leading to the house, and running away.'

The original description was given of the first man. The Mary Barrowman description of the second man was 'A man from twenty-eight to thirty years of age, tall and thin, clean shaven, nose slightly turned to one side (thought to be the right side); wore a fawn-coloured overcoat (believed to be a waterproof), dark trousers, tweed cloth cap of the latest make, and believed to be dark in colour, and brown boots.'

These descriptions were published in the evening news-papers on Christmas Day. On that same happy festival the

Glasgow police got their second present – a visit from a bicycle dealer named Allan McLean. Mr McLean had read all about the missing brooch. He now told the police that he was a member of the Sloper Club in India Street (where Madeleine Smith used to live, you may remember). This club was not so much devoted to the famous cartoon figure Ally Sloper, as it was to gambling. Ally Sloper was the Andy Capp of his day, though higher, ostensibly, in the social scale.

McLean said that a fellow member of the Club, a German Jew whom he knew only by his first name, Oscar, had been trying to sell a pawn ticket for a diamond crescent brooch, and he wondered if this was the brooch the police were looking for. He didn't know Oscar's address, but he could show the police the house that Oscar lived in. He had walked home behind Oscar and his friends from the Sloper Club one night and marked where this German Jew left them.

The Disappearing Dentist

The police followed this lead gladly. Immediately they tasted triumph and disaster. The triumph was that the flat at 69 St George's Road where the mysterious Oscar stayed had a plate at the door saying 'A. Anderson, Dentist', but, so far from being a dental surgery, it was a place where a gambler and jewel dealer named Oscar Slater lived with his mistress, a Madame Andrée Junio Antoine, who was not Slater's mistress alone. This was the right kind of atmosphere for the police, especially as on that very Christmas Day Oscar Slater and Madame Junio (her professional name) had left Glasgow for Liverpool, then by the *Lusitania* to New York.

Why this sudden departure? – at least the police considered it sudden. Surely it was because of the second description of a wanted man which had appeared in the evening newspapers on that day. Besides, this man Slater lived less than four hundred yards from Miss Gilchrist's house. The servant that Slater had left behind, Catherine Schmalz, gave most unsatisfactory answers to the police questions. This Oscar Slater was just the kind of suspect who was wanted at that moment.

But then came disaster. The police traced the diamond crescent brooch that Slater had pawned and it was not in the least like the one said to be missing from Miss Gilchrist's home. They had started from a false clue. This brooch had been pawned by Slater as far back as November 18th.

Frailer men might have thrown up the case against Slater. But the Glasgow police were not frail. This disaster made them all the more determined. They decided that the journey of Slater and Madame Junio from Glasgow to New York was a flight from justice. This was all the more certain when they discovered that these passengers were travelling under the names of Mr and Mrs Otto Sando.

On Hogmanay, 1908, Chief Constable Stevenson issued another notice. It said:

GLASGOW CITY POLICE
£200 REWARD
MURDER

Whereas on Monday night, 21st December, 1908, Miss Marion Gilchrist, an old lady, was foully murdered in her house at 15 Queen's Terrace, West Princes Street, Glasgow, by some person or persons unknown.

Notice is hereby given that the above reward will be paid by the Chief Constable of Glasgow to any one giving such information as shall lead to the apprehension and conviction of the person or persons who committed the crime.

Such information may be given at any Police Office in the City, or to the Subscriber,

J. V. Stevenson,
Chief Constable.

The *Lusitania* passed the Statue of Liberty on January

196

2nd, 1909, and docked in New York. The Glasgow police had laid their plans, and Mr Otto Sando (alias Oscar Slater, alias A. Anderson, dentist) was arrested and put into a cell in the Tombs prison. Mrs Otto (alias Madame Junio) was deposited on Ellis Island.

And now Oscar Slater's name and photograph appeared in the Glasgow papers, with a great deal of speculation that would not be allowed today. Whether it was the photograph, or the £200 reward, or a combination of the two, I don't know, but the fact is that a host of witnesses came forward to say that they had seen such a man in and around West Princes Street before the murder, on the night of the murder, and on four days after the murder. And now it could be said that the Glasgow police were having a Happy New Year, and that trifling business of the wrong brooch was forgotten altogether.

The public were delighted to know that, at last, someone had been arrested for the murder of Miss Gilchrist, and, although the papers did not exactly say that Oscar Slater had murdered the old lady, their readers came to their own conclusions, and were glad to think that this dastardly deed had been committed by a foreigner.

Now it was necessary to extradite Oscar Slater from the United States. It was expected that he would resist extradition, and so the Glasgow police decided to send their three chief witnesses to New York to identify him – Nellie Lambie, Arthur Montague Adams and Mary Barrowman. They may have had some qualms about this, for Nellie Lambie had told two detectives that she would not be able to identify the man she saw in the lobby, Arthur Adams had admitted he hadn't his spectacles with him, and Mary Barrowman's man in Princes Street was obviously not the man they had seen. But the police repressed their qualms. They concentrated on the two girls. Indeed, they examined them every day for a fortnight, so that, by the time they sailed for New York with Arthur Adams, their descriptions of the mysterious man tallied. And, just for convenience, they put Nellie and Mary into the same cabin for the twelve days' journey across the Atlantic. Each swore at the trial that they had never discussed the case at all during the entire voyage!

On the morning these witnesses arrived in the New York court, they were waiting in a corridor when along came three men. One was well over six feet in height, one wore a badge about six inches long, and the man in the middle was short, square and very foreign-looking. The man in the middle was handcuffed to the giant. At Oscar Slater's trial Nellie Lambie and Mary Barrowman each said that she had said, 'That's the man!' before the other. But the giant, a New York detective, said nineteen years later that a man with the girls had asked, 'Is that the man?' and pointed to Oscar Slater, the man in the middle.

In court Nellie Lambie and Mary Barrowman identified Slater as the man they had seen, and Arthur Adams was more cautious. He thought Slater was *like* the man he had seen. (It's interesting to note that, many years later, when Slater was vindicated, Arthur Adams felt he had to justify himself and told friends that Slater *was* the man – an odd case of hindsight, when you remember that he didn't have his spectacles with him in Miss Gilchrist's lobby.)

Oscar Slater's American agent proved that the brooch clue was worthless and he felt much the same about the 'identification'. He recommended his client to resist extradition. But Slater said that he was innocent, he had never heard of Miss Gilchrist until he read about the murder in the newspapers, and that he was going back to Scotland to prove his innocence.

To one of his Sloper Club friends, Hugh Cameron, he wrote a letter on February 2nd, 1909. Hugh Cameron was a peculiar character, known in Glasgow as 'The Mowdie' (The Mole). He was a bookie's clerk, a dealer in jewellery, and a gambler. It's difficult to say whether he was really a friend of Oscar Slater's or not, although he did appear at the trial as a witness for the defence. At any rate, that is what Oscar Slater wrote to Hugh Cameron – and I give Slater's own spelling and grammar:

'Dear Friend Cameron,

'Today it is nearly five weeks I am kept here in prison for the Glasgow murder.

'I am very down-hearted my dear Cameron to know my friends in Glasgow like Gordon Henderson can tell such liars about me to the Glasgow police.

'I have seen here his statement he made in Glasgow telling the police that a German came up to him and had told him Oscar Slater had committed the murder, and also that I have been on the night of the murder in his place asking him for mony, I was very excited and in hurry, I didn't think it was very clever from him, because he like to make himself a good name by the police to tell such liars.

'I don't deny I have been in his place. [It was the Motor Club, next door to the Sloper Club] asking him for mony because I went brocke in the Sloper Club. Only I will fix Mr Gordon Henderson, I will prove with plenty of witnesses that I was playing there mucky [a card came], and I am entitled to ask a proprietor from a gambling house when I am broke for mony.

'He would not mind me to get hangt and I will try to prove that from a gambling point I am right to ask for some money. *I hope nobody propper mindet* will blame me for this.

'The dirty caracter was trying to make the police believe I done the murder, was excitet, asking for mony to hop off.

'I think you know different remember whe have been in the Cunard Line office trying to change for a £5:0:0 note, we have been in three or four differend place after found some change in the Grosvenor have posted with you on Hope Street office a registered letter.

'I shall go back to Glasgow with my free will, because you know so good than myselfs that I am not the murder.

'I hope my dear Cameron that you will still be my friend in my troubel and tell the truth and stand on my side. You know the best reason I have left Glasgow because I have shown to you the letter from St Francisco.

'I reely was surprised I don't have seen your statement because I think you was too strait forard for them. They only have taken the statement against me and not for me. Likely I will be in Scotland in fourteen days and so quicke you hear that I am in prison in Glasgow send me the best criminal lawyer up you get recommendet in Glasgow I stand on your dear Cameron.

'Keep all this quiet because the police is trying hard to make a frame up for me. I must have a good lawyer, and after I can proof my innocents before having a trial, because I will prove with five people where I have been when the murder was committed.

'Thanking you at present, and I hope to have a true friend on you, because every man is able to get put in such a affair and being innocent.

'My best regards to you and all my friends. – I am, your friend,

Oscar Slater.'

'Tombs, New York.'

Now, before we follow him back across the Atlantic, a word about the writer of this letter. First of all, Oscar Slater knew so little about the murder of Marion Gilchrist that he thought it had taken place on December 22nd, and not December 21st. And when he told Cameron he would 'prove with five people where I have been when the murder was committed', he was writing about the wrong night. He had, as it turned out, a very strong alibi indeed for the real night of the murder, but that was not brought out at his trial.

Oscar Slater used a number of names – Anderson, Sando, George and Schmidt. His real name was Oscar Joseph Leschziner but, when he left his native Germany for London, he realised that was too difficult a name for the English, so he simplified it in various ways. He remained most faithful to Slater, and, since he spent most of his life under that name, that is the one we shall use.

His father was a Jewish baker. Oscar was, in turn, an apprentice to a timber merchant and a bank clerk in Hamburg. As he did not want to serve in the German Army, he left his country before he was called up and came to London. There he was a bookie's clerk, and later a bookie in his own right. He ran, or assisted to run, 'social' clubs, which were really gambling clubs.

Oscar moved about the country, and sometimes across to America, as opportunities presented themselves to him. For, example, when the great Glasgow International Exhibition was held in 1901, he felt Glasgow would be a good place to be in. But Glasgow was to turn out his unlucky city. He did fairly well in its night life, but he met a Scottish girl and married her and she became the bane of his life. She was an alcoholic and a wild spender. He left her, but there was no divorce, and every now and then she pursued him for money. That was one reason, he said, why he used so many names.

At the Empire Theatre in London he met Andrée Junio Antoine. They became very much attached, and went off together to New York as Mr and Mrs A. George. Oscar Slater had already helped to run the Italian-American Gun Club on Sixth Avenue, New York. Now he spent a year in partnership with a man named Devoto running a club on West Twenty-sixth Street.

A Gambler's Luck

In the autumn of 1908 Oscar Slater and Madame Junio returned to Britain. They were in London when Glasgow seemed to call once again. Oscar Slater arrived in Glasgow on October 29th and lived in the Central Hotel for a few days. He was always a very well-dressed man and had his shirts specially made for him. He was very broad-shoul-dered, had a prominent nose and a small moustache, and was a distinctly foreign-looking man at a time when there were comparatively few foreigners in Glasgow.

Madame Junio and her maid, Catherine Schmalz, came to Glasgow a week later, and they went into lodgings at Renfrew Street. But a couple of days after that Oscar Slater took the flat at 69 St George's Road in the name of 'A. Anderson, dentist'. Just below the flat was Stuart and Stuart's furniture shop (it is still there) and there Slater furnished his flat on the hire purchase system. Around that time he also bought a card of household tools, costing about half-a-crown. It included a hammer nine inches long, a hammer destined to become famous.

Oscar Slater seemed to settle down in Glasgow right away. He opened a Post Office Savings Bank account and bought some Consols in the name of Adolf Anderson. He picked up some of his old friends, and his daily routine was to go out around lunch-time and meet his friends in certain pubs and billiard rooms. He was dealing in jewellery when he could. He always arrived back at 7 p.m. for dinner at 69 St George's Road, and some time after eight o'clock, he'd go out for the evening. His evening consisted usually of more pubs and billiard rooms, often a music hall, and then one or two of those odd gambling clubs which proliferated in later Victorian and Edwardian Glasgow.

Madame Junio stayed at home for most of the day, receiving gentlemen visitors, but sometimes she went out to the music hall in the evening too. And, however else they spent the week, they always took Sunday as a day of rest. They didn't go out at all on that day, and usually entertained friends in the evening.

On November 18th Oscar Slater pawned the diamond crescent brooch which was later to send the police off on a false clue. It was, actually, a brooch which he had given Madame Junio as a present, but, as gamblers so often are, he was temporarily embarrassed. He raised £20 on the brooch.

He may also have been embarrassed at having to be

introduced to so many of the gambling clubs as a guest. At any rate, he was elected a member of the Sloper club on December 1st. According to the prosecution theory at the trial, it was about this date that he learned of Miss Gilchrist and her jewels and started watching her flat in West Princes Street, to find out what the movements of the occupants were so that he could plan a robbery. The Lord Advocate, for the prosecution, held up Slater as a keen-eyed, practised criminal, who was quite ready to commit murder to gain his own ends. If Slater were the murderer in this case and the criminal he was supposed to be, then he was one of the most inefficient ever known.

Incidentally, Oscar Slater had only two convictions that we know of – he had been fined £1 for being in a fight (the other man was fined £1 as well), and 5s. for being found in a gambling club when the police raided it. That was his criminal record.

In actual fact, so far from planning robbery and/or murder, Oscar Slater was deciding in December to leave Glasgow for America. It had not turned out to be the gold mine he had hoped it would. Maybe he was unlucky, or maybe the Glasgow gamblers were a bit too good for him. At any rate, he wrote to one of his American friends and arranged to return to the land of the free. The idea was to start up a club in San Francisco. He mentioned this to his friends as early as December 7th, but didn't give a date when he might leave.

Obviously he had no intention of leaving Glasgow in a hurry, for he sent his watch to a London firm for repair. Watch repairs took quite as long then as they do now. This was on December 9th and on that same day he raised £10 more on the famous pawned brooch.

On the Saturday before the murder Oscar Slater went to More's shop in Sauchiehall Street and ordered his Christmas cards. Although he was a Jew, he always observed Christmas and sent his old father and mother in Germany a present every year.

On the Sunday he spent the day at home as usual, and a friend named Reid came up in the evening with his little boy and had dinner with him and Madame Junio. But, according to two witnesses at the trial, he, or a man like him, was seen in West Princes Street at 7.40 and 9.15 that night.

And now comes the fatal day – truly so for Miss Marion Gilchrist, and nearly so for Oscar Slater. On December 21st Slater received word that his wife was after him for more money. She had caused him trouble before and he was afraid that she would smoke him and Madame Junio out in Glasgow. So he decided to get out of Glasgow and take up the American club prospect sooner than he originally meant to. He had given the London watchmaker's till December 30th to repair his watch, but now he sent a telegram to them, asking that it should be returned as soon as possible.

Shortly after noon that day he raised a further £30 on the diamond brooch. He was seen by various friends during the afternoon, and in particular by his two German cronies, Rattman and Aumann, in a billiards saloon in Renfield Street.

Slater wasn't playing that afternoon. He just dropped in and watched his friends playing for a while, and then he left them about 6.30. You'll recollect that his regular dinner hour was seven o'clock. According to the Lord Advocate he then went by back streets to the scene of the crime. He avoided brightly lit Sauchiehall Street in case he should be recognised. He got to 49 West Princes Street just before seven, watched Nellie Lambie leave the house, got into the place himself, murdered Miss Gilchrist, and was just collecting the loot when Arthur Adams rang the bell. Then, when Nellie Lambie opened the door, he walked boldly out and bolted down the stairs. All this happened in about ten minutes.

Well, I have followed in Slater's footsteps – I should say the footsteps which the Lord Advocate said Slater took. I worked out on a street map the quickest way to get from the site of the billiards saloon to 49 West Princes Street. The billiards saloon no longer exists and the Apollo Centre now covers its site. I walked from the cinema, over Garnethill, by a route which you cannot take today, owing to the fact that a motorway has been built between the hill and West Princes Street. When I did it, however, I arrived just before five minutes to seven at the scene of the crime, considerably out of breath. I should not like to have been asked to commit a murder there and then.

After the murder, again according to the Lord Advocate, Slater bolted along West Princes Street, turned sharp left at West Cumberland Street and then took a circuitous route among the terraces and streets between Woodlands Road and Great Western Road, finally arriving about 7.30 at Kelvinbridge Subway Station. He took a train to the south side of Glasgow and then strolled back to his home in St George's Road some hours later.

But, according to Madame Junio and Schmalz, the servant, Oscar Slater came home for dinner at seven as usual, and stayed in the house until some time after eight. At the trial the Lord Advocate plainly did not believe these two witnesses and, when it came to his summing-up, the judge just ignored them. But there was one witness who could prove that Oscar Slater was standing at his close-mouth at 8.15 that night, standing quietly there having a smoke and looking much more like a man who had just had his dinner than a man who had just committed a particularly atrocious murder.

This witness was a grocer who worked in a shop at Charing Cross. He knew Oscar Slater as a customer, so there was no doubt about the identification here. He was not called as a witness by the prosecution and, as the defence didn't know of his evidence, they couldn't call him.

Later that night Slater was seen in the Sloper Club. He was having his usual bad luck. At 9.45 he called on Gordon Henderson, the manager of the Motor Club next door and said, 'Have you any money in the club, Mr Henderson?'

When Henderson said he hadn't, Slater said, 'Give me what you have and I will give you a cheque for it.' But Henderson said that his committee did not allow him to lend money and Slater left.

The day after the murder seems to have been quite a normal one for Oscar Slater. He had succeeded in getting a friend in London to take over his flat in St George's Road, and expected his friend's 'girl' to arrive about the end of the month. He was having a bit of trouble with Madame Junio. Slater wanted her to return to her family in France and join him in America when the sailing weather was better. But Madame Junio wanted to be with Oscar Slater and she cried until she got her way. He was still afraid that his wife would appear, so he told some people that he was going to the Continent and others that he was going to America.

Now he had to collect all his money for the American trip, so he closed his Post Office Savings Bank account and collected the balance on December 23rd, and next day sold his Consols. On December 23rd, too, he sent a second telegram to the London watchmakers asking for his watch back by return. He called at Cook's office and asked about booking a cabin on the *Lusitania*, due to sail from Liverpool on Boxing Day. He asked his friend The Mowdie to see if he could sell the pawn ticket for the diamond brooch.

The Mowdie met Oscar Slater on Christmas Eve just as Slater was trying to get five Scottish pound notes changed for a Bank of England fiver. He wanted to send his parents £5 as their Christmas present, and he knew that Scottish bank notes would not be changed into marks in Germany. He and The Mowdie went to various places ere they succeeded in the transaction at the Grosvenor Restaurant. That same day Slater paid a second call on Cook's, but he couldn't get the cabin he wanted and told the clerk that he'd see if he could do better when he got to Liverpool.

Oscar Slater and Madame Junio spent most of Christmas Day packing for the voyage. A Mrs Freedman had arrived to take over the flat, and they sent word to her hotel that she could move in that evening. They packed nine trunks and cases, very carefully indeed. They even put camphor tablets among the linen so that it would keep fresh during the trip to America. And this, you will remember, was what the police were to call 'a flight from justice'!

On Christmas night Oscar Slater engaged a man to take the luggage by barrow to the Central Station, and he and Madame Junio followed in a cab. He bought tickets to Liverpool. Later the police were to claim that he bought tickets to London and got off at Liverpool, so as to throw any followers off his track. But the fact was that only two Liverpool tickets were sold that night, and the only people who got off at Liverpool, apart from some short-distance travellers, were Oscar Slater and Madame Junio. Of course there could have been a most unwelcome follower. The first Mrs Slater might have been on their track, and that is why Oscar Slater gave the names of 'Mr and Mrs Otto Sando' to the booking clerk. He even made a little joke about it, saying there was no 'w' at the end of the name. 'I'm not the strong man,' he said.

Well, they sailed for New York and we know the rest. The police found the wee hammer from the half-crown card of tools and decided this was the murder weapon, especially as it had some stains about the head. They also found, among the luggage, a light raincoat with stains on it and decided this was the coat which Oscar Slater wore when he did Miss Gilchrist to death. The stains on the hammer were later found to be rust and the stains on the coat were due to weather.

How to Run an Identification Parade

You may well wonder by this time how Oscar Slater could possibly be connected by the police with the murder of Miss Gilchrist. But in those days the Glasgow police had their own methods. In all fairness I must say that, in later days, when police recruits were being trained in Glasgow they received a lecture on 'How not to do it', and the case taken as an illustration was the Oscar Slater case.

The public were certainly behind the police in February, 1909. The newspapers made it plain that Slater was a dirty dog and, in the immortal words of a Scottish judge, 'nane the waur o' a guid hangin' '. When they heard that Slater was aboard the liner *Columbia* coming up the River Clyde on February 21st the crowds rushed to the riverside which was lined wherever people could get access. The police were worried about Slater's reception in Glasgow, so they had the liner stopped at Renfrew, took him ashore there and then by car to Glasgow. Just as two detectives were leading him off the *Columbia*, a brave member of the crew rushed forward and kicked Slater. That was an earnest of what was to happen to him in Scotland.

He was taken to the Central Police Station and on that day and the next identification parades were held. These identification parades were a disgrace to the Glasgow police. Slater, an obvious foreigner, was put among nine policemen and two railway officials, all Scots. You will be glad to know, though, that they were not wearing their uniforms! The witnesses had not the slightest difficulty in pointing Slater out as the man they thought they had seen in and around West Princes Street for three weeks before the murder and immediately after it. When Slater's counsel asked a police witness at the trial if it would not be fairer to put an accused man among men more or less like him, the witness replied, 'It might be the fairest way, but it is not the practice in Glasgow.'

Over the years there has been a good deal of criticism of the police action in the Slater case and I feel it's only fair to them to make one point clear. Their job was to find the murderer of Miss Gilchrist and provide evidence to show that he had committed the deed. All their evidence went to an official called the Procurator-Fiscal, and he was the person who decided whether the case should be proceeded with or not. In those days the Procurator-Fiscal was

208

regarded as part of the prosecution and he was out to help the police in any way he could. Things have changed considerably and the connection of the Procurator-Fiscal with the police was dropped many years ago.

The trial of Oscar Slater was fixed to start on Monday, May 3rd, in Edinburgh. Lord Guthrie was appointed to be judge, and the Lord Advocate, Alexander Ure, decided to conduct the case for the Crown himself. It was said in lawyers' circles that the Crown were for dropping the case against Slater at one point, because the evidence against him was so poor. But the Lord Advocate was as determined as the Glasgow police to get his man. He swept all doubts aside.

Slater's counsel was Mr A. L. McClure, K.C. He made a good defence, but it could have been better. After the trial it was suggested that he had been unwell throughout the four days in the High Court. But perhaps Mr McClure's trouble in this case was that he believed in sweet reasonableness, and that was no counter to the Lord Advocate's passionate belief that Slater was guilty.

The whole crux of the case lay in identification. Was Oscar Slater the 'watcher' seen in and around West Princes Street between December 1st and the night of the murder? Was he the man who walked through the lobby of Miss Gilchrist's house, past Arthur Adams and Nellie Lambie? Was he the man Mary Barrowman said she saw running from 49 West Princes Street just after the murder?

In the witness box Arthur Adams was still doubtful. But Nellie Lambie and Mary Barrowman were now quite positive that Oscar Slater was the man. Then there were the dozen people who saw the 'watcher' and came forward after they had seen Slater's photograph in the newspapers. Only one had actually spoken to this 'watcher' and she said that she noticed nothing odd about his accent, and did not think he was a foreigner. The jury could not know it, but Slater's accent was so strong that his counsel decided not to put his client in the witness box in case his foreign accent put the jury against him.

Arthur Adams' sister, Mrs Liddell, had said nothing on the night of the murder of seeing a man standing against the railings at Miss Gilchrist's door at five to seven, but remembered this incident some days later. She said Oscar Slater was the man and identified him by his profile. But she also added that he was wearing a heavy tweed overcoat and not a waterproof, and that he 'had the appearance of a delicate man'. Everybody else said he was wearing a waterproof and it was very obvious indeed in the court that Slater was anything but a delicate man.

We have no means of knowing now how the jury were affected by this sort of evidence. But it is clear that the Lord Advocate's address affected them deeply. When Ure died, as Lord Strathclyde, a fellow judge said of him: 'Some advocates are obsessed by doubts and difficulties. Ure had none. Some are perturbed by considerations of the strength of the other side. For Ure there *was* no other side. He believed implicitly and invincibly in the strength of his own case. He could not see that any other view than his was possible.'

Such single-mindedness may be a good thing, but it should not result in misleading the jury. Never at any time in the trial did the Lord Advocate attempt to show that Slater knew anything of Miss Gilchrist's hoard of jewels. But near the start of his speech, Mr Ure said, 'We shall see in the sequel how it was that the prisoner came to know that she was possessed of these jewels.' Then he didn't mention the subject again.

There was the question of how the murderer got into Miss Gilchrist's house. After all, she was afraid of burglars and had the signalling arrangement with the Adams family downstairs. She had three locks on the door, and also, if the close door was shut and someone rang the bell, she could see that person from her windows, and decide whether or not to pull the lever which would make it possible for him to open the outer door. The Lord Advocate did not prove any association between Slater and Miss Gilchrist. He made no suggestion whatever as to how Slater got into the house, and no-one else mentioned it either.

The Lord Advocate leaned heavily on the theory that the 'watcher' was Oscar Slater. He said that the murderer 'required as part of his elaborate precautions to familiarise himself with the inmates of the house, with their movements and their habits, and also with the movements of the police. There was one method, and one only, by which that object could be accomplished, and that was by careful, prolonged, and steady watching with a skilled eye.'

Fine! But if Slater was as skilled as all that, why did he finally decide to commit his crime when Nellie Lambie was out on a casual errand? Surely a skilled watcher would know, after three weeks, that the servant had a regular afternoon and evening out twice a week.

The Lord Advocate described Slater as 'gasping and panting for money'. But that very day he had raised £30 on his pawned brooch. He had money in the Post Office Savings Bank and in Consols.

Several times the Lord Advocate stated that Slater made his 'flight from justice' on Christmas night because his name and description had been published in the Glasgow evening newspapers. But, while it was true that Mary Barrowman's description of a second man appeared that evening, Slater's name did not, for the very good reason that the Glasgow police had not heard of him until his fellow member of the Sloper Club went to them on Christmas Night.

The Lord Advocate's speech to the jury lasted for two hours. William Roughead was at the trial and after it was over he told Sir Edward Marshall Hall how amazed he'd been at the Lord Advocate making this prodigious speech without a single note. 'Possibly,' said Sir Edward, 'that accounts for its manifold inaccuracies.'

For the defence Mr McClure quoted the famous case of Adolf Beck. Ten women in London swore that Beck was the

man who had got jewellery from them on various represen-
tations. Two policemen also identified him. Beck was sen
to prison for seven years. In actual fact the criminal was
man named Smith, who did not look at all like Beck. After
Beck had done his seven years, he came out of prison bu
was soon charged again with the same sort of crime. Again
women identified him, and again he protested his innocence
This time he got five years, and again the real criminal wa
Smith. Fortunately the judge who tried Adolf Beck a second
time felt there was something strange about this case. A
Parliamentary inquiry was held and it was found that Beck
had been wrongly convicted. The Government gave him
solatium of £2000.

Mr McClure asked the jury to be very careful in accepting
the identification evidence in this case. But Lord Guthrie, in
his summing up, said, 'Now, in this case there is one thing
quite clear – the prisoner is like the murderer. But, then he
is not charged with being like the murderer; he is charged
with being the murderer. Yet I do not think you can doubt
after the body of evidence led before you, that he has at leas
a marked resemblance to the man who haunted the stree
outside Miss Gilchrist's house, and to the man who wa
seen coming from the house.'

Lord Guthrie made his own position quite plain with on
statement after another. Talking of Oscar Slater he said
'He has maintained himself by the ruin of men and on th
ruin of women, living for years past in a way that many
blackguards would scorn to live.' And later: 'The man's lif
has been not only a lie for years, but is so today.' And then
'We do not know whether he ever did an honest day's worl
in his life. The man remains a mystery as much as when thi
trial began.'

And what were the jury to make of this statement of Lor
Guthrie's? 'The Lord Advocate,' he said, 'founds on th
prisoner's admittedly abandoned character as a point in
support of the Crown. He is entitled to do so, because a man
of that kind has not the presumption of innocence in hi

favour which is a form in the case of the ordinary man. Not only is every man presumed to be innocent, but the ordinary man, in a case of brutal ferocity like the present, has a strong presumption in his favour. In addition, a man with the prisoner's sinister record may be capable of exhibiting a callous behaviour even immediately after committing a murder.'

It was at 4.55 p.m. on Thursday, May 6th, that the jury retired to consider their verdict. Oscar Slater was so certain that they could not possibly find him guilty that he remained in the dock. They returned after an hour and ten minutes.

'What is your verdict, gentlemen?' asked the Clerk of Court.

'The jury,' said the foreman, 'by a majority find the prisoner guilty as libelled.'

Oscar Slater rose in the dock. 'My lord,' he cried, 'may I say one word? Will you allow me to speak?'

'Sit down just now,' said Lord Guthrie.

But while the verdict and sentence were being recorded, Oscar Slater rose again. 'My lord,' he said, 'my father and mother are poor old people. I came on my own account to this country. I came over to defend my right. I know nothing about the affair. You are convicting an innocent man.'

'I think' said Lord Guthrie to Mr McClure, 'you ought to advise the prisoner to reserve anything he has got to say for the Crown authorities. If he insists on it, I shall not prevent him now. Will you see what he says?'

'My lord, what shall I say?' burst out Oscar Slater. 'I came over from America, knowing nothing of the affair, to Scotland to get a fair judgment. I know nothing about the affair, absolutely nothing. I never heard the name. I know nothing about the affair. I do not know how I could be connected with the affair. I know nothing about it. I came from America on my own account. I can say no more.'

Lord Guthrie made no observation on this statement. He assumed the black cap and sentenced Oscar Slater to be hanged on Thursday, May 27th. Slater was hustled downstairs from the court and the spectators, considerably shaken by the scene, went home to wonder. They wondered if the police, the Lord Advocate, the judge and the jury had been right after all. The voting of the jury was: Guilty, nine; Not Proven, five; Not Guilty, one. As William Roughead says, 'Had two more jurymen been able to withstand the eloquence of the Lord Advocate, Slater would have been set free.'

On the other hand, there was the newspaper leader next day which said, 'The trial has cast a lurid light in the dark places of our great cities, in which such wretches ply their calling. It shows a brood of alien vampires, lost to conscience and to shame, crawling in black depths at the basement of civilised society.'

Many Glasgow people did not see the leader writer's point of view at all. They lined up at street corners to sign a petition for the commutation of Slater's sentence. More than 20,000 people signed that petition. But some of the petition sheets never reached Lord Pentland, the Secretary for Scotland, because sometimes the petition tables were over-turned and the sheets destroyed. Miss Mary Cleary told me that she went to sign the petition at a table at the corner of Gordon Street and Buchanan Street, when an elderly, well-dressed man in a top hat raised his umbrella in remonstrance and said, 'Why are you signing that? The man wanted to ruin young women like you.'

Miss Cleary replied that she was signing the petition because she did not believe that Oscar Slater had committed the murder. Retirement of Elderly Party! The two points the petition made were, first, that the identification of the prisoner with the murderer was insufficient; second, that the alleged immoral character of the prisoner should not have been brought before the jury and must have influenced their judgment.

Mr Ewing Speirs, Oscar Slater's law agent, sent the petition to the Secretary for Scotland, and he added to it a Memorial of his own which went into the story as we know it up till now. But one new fact emerged. One of the Crown witnesses who was not called to give evidence was a Miss Agnes Brown, a thirty-year-old school teacher who lived near Miss Gilchrist's house.

Agnes Brown said that, just about ten minutes past seven on the night of the murder, she had come up West Cumberland Street into West Princes Street when two men rushed past her. They came from the direction of Miss Gilchrist's flat but, unlike the mysterious man who Mary Barrowman said she saw run *down* West Cumberland Street, this pair turned up Rupert Street towards Great Western Road. Miss Brown said that one of these men wore a navy blue coat with a velvet collar, and later she identified Oscar Slater as that man.

It was very obvious indeed that, if the Lord Advocate had produced Agnes Brown as a witness, his prize silver teapot – Mary Barrowman – would be shown to be base metal. So he did not produce Miss Brown.

Just Rewards

Oscar Slater was to be hanged on May 27th but now the Lord Chancellor, the Minister for War (Mr Haldane), and Lord Guthrie himself had a consultation. And two days before the date of the hanging the Secretary for Scotland sent a message to Glasgow saying that the capital sentence on Oscar Slater was commuted to penal servitude for life.

And so Oscar Slater, a bewildered, innocent man, was taken to Peterhead Prison, in the north-east of Scotland. The people who had helped to send him there got their just reward. Of the £200 offered for information leading to the discovery of the murderer, John Forsyth, manager of the second-class department of the Cunard Company in Liverpool, who had identified Slater as the Otto Sando who travelled aboard the *Lusitania*, received £40; Allan McLean, who brought the information about the brooch, received £40; Gordon Henderson, manager of the Ally Sloper Club, received £20; and the imaginative message girl, Mary Barrowman, got £100.

I described Oscar Slater as 'bewildered'. You have only to read his letters from Peterhead to his lawyers, first Mr Ewing Speirs and then Mr Shaughnessy, to see that he was butting about wildly in an endeavour to solve a murder case of which he knew nothing except what he had heard in court. He fastened on the idea that a sweetheart of Nellie Lambie's named Nugent was either the murderer or had some connection with the crime – although Nugent, in fact, was completely cleared by the police.

'My firm opinion,' wrote Slater to Mr Speirs, and I keep to his own spelling, 'is that the murder was one of Nugent friends or a other sweethearth of Lambie, a old, story, and allwise true, is whe murder is committed and the reason was robbery, and a servant was staying in the house like Lambie, knowing so many boys, the murder is most times the sweethearth, or a friend of the sweethearth.'

He suggests that a private detective might be engaged to go into the case on his behalf. He wants bills posted up in various towns asking for information that he thinks will help. Although he complains in some of his letters that they are read before they leave Peterhead, he keeps saying that the police framed him.

When William Hodge and Company, Ltd., of Edinburgh, published *The Trial of Oscar Slater*, edited by William Roughead, in April, 1910, Slater wrote immediately to his lawyers and asked for a copy. For some reason the prison authorities decided to cut out the whole of Mr Roughead's introduction before the book was passed to Slater, Convict No. 1992. Maybe they thought he wouldn't have time to read it all. Or maybe they didn't appreciate the masterly fashion in which William Roughead dealt with the weaknesses, the peculiarities and the shortcomings of the case against Oscar Slater.

The reviews of the book, especially those published in the

English newspapers, made it clear that an injustice seemed to have been done. In a private letter to Roughead the novelist Andrew Lang wrote that, on such evidence as that led against Slater, 'a cat would scarcely be whipped for stealing cream'.

Sir Arthur Conan Doyle, that doughty paladin for truth and justice, sailed into the attack in *The Times*. Their Letters to the Editor, and those of *The Spectator*, were full of the case. Most of these letters cannot have been happy reading for the Glasgow police or for the Crown authorities in Scotland.

In Peterhead Prison Slater read the account of his own trial and found for himself the errors and omissions which ran through the prosecution evidence and the Lord Advocate's address. He brought all these up painstakingly in letters to Mr Shaughnessy. He now regarded himself as the 'Scottish Dreyfus'.

One of his letters pleads, 'Don't say Mr Shaughnessy: yes Slater, surely you are right, I believe you, I am awful sorry for it, only everything is over now. I know this, Mr Shaughnessy, it is over, only I am still alive, and I have very strong hope, something may turn up, without the murder is found.'

And again: 'I will fight so long as I live in here, I am not crying to get liberated; I want justice and this I will get at last, *we have some straight in Scotland too*. I am glad to hear Mr Shaughnessy you write to me not to bother my head, this naturally means you are doing everything in your power what a honourable lawyer would do. Hoping that nobody *shall be able* to poison you against me, I wish you to come out as a 'Labory' in my case. [Labory was Dreyfus's Agent in Paris.]

Yours faithfully,
Oscar Slater.'

Perhaps the most poignant paragraph in his letters from prison was this:

By going slightly over the contents of my unfair trial, I find

Lord Guthrie's charge to the jury, which have grieved me *very much*, and I cannot deny, that I had not a good cry over it, and now I feel better. How is it possible Mr Shaughnessy an honourable man, like Lord Guthrie, could sum up, as he did??? *In such a dangerous case.*'

On the surface, however, nothing was being done for Oscar Slater. Convict No. 1992 would have been amazed if he had only known that one man who fervently believed in Slater's innocence, and was already working to prove it, was a Glasgow policeman. His name was John Thomson Trench and he is the real hero of the whole Slater story.

Before he comes actively on the scene, let's return to August, 1912. In that month Sir Arthur Conan Doyle published a booklet at sixpence entitled *The Case of Oscar Slater*. It was meant to get the widest possible sale, and it did. The booklet was based on the Roughead trial volume and Roughead himself said, 'Over and above what have long since become the stock features of the mystery, the author made the new and interesting point that some *document*, such as a will – not jewels – was the object of the murderer's quest, the abstraction of the brooch – if it in fact were stolen – being but a blind.'

William Roughead does less than justice to that once great Glasgow newspaper, *The Evening News*. Two days after the murder of Marion Gilchrist, the *News* reported that not the brooch but a will was now concerned in the case. But such a document was not mentioned again until Sir Arthur Conan Doyle brought out his booklet.

This time the Slater case got into the House of Commons. In December, 1912, Sir Edward Marshall Hall (who had already, as we know, made his opinion of the Lord Advocate's speech quite plain) asked, 'Is the Scottish Secretary aware that the verdict upon which Oscar Slater was convicted was a majority verdict of three in a jury of fifteen? That certain witnesses to his identity whose precognitions had been taken by the Crown were not called at the trial?

That the speech of the counsel for the prosecution contained inaccurate statements of fact? And, in view of the general uneasiness as to the justice of the verdict, will he state what steps he proposes to take?'

Mr McKinnon Wood, the Scottish Secretary, did not propose to take any steps. But McKinnon Wood, like Oscar Slater, did not know what John Thomson Trench was doing.

Trench was an outstanding man in the Glasgow Police Force. He joined it as a constable in 1893 and in this year of 1912 had been commissioned as Detective-Lieutenant Trench. He was also a King's Medallist, an honour not easily won in the police. For this he had been specially recommended by the Chief Constable of Glasgow.

From the moment that the murder of Marion Gilchrist was reported to Central Police Headquarters on the night of December 21st, 1908, Trench was involved in the case. And, according to him, Nellie Lambie that very night named the man she saw in the lobby of Miss Gilchrist's flat as a man known to her and to the victim. Naturally, it wasn't Oscar Slater. At that time the police were going on the theory that the murderer was known to his victim. But then along came the clue of the pawned brooch, and Trench's superiors dropped everything in favour of pursuing Slater.

It was Trench's duty to obey instructions, so he did. He said nothing about his own suspicions, but he did feel that Slater had been wrongly convicted, and this continued to prey on his conscience. Then, in November, 1912, the Dundee police asked the Glasgow police for help in a most mysterious murder in a villa in Broughty Ferry. By this time Detective-Lieutenant Trench was regarded as the finest detective in Scotland, and he was sent to Dundee.

This Broughty Ferry murder was amazingly like the Marion Gilchrist case. The body of Miss Jean Milne, sixty-five years old and rich, was found lying in the lobby of the big house in which she lived alone. She had been killed with a poker. Although there was a great deal of money and jewellery about, nothing had been taken. There was no trace of any forced entry to the house, so it seemed that Miss Milne, like Miss Gilchrist, had admitted the murderer herself.

When a reward of £100 was offered, a number of people came forward and gave descriptions of a strange gentleman they had seen in the district and even in the garden of Miss Milne's house. A description of a wanted man was issued, and the police at Maidstone were sure they already had him in custody. He was doing fourteen days for having obtained from a Tonbridge hotelkeeper food and lodgings to the value of seven shillings by false pretence. He had given his name as Charles Warner, and his address as 210 Wilton Avenue, Toronto.

The Dundee police sent five witnesses to Maidstone to see if they could identify Warner as the man they had seen in Broughty Ferry. The two men and three women all identified Warner as the man. Trench also went to Maidstone and arrested Warner. But, as he travelled with the prisoner back to Dundee, he began to wonder if this was the wanted man. Warner's own story was that he had come across from Canada to the Continent and was wandering around England, France, Belgium and Holland.

Now it had been discovered that, though Miss Milne's body was not found until November, the murder must have been committed on October 16th. So Trench asked the accused man where he was on that day. Warner said he'd been in Antwerp. Could he prove it, asked Trench. No, Warner couldn't because he'd had no money and was sleeping out in parks. And then he remembered that, on October 16th, he'd pawned his waistcoat for a franc.

Trench went to Antwerp, found the pawnshop, checked the date, redeemed the waistcoat and brought it back to its owner — not just a garment but a perfect alibi. You can imagine with what feelings Dundee police received the news: to say nothing of the Dundee Procurator-Fiscal, who had sent to the Crown Authorities in Edinburgh his 300-page case against Charles Warner. Warner was liberated and the Broughty Ferry murder remains a mystery to this day.

Reflecting on this case, Detective-Lieutenant Trench worried about Oscar Slater more than ever. If it had not been for the pawned waistcoat, Warner might have been found guilty of murder on the identification of at least five witnesses who could not possibly have seen him. What about the identification of Oscar Slater?

As a police official, Trench's duty was to say nothing and leave Slater to rot in Peterhead Prison. But he felt that his duty as a man was more important than his duty as a policeman. He could not convince his superiors of Slater's innocence, so he went to a well-known Glasgow Lawyer, Mr David Cook, and told him the whole story. The lawyer advised him to tell it publicly, but Trench was worried about his position in the Glasgow police. He wanted some guarantee that he would not suffer for telling what he believed to be the truth.

Mr Cook approached Dr Devon, one of H.M. Prison Commissioners for Scotland, and explained the situation. Dr Devon wrote to Mr McKinnon Wood, and the Scottish Secretary replied on February 13th, 1914, 'If the constable mentioned in your letter will send me a written statement of evidence in his possession of which he spoke to you, I will give this matter my best consideration.'

Well, you could hardly ask for a better guarantor than the Scottish Secretary. Detective-Lieutenant Trench sent his information, and so started his own personal tragedy.

In March Mr David Cook, the lawyer, asked the Scottish Secretary to hold an enquiry into the Slater case. He raised five important questions:

'Did any witness to the identification on the night of the murder name a person other than Oscar Slater?

'Were the police aware that this was the case? If so, why was the evidence not forthcoming at the trial?

'Did Slater fly from justice?

'Were the police in possession of information that Slater had disclosed his name at the North-Western Hotel, Liverpool, stating where he came from, and that he was travelling by the *Lusitania*?

'Did one of the witnesses make a mistake as to the date on which she stated she was in West Princes Street?'

All these points were raised in Trench's statement, and I have raised most of them already in this book.

The Secret Enquiry

Though Mr McKinnon Wood had managed to dodge the issue up till now, he could not ignore Mr Cook's serious statements. He appointed the Sheriff of Lanarkshire, Mr Gardiner Millar, K.C., to conduct an enquiry and to report. The enquiry was to take place in private in the County Buildings, Glasgow, at the end of April. Judicial farces are not unknown in Scotland, but it would be difficult to find an enquiry more farcical than this one. William Roughead charitably describes it as Gilbertian.

Neither the prisoner nor his agent was allowed to be present at 'The Secret Enquiry', as the newspapers immediately dubbed it. The witnesses were not on oath. Indeed, they did not even need to appear if they felt disinclined. The Commissioner was instructed that his investigations 'should in no way relate to the conduct of the trial'. The only persons present were the Commissioner, his clerk, and the witnesses.

The actual words of the witnesses were not taken down. The Commissioner dictated a digest of each witness's evidence to his clerk. The result of the enquiry was later published as a Parliamentary Paper, and it was discovered that the Commissioner had used as many asterisks as Ethel M. Dell. When he felt that what a witness said was undesirable, he just left the evidence out and put in asterisks instead.

Most, if not all, of the asterisks replace the evidence which was given about the mysterious man who walked through Miss Gilchrist's lobby in front of Nellie Lambie and Arthur Adams. He was known in the report as A.B.

Detective-Lieutenant Trench stated:

'I am aware that on 22nd December, the day after the murder, Superintendent Douglas, along with Detective Pyper and Dornan, drove in a taxi-cab to the house of A. B. I am also aware that they did so in view of the information supplied by Nellie Lambie. I have endeavoured from time to time to elicit what took place in A. B.'s house, but I am without information.

'On 23rd December I was instructed by Chief Superintendent Orr to visit and take a statement from Miss Birrell, 19 Blythswood Drive. I had particular instructions to question her with regard to A. B. and as to what Lambie said when she visited her house on the night of the murder. I visited Miss Birrell and from her received the statement word for word as contained in her precognition.'

Let's have a look at Miss Margaret Birrell's precognition:

'I am a niece of the late Marion Gilchrist,' it goes, 'my mother was a sister of the deceased. Miss Gilchrist was not on good terms with her relations. Few, if any, visited her. [The Sheriff's asterisks come in here.] I can never forget the night of the murder. Miss Gilchrist's servant, Nellie Lambie, came to my door about 7.15.

'She was excited. She pulled the bell violently. On the door being opened she rushed into the house and exclaimed, "Oh, Miss Birrell, Miss Birrell, Miss Gilchrist has been murdered, she is lying dead in the dining-room, and oh, Miss Birrell, I saw the man who did it." I replied, "My God, Nellie, this is awful. Who was it, do you know him?" Nellie replied, "Oh, Miss Birrell, I think it was A.B. I am sure that it was A.B."

'I said to her, "My God, Nellie, don't say that. [Sheriff's asterisks.] Unless you are very sure of it, Nellie, don't say that." She again repeated to me that she was sure it was A. B. The same evening Detectives Pyper and Dornan visited me, and I learned from them that she had told them it was A. B.

We go back to Detective-Lieutenant Trench. He says:

'On receiving the statement I returned to the Central Police Office. I told Superintendent Orr and Superintendent Ord what Miss Birrell had said. Chief Superintendent Orr seemed impressed with the statement, and remarked, "This is the first real clue we have got." I was instructed to write out the statement. I did so. In handing that statement to Superintendent Ord, he said, "I have just been ringing up Douglas [Superintendent of the Western Police] and he is convinced that A. B. had nothing to do with it".'

Trench goes through the case against Slater, showing how little evidence there is against him, and then returns to Nellie Lambie.

'On 3rd January, 1909, along with Detective Keith, I visited Nellie Lambie at 15 South Kinning Place, at the house of her aunt. She was lodging there. I had with me a sketch of Oscar Slater which I had received from Superintendent Ord. I showed the sketch to Lambie. She could not identify. She said she did not know him. The sketch was a fair representation of Slater, and had evidently been drawn by someone who knew him. Although I had not spoken to Lambie, I was aware, having taken Miss Birrell's statement, that she had declared that A. B. was the man. I touched on A. B., asking her if she really thought he was the man she saw. Her answer was, "It's gey funny if it wasn't him I saw". [Sheriff's asterisks.] My first conclusion after meeting Lambie was that if she had had anyone to support her she would have sworn to A. B.

'So much impressed was I that I mentioned the fact to Superintendent Ord next morning, asking if he thought that

A. B. might not be the man. His only answer was, "Douglas has cleared up all that, what can we do?" '

Dealing with the imaginative message girl, Trench says, 'I am forced to the conclusion that Mary Barrowman was not at or near Miss Gilchrist's close at the time the murderer rushed therefrom. I have had from her employer and his sister an emphatic statement that Barrowman did not deliver a message on the night of the 21st.'

Trench goes on at quite a length about Mary Barrowman but, for reasons which will emerge later, we'll not bother with Barrowman. I must just agree with Trench's last statement on the subject, 'Everything goes to prove that her statement of having seen the man was a cock-and-bull story of a young girl who was somewhat late in getting home and who wished to take the edge off by a little sensationalism.'

One other point that Trench mentioned showed later how lax the police had been once it was decided that Oscar Slater must be the man. I have mentioned that a box of matches, *Runaway* by name, was found beside the broken casket in Miss Gilchrist's back bedroom. Trench searched Oscar Slater's house and found no *Runaway* matches there. But he discovered that this particular match was sold not by the box but by the gross. It would surely have been a simple matter for the police to have followed this clue and find out who bought *Runaway* matches in bulk in the city of Glasgow, especially in the West End.

Well, you either believe Detective-Lieutenant Trench or you don't. It seems inconceivable to me that a man would put himself up against the whole Glasgow police force for any other purpose than to tell the truth. What could he possibly gain by this action? I only wish that, in similar circumstances, I could be as brave a man as John Thomson Trench.

I think Trench told the truth. But Miss Margaret Birrell said that Nellie Lambie had never mentioned the name of A. B. to her. Nellie Lambie, by now married to a miner and known as Mrs Gillon, said the whole story, as far as she was concerned, was absolutely false. Detective-Inspector Keith had no recollection of Trench ever mentioning A. B. to Nellie Lambie in his presence. Mary Barrowman's employer and his sister couldn't be quite sure whether she went a message or not on the night of December 21st, 1908, because their books 'had gone amissing'.

Assistant Chief Constable John Orr (the Superintendent Orr of Trench's statement) said he could not recollect that Trench had said anything to him about A. B., but the enquiries were conducted by Superintendent Ord and he (Orr) just signed the letters that were put in front of him.

And what did Superintendent Ord say? For one thing he said, 'The police satisfied themselves at the time that A. B. had nothing to do with the murder.' And then he made a statement which puzzles me somewhat. No doubt the Sheriff knew what it meant and why it came up at all.

'On account of the importance of this case,' he said, 'all the officers were requested to make their reports in writing, and these were filed and ought to be available now. Those that were forwarded to the Sheriff's Fiscal were copied in the Copying Book. If Detective-Lieutenant Trench states that he supplied to me a statement to him by Miss Birrell on 23rd December, 1908, then it should be on the file.

'I cannot trace such a statement and the numbers on the file are consecutive. With regard to the copying Books that were used at the time of the murder, the Copying Book at the time was near an end and I started a new book in order to keep the statements on the Gilchrist murder together, although finishing off the old book with other cases. When it was necessary to get the papers together for extradition some of the officers' statements were recopied.'

One Glasgow policeman after another appeared before the Commissioner and stated that what John Thomson Trench said, as far as each was concerned, was untrue.

This farce concluded on April 25th. The Sheriff of Lanarkshire sent his report to the Scottish Secretary, and that Hon. gentleman was able to state in the House of Commons on June 17th, in reply to a question, that no case had been established which would justify any interference with Oscar Slater's sentence.

The Government put out a White Paper on the 'Secret Enquiry' on June 27th, 1914. The only people who seemed to like it were the Glasgow police. The newspapers certainly didn't.

As for Detective-Lieutenant Trench, it soon became necessary for him to invoke the protection of the Scottish Secretary. He was suspended from duty on July 14th, and the Chief Constable of Glasgow reported his case to the Glasgow magistrates, stating, 'It is contrary to public policy and to all police practice for an officer to communicate to persons outside the police force information which he has acquired in the course of his duty, without the express sanction of the chief officer of his force.' Trench had communicated with Mr Cook, the lawyer, and so he was suspended.

Trench wrote out a full statement for the magistrates, and produced the letter from the Secretary for Scotland which had asked for the information. He did not budge one inch as far as the truth of his story was concerned. He said he had acted solely in the interests of justice but, if he had erred, he trusted the magistrates would bear in mind his long and useful services to the city.

The magistrates heard the Chief Constable, Trench, Cook, and Dr Devon, and decided to dismiss Trench from the Glasgow police. The respectability of the Force was justified.

Trench wrote to Mr McKinnon Wood in appeal. He said he looked on the Scottish Secretary's invitation to send the information, and his acceptance of that information, as ample protection against any breach of discipline that might be alleged against him. Mr McKinnon Wood did not even reply to Trench's letter.

Maybe the Scottish Secretary was worrying about the

rumours of war that were steadily growing. What we optimistically called the Great War broke out on August 4th, 1914. It was the end of any hope for Oscar Slater in Peterhead. As a one-time companion of his has since said to me, 'Who was going to bother about a German Jew in 1914?'

Trench, who had been in the Black Watch before he was in the police, joined the Army in November, 1914. He was then forty-five years of age. He enlisted in the Royal Scots Fusiliers and was sent to Stirling as a drill instructor. He was thought of so highly by the Army that he was appointed Provost Sergeant of Stirling and attached to the Brigade office.

It's possible that Trench had forgotten about the Glasgow police by the second year of the war. But the Glasgow police had not forgotten about him. The Royal Scots Fusiliers were due to leave for the Dardanelles on May 14th, 1915. On the previous day Trench was getting his field kit ready, when representatives of the Glasgow police arrived in the barracks and arrested him on a charge of resetting stolen jewellery. When he got to Glasgow, Trench discovered that Mr David Cook, his lawyer friend, had been arrested on the same charge.

This case was, to put it politely, a very strange one. The charge against Trench and Cook was that they had reset the jewellery on January 19th, 1914. But they were not arrested until May 13th, 1915. They were granted bail, but not brought to trial until August 17th of that year. Even the judge at their trial thought there was something odd about the law's delay and mentioned it to the jury. But the Crown did not explain.

The case was that a jeweller's premises in Argyle Street, Glasgow, were burgled on the night of January 13th–14th, 1914. The stolen goods were valued at £900, and the loss had to be borne by the Guardian Insurance Company. Detective-Lieutenant Trench was given the investigating job and soon found that it was the work of a gang of experts.

Then he was approached by a dealer named John McArthur, who might better be described as a double-dealer, for he specialised in the recovery of stolen goods. McArthur's proposition was that Trench should put him in touch with Mr Buchanan, the manager of the Guardian Insurance Company. This was done and McArthur explained that he could get back the jewellery for £400.

Trench reported this to the Chief Constable, who said that Buchanan would have to make his own arrangements. Then Trench contacted Mr Cook and, through the lawyer, Buchanan got the jewellery back. The Argyle Street jewellers put up a big poster saying, 'Great Capture. Whole stock of £1,756 recovered by the City Police,' which indicates that the jewellery must have doubled itself in value by being stolen! The Guardian Insurance Company were delighted and wrote to the Chief Constable thanking him for 'the good offices of Detective Trench' and suggesting that Trench should receive a reward. This charge, presumably, was his reward.

At the time Trench explained the case to the Procurator-Fiscal, who said it was a fishy sort of business but, if Trench could get evidence against the gang, he was to let him know. All this was corroborated by Mr Cook and Mr Buchanan, but at the trial the Procurator-Fiscal denied that he had ever heard anything from Trench about the case. The police witnesses concerned gave very shifty evidence indeed, and the Lord Justice-Clerk summed up in the entire favour of Trench and Cook.

'What the accused did,' he told the jury, 'was done with an innocent or even meritorious intention. The question is, have these two panels been proved guilty of reset of theft? I think, on the facts, that they have not; and I direct you, on the law, that you cannot and ought not to return a verdict of guilty, but on the contrary that you should acquit both prisoners of the charge laid against them.'

Amid applause from the spectators in court, the jury did as they were told, and the judge discharged the prisoners.

According to legend in Glasgow, Trench was so affected by this police persecution that, when he rejoined the Army and went to France, he deliberately led a bayonet charge across No Man's Land and so virtually committed suicide. But that was not true.

It *is* true that both he and Cook were very much affected by their trial. But Trench rejoined his regiment in Egypt, and then served in France with the rank of quartermaster sergeant. He was discharged from the army in October, 1918 and he died at the age of fifty in the following year, actually on the fourth anniversary of his arrest. Mr Cook, an older man who never really got over the effects of the trial, died two years after Trench.

But Trench was not forgotten. He had a journalist friend in Glasgow named William Park and to Park the detective had told the story of the murder of Marion Gilchrist as he thought it had occurred. Some eight years after Trench's death, William Park's book, *The Truth about Oscar Slater*, was published. We shall come to it at the proper time, but meanwhile you might like to read Park's dedication at the beginning of the book. Park wrote:

'Dedicated to the memory of the late Lieutenant John T. Trench, King's Medallist, Glasgow, who, as a public officer of the police force, actuated by an inspiring sense of justice, sacrificed his career and pension in a personal attempt to rescue from a life's detention in prison, and with a desire to save others from the risk of a similar cruel fate, a man whom he believed on his conscience to have been wrongfully convicted in the Scottish High Court of Justiciary, and for which noble act he was dismissed and ruined.'

A Voice from the Pit

In Peterhead Prison the man whom Trench tried to save must have heard of the efforts being made on his behalf. Even if Oscar Slater was not told directly about what was happening outside, the prison grapevine would relay the news to him. But, what with the Great War and its aftermath, people had forgotten that Slater was still in prison. Sir Arthur Conan Doyle wrote, 'From time to time one hears some word of poor Slater from behind his prison walls, like the wail of some wayfarer who has fallen into a pit and implores aid from the passers-by.'

It was the custom then in Scotland to release life-sentence prisoners after fifteen years. But the fifteen years went by and there was no word of Oscar Slater being released. There has never been any official explanation of this, but a fellow-convict of Slater's told me that he was certain that Slater was kept in prison because he was so intransigent. From the moment he had arrived in Peterhead, Slater had asserted that he was innocent, and consequently he was loudly resentful of prison discipline. According to my informant, Slater had also reported warders for ill-treating other convicts, and that did not exactly add to his popularity with the authorities.

One night in February, 1925, Sir Arthur Conan Doyle received a strange visitor in his London home. The visitor was a released convict who had come straight from Peterhead with a message from Oscar Slater to Sir Arthur. He explained that he worked alongside Oscar Slater in the prison bindery at Peterhead. Slater had written his message on a scrap of the glazed paper which was used to fix the spines of books that were being bound, and his friend had rolled it into a pellet and kept it hidden under his tongue so that he could smuggle it outside the prison walls when he was released the following day.

The message asked Sir Arthur, for God's sake, to try once again, and it was signed 'O.S.'

Conan Doyle did try again. One result was an article by Sir Herbert Stephen, an English man of law who had already championed Slater. 'I still hold,' he wrote, 'that no English judge would have allowed the case to go to the jury. I do not doubt that Slater was sentenced to death, and has been punished ever since, because he did not appear as a witness, upon evidence which I suppose that no bench of magistrates in England would make an order for the destruction of a terrier which was alleged to have bitten somebody.'

Then Sir Arthur Conan Doyle wrote to Sir John Gilmour, Secretary of State for Scotland, pointing out that Slater had already served more than 'the usual limit of a life sentence in Scotland when the prisoner behaves well', and asking that Sir John should give his personal attention to the case.

But Sir John seemed as little impressed as did his predecessor, McKinnon Wood. The Scottish Office replied that the Secretary did not feel justified in advising any interference with Slater's sentence. In answer, Sir Arthur wrote, 'I have done my best to set this injustice right. The responsibility must now rest with you.'

Conan Doyle, however, did not shirk his own responsiblity. In July, 1927, William Park's *Truth about Oscar Slater* was published by the Psychic Press at Conan Doyle's instigation. Park's book not only brought out all the points in favour of Slater and emphasised all the weaknesses of his trial, but, also, for the first time, gave Detective-Lieutenant Trench's theory of what really happened on the night of December 21st, 1908, in Miss Gilchrist's flat.

Park wrote that the man who called on Miss Gilchrist that night 'was on intimate terms of relationship with the victim'. He arrived without intention to murder and carried no weapon with him. He wanted a document which Miss Gilchrist possessed. They had a quarrel over this and he struck her. When she fell, her head hit the coal-box. 'He stooped down, quickly examined her, and judged there was a grave danger of fatal consequences, but not just at once. He was aware that if she survived beyond ten minutes, which seemed a certainty, and the maid were to reappear, his name would be disclosed, and in the event of death ensuing, he would be accused of murder.'

And so he seized a chair and used it to kill Marion Gilchrist. Then the bell rang. He went into the bedroom and broke open a casket to secure the document. 'He then slipped out unchallenged – because the servant knew him, and his presence allayed rather than excited her suspicion.'

Trench's theory was a good one but, as I hope to show you when I reconstruct what I think did happen that night, it was only half the truth.

The Truth about Oscar Slater created an immediate sensation. *The Morning Post* not only engaged the great crime writer, Edgar Wallace, to review the book, but also printed a leading article which cannot possibly have pleased the Secretary of State for Scotland.

Writing of Nellie Lambie and the man in the lobby, Edgar Wallace said, 'Obviously she knew him. As obviously, to my mind, the murderer was in the house when she left, ostensibly to buy a newspaper.' Later, discussing the trial, Wallace observed, 'Nothing was said of the bloodstained chair, because it did not fit in with the case that had been manufactured against Slater. No questions were asked of Lambie that were in any way inconvenient to the prosecution.'

And Edgar Wallace was yet another writer to have a swipe at the Scottish judge and jury of 1909. 'An Old Bailey jury,' he wrote 'would have stopped the case halfway through and dismissed the prisoner. In no other place in the British Empire would such a trial and such a conviction be possible. Slater is still in prison. He has served nineteen years for a crime of which anybody but a fool might know he was guiltless.'

A copy of Park's book was sent to the Secretary of State for Scotland. In the House of Commons the Lord Advocate, the Right Hon. William Watson, K.C., was asked what truth there was in a press report that an enquiry was to be granted. The Lord Advocate replied that he would be very much surprised if it were.

Among the newspapers which took an interest in the case, the outstanding was the *Daily News*. They sent their famous special commissioner, 'The Pilgrim', to Scotland and from September 16th to October 19th he analysed the case day by

233

day. At the end of this remarkable series, the *Daily News* commented, 'That nothing should have been done in all these years, when the truth could have been so easily elicited through official channels, is a grave reflection on the British system of justice.'

'One of the most dramatic developments in a criminal case ever recorded,' shouted the *Empire News* for Sunday, October 23rd, 1927. This was an alleged statement by Nellie Lambie. It was not revealed how it came into the hands of the *Empire News*, nor where Nellie Lambie (now Mrs Gillon) was, but Sir Arthur Conan Doyle wrote, 'I have read the document, which, I understand, comes direct from Helen Lambie, and can be certified by an affidavit from the interviewer. The matter is of enormous importance. Indeed, it is not too much to say that it must mark the end of the Oscar Slater case.'

In this statement Nellie Lambie admitted that she did know the man in the lobby. She said she had told the police, but they told her it was nonsense and persuaded her that she had made a mistake. Slater was not unlike the man, so she was also persuaded to identify him. She also said that Miss Gilchrist was visited by a number of men, whom she let in and out of the house herself so that the servant could not see them. And once Nellie Lambie heard a quarrel between Miss Gilchrist and one of these visitors.

The irrepressible Mary Barrowman had to have *her* word. 'The Pilgrim' of the *Daily News* tracked her down, now married and middle-aged, and still living in Glasgow. Her signed statement appeared on November 5th and she now said that she never meant to go any further than saying Slater was 'very like the man' she saw in West Princes Street. But the Procurator-Fiscal had her in his office every day for a fortnight before the trial, rehearsing her evidence. And gradually 'he was very like the man' became 'he was the man'.

Sir John Gilmour gave in. When he was asked a question about the case in the House of Commons on November 10th, he replied 'Oscar Slater has now completed more than eighteen and a half years of his life sentence, and I have felt justified in deciding to authorise his release on licence as soon as suitable arrangements can be made.'

If Sir John was expecting loud cheers for his kind action, he was very much mistaken. The uncharitable Press said quite bluntly that they thought that releasing Oscar Slater was an attempt to circumvent the demand for an enquiry into the whole case.

Oscar Slater was released from Peterhead four days later. A Jewish Rabbi, the Rev. Mr Phillips, who had worked unceasingly on Slater's behalf, was at the gate to meet him. He took the ticket-of-leave man to his home in Glasgow.

Newspaper reporters were waiting for him at Peterhead, followed him on the train, and besieged him at Rabbi Phillips' home. But all that Oscar Slater would say was, 'I am tired. I have not slept for the last five nights, since I heard I was coming back again. I want rest. I want rest.'

He was treated with such kindness in the Rabbi's house that he burst into tears. But even the sight of a tablecloth on a table was wonderful to a man who had spent nineteen years in jail.

Sir Arthur Conan Doyle charged into the fray once again. He sent a circular letter to all M.P.'s stating the case for an enquiry into the trial of Oscar Slater. This time Sir John Gilmour did the handsome thing. He arranged that the enquiry would be conducted by the Scottish Court of Criminal Appeal.

The appeal of Oscar Slater against His Majesty's Advocate was not held until June 8th, 1928. The delay was mainly due to the immense amount of work which had to be done by Slater's agents in tracing witnesses and documents and statements of some twenty years before. Slater was represented by one of the greatest pleaders Scotland has ever produced, Mr (later Lord) Craigie Aitchison, K.C. He was known as the Edward Marshall Hall of Scotland.

The five judges of the Appeal Court sat in the High Court

of Edinburgh where Oscar Slater had last seen Lord
Guthrie. And Slater himself sat among the spectators in
court, instead of in the dock. He was well dressed and, as
one reporter with a turn of phrase put it, looked bronzed
and fit. Sir Arthur Conan Doyle was there, and also William
Roughead, but he was a witness this time and not a
spectator.

Mr Craigie Aitchison explained to the bench that he
proposed to call a number of witnesses, including Oscar
Slater himself. The Lord Advocate replied that there must
be no attempt to re-try the case, and only new evidence
could be allowed. The arguments lasted for two days, and
then the five judges, after considering them, announced
which witnesses they were prepared to hear. And then:

'With reference to the appellant himself, his counsel had
stated he had nothing new or additional to say, and that his
evidence would amount to no more than a repetition of his
plea of Not Guilty. In these circumstances it would be quite
unreasonable to spend time over his examination now, and
the Court therefore is not prepared to allow his evidence to
be heard.'

The judges fixed the hearing of the appeal for July 9th.

Oscar Slater was filled with anger and despair when he
heard that he was not to be allowed to give evidence. He felt
that the old conspiracy against him was still in existence.
After all, he *knew* he was innocent. Why shouldn't he go into
court and say so? He brooded over this for some days and
then, without consulting his lawyers or counsel, he told the
newspapers he was withdrawing his appeal. He wrote to the
same effect to his friends, William Park, Rabbi Phillips, and
Sir Arthur Conan Doyle. And the same letter went to the
Lord Justice-Clerk.

They were horrified and lost no time in persuading Slater
that he was wrong. The very next day the papers printed a
second statement: 'The appeal of Oscar Slater will proceed.'

he letter to the Lord Justice-General was written because
f the appellant's great anxiety to enter the witness box, and
ecause his failure to do so would be misrepresented. The
ppellant has agreed to leave his case unreservedly in the
ands of his advisers.'

When the Appeal Court met again on July 9th, Mr
raigie Aitchison had to admit a defeat. He wanted to call
ellie Lambie. She was traced to Peoria, Illinois, but she
efused to attend the court and there was no machinery by
hich she could be brought. However, he called his other
itnesses, whose evidence had already been told in various
orms here. His address to the bench lasted for fourteen
ours, not counting the inevitable intervals.

The Lord Advocate did his best in his two hours' reply,
ut he was subjected to a good deal of heckling from the
ench. Typical is this statement and question by the Lord
ustice-Clerk: 'In this case Slater made no attempt whatever
o prove that he led a moral life, and for the very good
eason that such evidence would have been irrelevant.
otwithstanding that fact, the Lord Advocate brought out
at Slater did not in point of fact lead a moral life, and in
is speech to the jury he used that in explicit support of
roof of the charge of murder. Now, is that justifiable?'

On the morning of July 20th the Court met to hear
dgement given. The Lord Justice-General read out the
nanimous findings of the five judges. To the surprise of
any in court the judges had decided that the appeal had
iled on its first three points: That the jury's verdict was
nreasonable or unsupported by evidence; that any new
cts had been disclosed material to the issue; that the
ppellant had suffered prejudice by non-disclosure of evi-
ence known to the Crown.

But finally he dealt with Lord Guthrie's address to the
ry, and said, 'It is manifestly possible that, but for the
rejudicial effect of denying to the appellant the full benefit
f the presumption of innocence, and of allowing the point
f his dependence on the immoral earnings of his partner to

go to the jury as a point not irrelevant to his guilt of Miss
Gilchrist's murder, the proportion of nine to five for Guilty
and Not Proven respectively might have been reversed. In
these circumstances we think that the instructions given in
the charge amounted to misdirections in law, and that the
judgement of the Court before whom the appellant was
convicted should be set aside.'

Slater, not surprisingly, had some difficulty in following
this. When he learned that his conviction had been quashed
on a technicality he was most disappointed. He had expected
that the Court would pronounce him Not Guilty.

However, he took the same view as the one expressed by
Nellie Lambie in Peoria. When a newspaper reporter there
told her of the result of the appeal, she said, 'I am glad it is
all over.'

Now the question of compensation to Slater came up in
the House of Commons. 'I think it proper,' said Sir John
Gilmour, 'that the person concerned ought to have a
reasonable opportunity of putting forward any claim he may
wish to make.' Slater's public reply to that was: 'As far as I
Oscar Slater, am concerned, there will never be a bill for
compensation sent in.'

That was all very well, but what about the cost of his
appeal? The expenses were between £1000 and £1500, and
the defence fund raised on Slater's behalf was only £700.

However, Sir John Gilmour wrote to Slater that the Lords
of the Treasury 'have assented to an *ex gratia* payment to
you of £6000 in consequence of your wrongful conviction in
May, 1909, and subsequent imprisonment'. Slater should
have left the whole question of compensation to his lawyers.
Undoubtedly they would have arranged better terms, and
the vexed question of costs would have been settled. But
once again without consulting anybody, he took matters into
his own hands and accepted the £6000.

Later, when he understood the position about the costs,
Slater wrote to Sir John, 'I should have thought that the
Government, in common fairness, ought not to expect me to

bear the costs of this case.' But, as the Lord Advocate was
kind enough to point out, even if £1500 were deducted from
the total, Mr Slater would be able to buy an annuity from
the Post Office of £351 a year, or nearly £1 a day for the rest
of his life.

Oscar Slater and Sir Arthur Conan Doyle fell out over
this question of costs. Slater's point of view was that Sir
Arthur had been making money out of articles about Slater
for years, so he could afford to pay the balance. On the
other hand, quite unasked, Slater sent £200 to William
Park, author of *The Truth about Oscar Slater*.

Around this time Oscar Slater was approached, like
Madeleine Smith, by an American film company. They
wanted him to appear in a picture about himself. But, again
like Madeleine, he turned it down. All he wanted was to live
a quiet life. He soon found he couldn't do that in Glasgow,
where he was always recognised. So he went to the county
town of Ayr and settled there. And there, too, he married,
very happily indeed.

Who Really Did It?

Oscar Slater died on February 3rd, 1948. He was seventy-
five and, from the time he was released from Peterhead, he
lived a comfortable, pleasant life, broken only by the
internment at the start of World War Two. He was popular
among the people who knew him. He achieved, in fact, the
respectability which almost sent him to the gallows.

And now, before I reconstruct the murder of Miss
Gilchrist, I should tell you of the two star witnesses – Mary
Barrowman and Nellie Lambie. Many years after the trial
of Oscar Slater, Mary Barrowman turned up at a certain
house in Glasgow. She said she wanted to confess. She had
not been in West Princes Street at all on the night of the
murder. Her mother, who was an alcoholic, had made her
tell the story so that she could share in the reward.

As for Nellie Lambie, she did return to Britain. She and

her husband went to live in a small town in the North of England. Two reporters of the long dead *Daily Herald* traced her to her new home and tried to interview her. Her husband came to the door and, as they were talking to him, they saw Nellie Lambie in the background. But her husband would not allow them in and said that his wife had nothing to say about the Oscar Slater case.

One night, when I was at the Citizens' Theatre in the Gorbals district of Glasgow, the doorman revealed to me that he was a nephew of Nellie Lambie's. He assured me that his Aunt Nellie had prepared a statement which would be released to the world on her death. But Nellie Lambie died several years ago, and as yet, there is no word of any statement.

Every now and then someone comes out with a new solution of the Gilchrist murder. There was a Glasgow character whom I call the Imaginative Liftman. Every time the Oscar Slater case was mentioned, he would write to the newspaper concerned and tell the 'truth' about the murder. He said it was done by a gang. Slater was a member of this gang but did not commit the murder. But he was made the scapegoat.

The Imaginative Liftman's accounts were so riddled with inaccuracies that I was amazed when one Glasgow newspaper actually printed a version of his story.

The Slater case never seems to die. The *Paris Soir* made a strip cartoon out of it, and a study of the drawings shows that most Glaswegian wore the kilt in 1908! I had a visit from a Swiss journalist who had been commissioned by a German newspaper to write a series about Oscar Slater. And there is still an enterprising film entrepreneur who has been working for some years on a script about the case.

So now we come to the question: What did happen at 49 West Princes Street on the night of December 21st, 1908? Nobody really knows, but theories abound. Some people even believe that Oscar Slater *did* murder Miss Gilchrist, though they cannot produce a shred of evidence that he knew her, far less that he was ever in the house. When this book was first published in 1961 I put forward my theory. Since then I have realised that I was wrong.

The difficulty with this case is the identification of A. B., the mysterious man who walked through the lobby past Nellie Lambie and Arthur Adams and was supposed to have done the murder. He has been identified over the years with a Dr Charteris, a nephew of Miss Gilchrist's, and later a distinguished Professor of St Andrews University. When, many years after the murder, he was asked if he was A. B., he denied it completely. But, of course, what he was denying was that he had murdered Miss Gilchrist, because all through the case, A. B. is supposed to have been the murderer. Sir Arthur Conan Doyle believed it, so did William Park, John Thomson Trench and Edgar Wallace, to say nothing of the greatest of them all, William Roughead.

But, if you think it out carefully, you must realise that the man who walked through the lobby, call him by any initials you like, was not the murderer. Let me spell out the theory I have come to over many years.

First, we have to take into consideration the strange character of Miss Marion Gilchrist. This elderly lady, living alone with her young servant in a West End flat, was on bad terms with the rest of her family. Her father had left a fair amount of money and there were constant family squabbles between Miss Gilchrist and her married sisters about that money. This was exacerbated by the fact that Miss Gilchrist had had, when young, an illegitimate daughter, and she proposed to leave most of her money to her daughter and grand-daughter.

The reason that some people said that Nellie Lambie was Miss Gilchrist's illegitimate daughter was that they had got slightly mixed up with their dates. If Nellie was Miss Gilchrist's daughter then Miss Gilchrist gave birth to her when she was sixty-five! Miss Gilchrist *had* employed her real illegitimate daughter as her servant many years before Nellie Lambie came on the scene.

Now, as I see it, two men called together on Miss Gilchrist on the night of the murder. They were, I believe, relatives – the aforesaid Dr Charteris and a man named Austin Birrell. It's not real proof, of course, but I have met a nephew of Austin Birrell's who told me, seriously, that the whole family knew that Uncle Austin had done the murder.

When they arrived at 49 West Princes Street, either Nellie Lambie let them in before she went out, or else they arrived soon after she left. The point is that they were well-known to both Miss Gilchrist and her servant. It was virtually impossible to get into that house without being known to the occupants.

Charteris and Birrell were determined to get hold of a document in Miss Gilchrist's possession. They knew it was kept in the casket in the spare bedroom. So, once they were in the lobby, Birrell hustled Miss Gilchrist into the dining-room, while Charteris went into the back bedroom to find the document.

Miss Gilchrist, suspecting what they were about, took the harsh edge of her tongue to Birrell. Now Birrell was subject to epileptic fits – not the serious kind, but rather the sudden rage that overtook the late Adolf Hitler at times. If he took one of these fits he might do anything and not be aware of what he'd done until he recovered.

Enraged by Miss Gilchrist's taunts, Birrell struck her. As Detective-Lieutenant Trench surmised, she fell and her head struck the coal-box. It was the sound of this fall which alerted the Adams family in the room below. And then, either because he was in a fit or because he suddenly realised she might be dying and he could be caught for her murder, Birrell seized the chair by the dining-room table and showered blows on her head and chest with one of the legs of the chair.

As we know, there was blood everywhere about the fireplace. But the murderer, holding the chair in front of him, would keep some of it off his clothes. He could not keep it off his hands, however, and William Roughead had a photograph of that chair showing quite plainly the print of a hand in blood. Unfortunately, although the Glasgow police had already gone in for finger-printing, they did not use it in this case.

But this is why we know that two men were involved. If the man who lit the gas in the back bedroom with the *Runaway* matches was the murderer, his hands would be bloodstained. No marks of blood whatever were found on the casket, the matchbox, or anywhere else in that room.

So, as Birrell was killing Miss Gilchrist in the dining-room, Charteris was breaking open the casket and searching for the document. Up the stairs came Arthur Adams and rang the bell. Birrell stopped for a moment. Then, as nothing more happened, continued his attack. The bell rang again. But Birrell maybe realised that it could not be Nellie Lambie and therefore he could ignore it. He threw a rug over Miss Gilchrist's head. Then he made sure the coast was clear, left the house, and went upstairs to the landing where the flat was unoccupied.

Arthur Adams had reported to his family and had been sent back up to try again. Nellie Lambie arrived and opened the door. In the back bedroom Charteris had found the document at last. So he just strolled out and past the servant, whom he knew well and who recognised him, and he astonished Adams, and hurried down the stairs. Birrell, waiting on the landing above, saw Charteris leave, followed him, and the two ran along West Princes Street to Charteris's house. They were not seen by Mary Barrowman, because Mary Barrowman, as we know now, was never there. They *were* seen by Agnes Brown, the schoolteacher who was not called by the prosecution.

They reached Charteris's house and had plenty of time to compose themselves and for Birrell to change his clothes before the police arrived. And then they could swear that they had been in the house all night and not only knew nothing about the murder but were horrified that it had happened.

But all this is theory and the fact is that we can be sure of one thing only in this most mysterious of murder cases. And that is that — whoever murdered Miss Gilchrist, it wasn't Oscar Slater.

With these words I ended *Square Mile of Murder* in 1961. Ever since then I have been involved, in one way or another, with the Oscar Slater case and this new edition sums up all that I have learned about it.

In the course of my later investigations I met a remarkable man named George Jacobs, who had been a very young reporter when Oscar Slater was released from Peterhead and met him soon afterwards. George was as bound up in the case as I was, and his hero was John Thomson Trench.

He discovered that Trench's widow was still alive, living with relatives in Berwick and over ninety years of age (Mrs Trench died recently at the age of 100). George Jacobs proposed that a fund should be set up to make a presentation to Mrs Trench to honour the memory of her husband. It was also proposed to approach the police in an endeavour to seek the rehabilitation of Trench's reputation. John Mack, the crime expert of Glasgow University, joined us in this project.

Two Glasgow Town Councillors raised the question of rehabilitation, but the Town Clerk reported that, legally, it was not possible. However, we went ahead with raising the fund in Trench's honour. I attended the presentation to Mrs Trench, a most remarkable old lady whose only trouble was a slight deafness. She decided that the money should go to some cause in memory of her husband.

And so now there is a John Thomson Trench Prize in Civics at Glasgow University, and the hero of the Oscar Slater case will be remembered as long as Glasgow and its University last.

When Mrs Trench died, a writer in *The Glasgow Herald* announced that 'the last word' on the Oscar Slater case would now be spoken. With respect I disagree. I do not think we shall ever hear the last word on the Oscar Slater case.

A Respectable Postscript

Now that we have examined these four famous cases in our square mile of murder, let's see if my theory is true that respectability was at the root of each. Doubtless real respectability is a solid virtue. Even today how often do we see newspapers commenting with surprise that the murderer (or the victim, if he or she has more or less invited the murder) comes from a 'respectable working class' district?

Of course, in England (as opposed to Great Britain), the working class are still supposed to take respectability as their ideal. In Scotland it is expected that all classes, except those completely beyond the pale – such as aristocrats and tinkers – will cleave to respectability. This is partly because Scotland is a much more democratic country than England, and there are fewer differences between the classes. And it is also partly because the Scots are still concerned to keep up a front, which is not in the least like 'keeping up with the Joneses'.

Another word of this type of respectability is hypocrisy, but it would be unfair to apply that word to the respectable condition of Scotland today. It would be quite fair, however, to apply it to Victorian Scotland, and our four murder cases, riddled with respectability, prove that.

Over Glasgow in Victorian times, and on into the Edwardian era, hung a miasma of respectability. Crime, compared with population, was much worse then than it is now. Poverty was indescribable. Disease, even up to Oscar Slater's day, was rampant. But ever-growing Glasgow, with its solid Victorian buildings, its immense industry, its pushing business-men who realised that London was ripe for a take-over bid, kept up its front. And anyone who punctured that facade was likely to be roughly handled.

The Victorians were horrified that Madeleine Smith should have behaved in the unrespectable way she did – or, at least horrified that she should have written about it, even in private letters. The Smiths were the acme of respectability in Glasgow, though even the outside of their house in Blythswood Square was a front, giving the impression of a mansion when it was merely the ground floor and basement. Obviously the respectable daughter of a respectable architect was deranged when she sinned with a common clerk, and a Frenchman at that. It seems to me that the whole desire of the judges and the jury in this case was to return Madeleine to a respectable life, so that she could wed the respectable Mr Minnoch.

For this reason it was necessary for the defence to mount an all-out attack on Pierre Emile L'Angelier as a cad, a scoundrel, a blackmailer, a womaniser, a drug-taker and a liar. Any man who took advantage of a respectable female could easily be all that. And it was noticeable that the prosecution did not take much trouble to contradict this view.

But the real problem for L'Angelier was that he was respectable too! He was known to his fellow clerks as a man who set great store by respectability; he was a pillar of the Episcopal Church (which, in Victorian circles, was regarded as even more respectable than a Scottish kirk); and we have seen ourselves in what a respectable tone he wrote to Madeleine, and how concerned he was that the front should be kept up. What L'Angelier wanted was a respectable marriage: to be the respectable son-in-law of a respectable gent – that was his goal. And that is why, in my opinion, he either could not believe or did not know that Madeleine was poisoning him, and why he said nothing against her as he was dying.

Why did Madeleine murder L'Angelier? Well, I shall go

into one reason when I come to the case of our 'human crocodile'. But another reason is that Madeleine thought she wanted a respectable marriage, so that she had to get rid of a man she knew was not properly respectable, in order to wed Billy, a pillar of respectability.

No wonder she objected so much to the jury's verdict of Not Proven, when she was looking for a Not Guilty. For what does Lord Moncrieff say in *The Verdict 'Not Proven'?* He says, 'When, therefore, the verdict 'Not Guilty' being available, a jury contents itself with finding the modified verdict 'Not Proven', the verdict reflects, and is intended to reflect, unfavourably upon the character of the person acquitted.'

In other words, Not Proven is not a respectable verdict.

Well, if respectability got Madeleine Smith off, it certainly convicted Jessie McLachlan. Poor Jessie undoubtedly thought she was respectable – indeed, the respectability of the servants' quarters at 17 Sandyford Place is constantly stressed by the servants – but she was up against the respectability of the Fleming family and a judge who made it clear that he considered upper-class people incapable of committing a crime which would come quite easily to a lower-class person.

The Fleming family were protected in court almost as much as the Smith family (though both families were ruined afterwards by the notoriety), and never at any time was the question raised as to what the rest of the family thought of Old Fleming, the Aged P. What a character he is! Twice to the kirk every Sunday, quietly and neatly dressed, a great boy for the nice walk in the park. Indeed, the only bad mark against him was his broad accent. Yet he was a secret drinker, a libidinous old goat, and in the end (and here I agree with William Roughead) a murderer.

As we know, the Sandyford murder might have been solved if the people passing in Sauchiehall Street, who heard moaning from inside the house, had investigated the origin of the sounds. The seamstress who gave evidence said she was afraid. But isn't it likely that the ladies and gentlemen who heard the sounds and moved on were actuated by the feeling that this was a respectable house and therefore (*a*) nothing unrespectable could be happening in it; or (*b*) it was the respectable householder's own business (just, maybe a servant getting a beating)?

When we come to the case of Dr Edward William Pritchard, respectability operates on two levels. First of all, there's the respectability which attended all doctors in Victorian days. As I have said, most respectable people in Glasgow just could not believe that a Sauchiehall Street doctor could possibly think of murdering his wife and his mother-in-law. A minister of the kirk would be as likely a suspect.

And the second level in this case is Edinburgh respectability, which is Glasgow respectability super-distilled. Dr Pritchard's mother-in-law, Mrs Taylor, was an Edinburgh lady. She was a pillar of society and a drug addict. She kept going on her Battley's Solution, which was largely opium, and she was able to get large quantities of it at a cheap rate by ordering it in the name of her doctor son-in-law. How much was her opinion of Dr Pritchard as her idol affected by the fact that she was using him to satisfy her craving? Respectability has such dreadful pitfalls.

Then there was Dr Paterson and his respect for medical etiquette. He could see a woman dying of poison and do nothing about it because of medical respectability. And was it Dr Paterson who took the unrespectable course of writing an anonymous letter to the Procurator-Fiscal? Or did he think it was more respectable to send an anonymous letter than a signed one?

As for Dr Pritchard himself, he worked very hard at being respectable, and for the rest of his activities, well, he simply rationalised them to himself. In this I think he was like Madeleine Smith and other born murderers. Roughead, in an essay (written for his American public) entitled *Enjoyment of Murder*, gave the classic definition of the born murderers:

'All have this common characteristic: self-conceit, so abnormally developed as to become a sort of moral cancer – an overwhelming sense of their individual importance in the scheme of creation, and a corresponding indifference to, and disregard of, the claims and feelings of others. For them alone does the sun shine, the bird sing, the grass grow green; and money is provided merely to satisfy their peculiar requirements. The murderer lives in a little world of his own, in which whatsoever he may want is his of right, and woe to such as come between him and his desires.'

That describes Madeleine Smith and Dr Pritchard. But it does not describe either Jessie McLachlan or Oscar Slater.

And, when it comes to respectability, could you get a more perfect prisoner in a respectable society than Oscar Slater? He was right in the middle of all that rich, respectable, right-minded Edwardian Glasgow wanted to hide. He was – prize of all prizes – a foreigner, and a Jewish foreigner at that. I don't mean to suggest that Glasgow treats her Jewish citizens badly. On the contrary. But to the majority of Glaswegians in the Edwardian era the Jew was a ready scapegoat.

A respectable old lady had been foully done to death, and what was demanded by the citizens in 1908 was an eye for an eye, a tooth for a tooth, and a murderer on the scaffold. Oscar Slater was just made for the part. He had a sinister appearance, if you looked at him in the right way. He frequented gambling dens. He lived under an assumed name. He was known to pawnbrokers. And he shared a flat with Madame Junio, who was not only no better than she should be, but good-looking and well-dressed to boot!

In the conduct of the trial there was a clear line of demarcation between the respectable witnesses and Oscar Slater's friends. Nellie Lambie and Mary Barrowman were respectable. But the defence witnesses were all suspect, since they knew Oscar Slater, drank and played billiards with him, went to the same clubs, or lived in his flat in St

Square Mile of Murder

George's Road. Even Madame Junio's servant, Catherine Schmalz, was tarred with the Oscar Slater brush. It was as good as suggested that she helped her mistress to entertain the gentlemen who visited 'the dentist'. As far as anyone can tell, Fraulein Schmalz was just a maid, in every sense of the word.

The respectability of the murdered Miss Gilchrist was important, but not as important as the respectability of the Glasgow police. That had to be guarded at all costs. And that was why such a fate was meted to Detective-Lieutenant Trench. He left the shelter of respectability when he reported what he thought of the Slater case to the Scottish Secretary.

The respectability of the police was, of course, linked with the respectability of the two men who were responsible for the murder. The police investigated them soon after the murder had taken place. Each was a patently respectable person. Each had simply to say he knew nothing about the case. In the very nature of things, it was obvious to the police that a respectable elderly lady could not possibly be assaulted, far less murdered, by respectable relatives. It must have been done, they persuaded themselves, by some thug from the lower orders. When Trench suggested that respectable people might have murdered the respectable Miss Gilchrist, the police closed their ranks and absolved the respectable suspects completely.

What has intrigued me about this case is to speculate what might have happened to Oscar Slater if the jury had brought in a verdict of Not Proven or Not Guilty. Presumably he would have gone back to the United States, teamed up with Madame Junio once again and carried on with the odd life he led. But nineteen years in Peterhead Prison taught Oscar Slater to be respectable too. In his latter days he was a model of respectability, from the crown of his bowler hat to the tip of his rolled umbrella. I recollect very clearly the Ayrshire woman who said to me that she felt, the first time she met Slater, that here was a man who could be trusted.

So perhaps Oscar Slater found *real* respectability. At the risk of repeating myself, I trust I have made it clear that what I am objecting to is the Victorian idea of respectability, the front or facade. The Victorians and the Edwardians believed devoutly in the Eleventh Commandment: 'Thou shalt not be found out.' That meant that they were impelled to punish those who *were* found out.

Are we any better today? I think we are. The wrong idea of respectability still rears its ugly head, particularly in Scotland. But the police of today would never behave as the police did in the cases of Jessie McLachlan and Oscar Slater. In any case, scientific methods of detection would almost certainly have solved these two murder cases before they had gone very far.

We must not be self-satisfied, however. Miscarriages of justice can still occur. If you read that striking book, Ludovic Kennedy's *Ten Rillington Place*, you will maybe recall that Mr Kennedy quoted the Oscar Slater case as an example of how an innocent man can suffer.

Looking back on our square mile of murder, however, I feel that there is one simple, straightforward thing to be said. How much better it was that Madeleine Smith should go free than that Jessie McLachlan should be hanged by the neck until she was dead.